THE PGA CHAMPIONSHIP

THE SEASON'S FINAL MAJOR

John Companiotte

and

Catherine Lewis

Clock Tower Press, LLC
3622 W. Liberty
Ann Arbor, MI 48103
www.clocktowerpress.com

Printed and bound in Canada by Friesens, Altona, Manitoba.

10 9 8 7 6 5 4 3 2 1

Library of Congress Cataloging-in-Publication Data

Companiotte, John.
PGA championship : the season's final major / John Companiotte and Catherine Lewis.
p. cm.
ISBN 1-932202-08-0
1. PGA Championship. 2. Golf—Tournaments—United States.
I. Lewis, Catherine. II. Professional Golfers' Association of America. III. Title.
GV970.3.P43C66 2004
796.352′66—dc22
2003023301

For the members and staff of The PGA of America, past, present, and future.

For Betty and Richard Lewis, now more than ever.

ACKNOWLEDGMENTS

This book was born in the atrium of the Atlanta History Center in 2001, when Rebecca Szmukler, Julius Mason, and Professional Golfers' Association of America (PGA) President Jack Connelly engaged us in a discussion about writing a history of The PGA Championship. With the blessing of The PGA, we began what has proved to be an incredible journey. The book has since come to fruition, but not without a lot of assistance.

It is imperative that we begin by thanking the staff at The PGA of America. Julius and Rebecca helped us from beginning to end, and the book is in many ways the fruit of their labors. We received more assistance than we could ever acknowledge from Bob Denney. Bob fact-checked each chapter multiple times and offered helpful suggestions on how to improve the manuscript. He is a superb historian and a good friend. Ken Anderson read and commented on the manuscript, and for that we are eternally grateful. In addition, Kerry Haigh, Jim Awtrey, Joe Steranka, and Marty Kavanaugh agreed to interviews or read various versions of the manuscript. Annette E. Mongeau, Kelly A. McGrath, and Susan Hickman offered enthusiastic support for the enterprise. Jim Langford, John Zurek, Pete Lewis, Sandy Cross, Tom Galvin, Susan McMillan, Pat McCarthy, Rebecca Gaither, Vicki Ray Crist, Earnie Ellison, and Rich Williams attended the early meetings at the conceptual stage and offered useful advice. Trish Fairbanks designed the cover. Christine Garrity provided valuable assistance in the final stages of publication. Bill Cioffeletti, who oversees The PGA Historical Center in Port St. Lucie, Florida, arranged a very productive research trip by recruiting some wonderful volunteers, including Erich Fuerbeck, Linda Sorel, Paul Edler, Roy Porter, and Harriet Palmer.

Special recognition goes to photographer Montana Pritchard and his associates, Carey Huffine and Lauren Cobb. Carey arranged a photo shoot of many of the artifacts that appear in this book. Lauren proved to be an incredible resource throughout the whole process. She helped us locate, identify, and scan many of the photographs and cannot be thanked enough for her assistance and good cheer.

Many of The PGA of America's past presidents agreed to be interviewed for the book and offered insights and perspectives that we were not able to find anywhere else. Special thanks to Mickey Powell, James Ray Carpenter, Tom Addis, M. G. Orender, Jack Connelly, Dick Smith, Patrick J. Rielly, Ken Lindsay, William Clarke, Mark Kizziar, Will Mann, and Joe Black. In addition, Lloyd Lambert, former general counsel of The PGA, kindly offered his time to the project.

Many of the players who won or competed in the Championship and their families gave of their time as well. We would like to recognize, in particular, Dave Stockton, Ray Floyd, Chandler Harper, Bob Rosburg, Larry Nelson, Gary Player, and Bobby Nichols. Rick Nichols assisted us in the interview with his father. We would like to thank Roberta Nichols for helping us get in touch with Dorothy Hutchison, Jock Hutchison's daughter-in-law. She had great stories that give texture to the book. Jack Nicklaus deserves special recognition for his kind assistance with the Foreword. We would also like to thank his wife, Barbara, for her suggestion about which photograph to use to accompany it. As always, Scott Tolley helped make all of that possible.

Two PGA professionals provided us with stories that appear in Chapter Eight. Dick Murphy, who recently retired after many years as the head professional at Peachtree Golf Club, shared his memories of the 1991 PGA Championship with us. In addition, Keith Reese, the head professional at Valhalla Golf Club, told the story about the pairing of Jack Nicklaus and Tiger Woods in 2000.

So many of the host sites of the Championship played an important role in this book. We would like to thank Derek J. Intinarelli at Manito Golf and Country Club; Maxine D. Harvey at Congressional Country Club; Ken Limes at Columbine Country Club; Mark Gore at Firestone Country Club; Larry Appleby at NCR Country Club; Cindy A. Brooks and Judy Comotto at Baltimore Country Club; Nick Sidorakis and Nancy Acton at Southern Hills Country Club; Lynda Taylor-Autry and Pasquale LaRocca at Inverness Club; Michael Hyler at Riviera Country Club; Robert Bonner at Blue Mound Country Club; Donald M. Kladstrup at Oak Hill Country Club; Jon Davis at Shoal Creek

Country Club; Amy Frearer at Flossmoor Country Club; Tim Boyer at Columbus Country Club; Paul Ramee at Park Country Club; Nancy Sadler at Pinehurst Country Club; Richard Mercer at Pelham Country Club; Jerry McGlouthlen at Big Spring Country Club; John R. Manley at Portland Golf Club; Mary Shaw at Scioto Country Club; Jerry Mills at the Dallas Park and Recreation Department; Wade H. Miller and David Wigler at Plum Hollow Country Club; Barbara Vondra, Jerry McAuliffe, and Carl Patron at Birmingham Country Club; Rick Bayliss and Cindy A. Hauss at Oakland Hills Country Club; Jim Reed at Hershey Country Club; Vinnie DelZeppo at Blue Hill Country Club; Edward Cunneen at Canterbury Golf Club; Neal Hotelling at Pebble Beach Golf Links; Pat Gilmore at Wannamoisett Country Club; Kevin E. Carroll at Bellerive Country Club; Mike Wilcox at Tanglewood Park; Summer Harwood at PGA National Resort and Spa; Sue and Mark Ursino at Sahalee Country Club; Tom Dupont and Bill Zabowski at Minneapolis Golf Club; Ed Clark at Miami Valley Golf Club; Clayton Cole at Cherry Hills Country Club; Tom Brakke at Hazeltine National Golf Club; Brian Keelan at Dallas Athletic Club; and Dave Harner at French Lick Springs Resort.

Gwen Russell at Olympia Fields Country Club and Wally Hund and Anna Di Bartolo at Medinah Country Club offered us the warmest welcome during our visit in the fall of 2002, and we want to acknowledge their hospitality. We would like to offer a special thanks to JoAnn Jordan, Chris Borders, and Jennifer Mosely at the Atlanta Athletic Club. They are always so generous with their time and resources, and for that we are eternally grateful.

There are so many people to thank at various libraries, museums, universities, and archives around the country. Steve Auch, Gerald Goodson, and Barbara Hartley of the Jack Nicklaus Museum helped us locate photographs for Chapter Six. Andrea Felder, Robinson Gomez, and Beauval Aristide at the New York Public Library provided valuable research assistance for the first three chapters. Rand Jerris, Doug Stark, Patty Moran, and Maxine Vigliotta at USGA Golf House helped us locate information about some of the early Champions. Kerry McLaughlin and Steve Smith at the Historical Society of Pennsylvania researched information about Rodman Wanamaker. Peter Lewis at the British Golf Museum located information about the *News of the World* tournament. Rachel Wolgemuth of the Hershey Community Archives found a wonderful image of Milton Hershey at the 1940 PGA Championship. Tom Jablonsky provided valuable information about the history of Marquette University. At the Atlanta History Center, Betsy Rix helped locate information on J. Douglas Edgar.

There are a variety of other people who helped in innumerable ways. Furman Bisher of the *Atlanta Journal-Constitution* told some great behind-the-scenes stories. Sue Brill at The Golf Channel provided important information and images for Chapter Seven. Sharon Yates at Gaylord Sports Management was an enthusiastic supporter of the project. Debbi Allamong at Susan Jacobs Inc. helped us invaluably. Dave Lagarde at the New Orleans *Times-Picayune* provided research advice. Mathematician and author William Quirin helped with information about golf clubs and courses in New York. Karen Bednarski, a well-respected historian and museum consultant, tracked down information about The PGA of America's founding. Peter Sansone at Great Golf Resorts of the World provided the image of the first cover of *PGA Magazine* on behalf of The PGA of America. Jim Sanford, who worked on *A History of the Season's Final Major*, the traveling exhibition on The PGA Championship, offered encouragement and support. Richard Hold helped research the early history of golf.

Special thanks goes to Barry Watts of the Atlanta History Center for helping to scan and touch up many of the photographs. Even up against the tightest deadline, he assured us that "it's all good." Projects like this cannot survive without such friends. Kim Blass of the Lovett School and Karen Leathem and Frances Westbrook of the Atlanta History Center proved, once again, to be fine editors. Rich Skyzinski, our fact-checker, had a great eye for detail and made useful suggestions. We are particularly grateful to Marty Elgison and Andrea Bates of Alston+ Bird LLP who ably assisted us in the final stages. Erin Howarth, the designer, deserves special recognition and kudos for all of her hard work, as does John Bardsley.

We also have personal favors to repay. Dr. Ana Glick and Dr. Morton Hodas offered housing during one of our many research trips to New York. Betty and Richard Lewis provided support, good humor, and advice. Over the holidays, Betty gave her time and energy to transcribe numerous interviews. Tony Lewis and Shelley Andrew have been patient with a sister who always seems to be tucked in a book or in front of a computer. Blue and Smilla were cheerful throughout the whole process, even when it meant that they missed their walk. Finally, the authors would like to thank their spouses. It is no overstatement to say that this book would not exist without their love and support.

John Companiotte and Catherine Lewis

FOREWORD

Once, while watching a televised interview with my son Gary, I noticed a framed photograph in the background. It was black and white, aged, and a bit grainy, but the image brought back a flood of colorful memories for me. The scene was of me carrying Gary, then a precocious four-year-old, off the 18th green of Canterbury Golf Club during the 1973 PGA Championship. I found out later that Gary's oldest brother, Jack, a practical joker then and now, had coerced Gary into running on the green after my second round. Later in that interview, I heard Gary mention that the photo remains one of his favorites. I think I can safely say the same.

The memories I've built of PGA Championships are as much about family as they are about hoisting the Wanamaker Trophy. Five times, I've had the honor and pleasure of lifting that trophy in the sky. Yet I have countless memories of friends and family that surround those moments. Whether it is having Barbara by my side in 1963, when after surviving temperatures that topped one hundred degrees in Dallas, the trophy was so hot, I had to hold it with a towel. Or fast forward to 1980 at Oak Hill, when I had the opportunity to tie the great Walter Hagen by winning my fifth PGA crown. In the photos from the trophy presentation, you could see my youngest son, Michael, peering impishly from beneath the trophy table in between Barbara and me. Or perhaps it is two decades later in the year 2000, when I likely played my last PGA Championship, and by

my side on the stroll up the 18th at Valhalla was my son, Steve. All these moments—and more—simply frame wonderful memories I have of almost 40 years of PGA Championship appearances.

Many players, sports writers, and fans will tell you that the career of a professional golfer is most often measured by his performance in the major championships. I definitely agree, and that is why I always structured my year and preparation around those four events. Each major championship has its own challenges and charms, if you will. Among the many charms of The PGA Championship is that it is the only major open only to professionals, and each year I knew I was playing for the Championship of the association to which I belong—The Professional Golfers' Association of America. That in and of itself provides motivation going in and a great deal of satisfaction after. The event also provides club professionals—the caretakers of the game—an opportunity to compete at the highest level of competition, carrying forward a tradition from the founding of The PGA of America in 1916.

The challenges associated with The PGA Championship were even more numerous, and some of the toughest tests in my career came each year there. The PGA Championship annually boasts one of the most competitive fields in all of golf. On top of that, The PGA is typically played on some of the country's finest and most challenging venues. The PGA of America then takes those venues and sets them up in a demanding, yet fair, manner, crowning true Champions, usually in dramatic fashion.

To have won five times while almost winning several others, makes The PGA Championship a wonderfully special part of my career and my tournament memories. To be able to weave family and friends into each of my PGA memories, underscores what The PGA Championship has meant to my life.

Dozens of books have been written about the Masters, the U.S. Open, and the British Open, but this is the first comprehensive history of The PGA Championship. It is important because it tells the story of the major that professional golfers have come to consider "glory's last shot." I feel privileged to have been part of this history and am grateful to my family and my fans for many years of support. *The PGA Championship: The Season's Final Major* tells the story of a great Championship—a legacy that will last as long as the game is played.

Good golfing,

CHAPTER ONE

AN AUSPICIOUS BEGINNING

At nine in the morning on October 10, 1916, Thomas Kerrigan stepped up to the first tee at Siwanoy Country Club and made history. He was likely given the honor of hitting the first ball in the inaugural Professional Golfers' Association of America (PGA) Championship because he was Siwanoy's golf professional. Kerrigan first came to Bronxville, New York, in the fall of 1914, shortly after the new Donald Ross-designed course was completed. Prior to the 1916 gathering, qualification rounds for the first Championship had been held throughout the country, and 31 players arrived to play, although 32 had actually qualified. When Jack Pirie failed to appear, Jack Dowling drew the bye in a blind draw and sat out the first match.

To promote the newly established event, Siwanoy hosted a professional-amateur (pro-am) event, with four-ball stroke play in the morning, followed by foursome stroke play in the afternoon of October 9. The results foreshadowed things to come. Jim Barnes, identified by the *New York Times* as the "leading professional of the season," and Hamilton K. Kerr of Greenwich scored a 67 in the morning, helped by Barnes' record-breaking round of 69. Although an accomplished amateur, Kerr only helped on the first and the seventh holes. In the afternoon, Barnes and Kerr played well again and, with a 36-hole total of 144, were the winners. Henry J. Topping and Kerrigan took second place, followed by Walter C. Hagen and Frank H. Hoyt.

Because of the expense of cross-country travel, most of the players hailed from Philadelphia, Boston, New York, and Washington; a few traveled from as far away as St. Louis, Chicago, and Santa Barbara, California. Five days of 36-hole, single-elimination matches would decide the winner. The favorites, Jock Hutchison and Jim Barnes, had placed second and third, respectively, in the 1916 U.S. Open played in late June.

Kerrigan's opponent in the first 36-hole match was Charles Adams of Santa Barbara. Adams was a skilled driver, but his short game suffered, and Kerrigan won, 6 and 4. The match between Jim Donaldson and Bob MacDonald attracted the largest

> "THIS IS THE FIRST BIG TOURNAMENT OF ITS KIND THAT THIS COUNTRY HAS EVER SEEN, AND EVEN IN THE PLAY OF THE FIRST ROUND IT GAVE EVIDENCE THAT IT WILL BRING OUT SOME OF THE FINEST MATCHES EVER CONTESTED ON THE GOLF COURSES OF AMERICA."
>
> —*NEW YORK TIMES*, 1916

Jock Hutchison watching as Jim Barnes drives off the tee in the final of the first PGA Championship in 1916.

gallery and was declared "close and sensational from the first tee to the last green" by the *New York Times*. Near the end of the match, MacDonald won three holes, sealing his 3-and-2 victory on the 16th green. But his luck would not hold. At 9:25 the next morning he faced Hagen, who hoped to add The PGA Championship to his Metropolitan Open, Western Open, and Shawnee Open titles that year. In the second round, Hagen defeated MacDonald, 3 and 2, needing only nine putts on the last seven greens. Kerrigan defeated George McLean, 2 and 1.

> "ALL THAT BARNES NEEDS TO WIN A GOLF TOURNAMENT IS A GOLF COURSE, A PUTTER, AND A LIBERAL SUPPLY OF THE CLOVER-LEAVES THAT HE CARRIES IN THE CORNER OF HIS MOUTH."
>
> —NEW YORK TIMES, 1916

In the quarterfinals, Kerrigan faced a more formidable opponent, the eventual Champion. Despite playing the last 13 holes in even fours, Kerrigan lost, 3 and 1, to Jim Barnes, a native of Cornwall, England, who was known for his height, estimated at six feet, three inches, and his long drives off the tee. In the semifinals, Hutchison beat Hagen on the final hole. Writing for the December 1927 issue of *Metropolitan Golfer,* Hagen reflected on what he learned that day: "I got one of my early lessons in match play from Jock Hutchison in the first PGA at Siwanoy in 1916. Jock beat me in the semifinals, in more of a foot race than a golf match. We played the last eighteen holes in exactly one hour and thirty minutes. I lost. Neither one of us took time to study the shots nor to play them carefully. . . . Since that day, eleven years ago, I have never hurried myself out of a championship match." Hagen took to heart that earlier loss to Hutchison and thereafter compiled one of match play's greatest records. In the other half of the semifinals, Barnes easily defeated Willie MacFarlane, 6 and 5.

In the final, on the morning of October 14, Barnes got off to a poor start, unable to capture the lead until the 25th hole. But he did not seem disturbed by Hutchison's good fortune. The *New York Times* reported that "the tall Briton just sort of played along with him in a bored way, for he knew that things were a little topsy-turvy, and only time would set them right." Hutchison took a 2-up lead on the front nine. On the back, Barnes reduced the lead to 1-up. His declaration that "I always do better after lunch" proved true. He squared the match on the 21st hole, and on the 25th he took the lead. On the 27th, he made a 35-foot putt for a birdie to remain 1-up. For the next several holes, the lead shifted back and forth. As Barnes was walking to the final hole, a female spectator, unaware that he was a competitor, politely asked if he had a good view of the event. He replied, "Don't worry. I have a ringside ticket."

Barnes later remembered that, with the match all square on the final green, he and his opponent "had a little bit of an argument about who was away. Jock thought I should putt first. I didn't think so, but Jock insisted. Finally, John G. Anderson, who was refereeing, asked: 'Don't you think, Jock, you should ask me to decide?' John measured and Jock was away. Jock missed, and I holed out to win the hole. But, boy, if Jock had dropped his putt, that one of mine would have been plenty tough." By holing his five-foot putt, Barnes won the first PGA Championship, 1-up. He was awarded $500 and a diamond-studded medal; Hutchison was given a gold medal and $250. Bronze medals went to the semifinalists and the low scorers in the qualifying rounds.

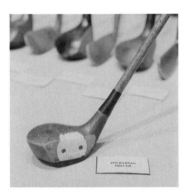

Jim Barnes, whose clubs are on display at The PGA Historical Center in Port St. Lucie, Florida, won all the significant majors of the day.

Nine months before Kerrigan hit the first shot in the 1916 PGA Championship, The PGA of America was founded over lunch. On January 17, 1916, Rodman Wanamaker, heir to the Wanamaker Department Store fortune, invited prominent professional golfers and businessmen to the Taplow Club in the Hotel Martinique on Broadway near Wanamaker's New York store. Thirty-five men, including such professional and

"ALMOST EVERY SEPARATE AND DISTINCT INDIVIDUAL IN THE MULTICOLORED THRONG THAT CHARGED WILDLY OVER THE HILLS AND DALES OF THE SIWANOY COURSE WAS HOPING THAT VICTORY MIGHT PERCH ON THE SHOULDERS OF THE PICTURESQUE SCOTSMAN."
—*NEW YORK TIMES,* 1916

amateur players as Walter Hagen and Francis Ouimet, convened on the blustery afternoon and lent support to Wanamaker's idea of forming a professional golfing organization. James Hepburn was named chairman of the organizing committee, with Herbert W. Strong as secretary. James Maiden, Robert White, Gilbert Nicholls, Jack Mackie, and Jack Hobens served as well.

A week later, on January 24, the group met again at the Taplow Club and, according to the meeting minutes, "It was decided to wait until a copy of the constitution and by-laws from Great Britain arrived. Mr. Jason Rogers

Barnes literally and figuratively towered over his opponents.

Mr. Herbert Strong,
   Secretary of the Organization Committee,
      Professional Golfers' Association of America,
         Inwood, Long Island, New York.

Dear Sir:
   The undersigned, a professional golfer regularly employed by a regularly constituted Golf Club, hereby makes application for membership in The Professional Golfers' Association of America as a Class "A" member, and agrees to remit $10 to the treasurer within ten days after notice of his election to membership by the Organization Committee.
   The undersigned further agrees that his signature to this application for membership shall be accepted as his formal signature to the Constitution and By-laws of the Association, binding him to agree to live up to and abide by all the rules adopted by the Association as indicated in the rough draft submitted and revised and adopted by the Organization Committee.

Signed *Walter C. Hagen.*
Dated *April 14* 1916   Club *Rochester Country Club.*
                           City *Rochester*
Approved *Yes*   County *Monroe*
                           State *N.Y.*
Rejected ....   Home Street Address *R.F.D. 1*

As his membership card shows, Walter Hagen was one of the original members of The PGA of America.

The Hotel Martinique in New York City was the site of the luncheon that launched The PGA of America.

kindly offered his services to the Committee relative to drawing up said constitution." On February 7, a constitutional committee consisting of Jack Hobens, Jack Mackie, Herbert Strong, and attorneys Jason Rogers and G. C. Ennever was established. In two weeks they drafted the document for approval at a February 24, 1916, meeting in New York.

Thirty-five men became charter members of the organization, and the first offices of The PGA of America were established at 366 Fifth Avenue in Manhattan. On April 10, 1916, the executive committee voted on 82 membership applications. Seventy-eight men were admitted at the rank of Class A, largely reserved for practicing golf professionals regularly employed by clubs, with annual dues of $10. On June 5, at a second meeting, 139 additional members were elected to Class A membership and three to Class C, reserved for golfers employed by sporting goods houses or equipment manufacturers.

On June 26, the members began their first organizing meeting at the Radisson Hotel in Minneapolis to coincide with the U.S. Open that was being played at the Minikahda Club. Of the 81 players in the U.S. Open field that year, 39 were members of the newly formed PGA. The attendees at the meeting elected Robert White of Wykagyl Country Club in New Rochelle, New York, as the first president. White, an immigrant from St. Andrews, Scotland, who came to America in 1894, was an appropriate choice, as he had sought to organize professional golfers in America as early as 1907.

Herbert Strong was elected secretary/treasurer, and George Fotheringham and James Maiden—the brother of Stewart Maiden, who so influenced Bobby Jones—were named vice presidents. A 24-man executive committee was selected, with nine members from the Metropolitan New York Section, six from the Middle States Section, three from the New England Section, three from the Southeastern Section, one from the Pacific Section, one from the Northwestern Section, and one from the Central Section. Unlike the commissioners who controlled baseball and football, The PGA of America devised a decentralized organizational structure. Rather than rely on a single leader, the association established an executive committee, which consisted of a president, secretary/treasurer (separated into two offices in 1928), and vice presidents who rep-

Framed at The PGA of America's headquarters, these minutes document the birth of the world's largest working sports organization.

resented various districts. On July 14, 1916, at a meeting at Garden City Golf Club in New York, Rodman Wanamaker agreed to donate $2,580 in prize money, a trophy, and various medals for the first Championship. Although that generous gift was enough to sustain The PGA of America, it was a mere fraction of Wanamaker's profits from the department store, which averaged $1,745,358 annually from 1914 to 1918.

The desire to organize professional golfers was not new, so why was The PGA of America so successful? Many historians credit Rodman Wanamaker's foresight. Prior to his decision to organize lunch at the Taplow Club in 1916, golfers and promoters around the country had tried to establish a national professional circuit. Although those early efforts were limited in scope, golfers in New York, Boston, Philadelphia, Baltimore, Washington, Chicago, and St. Louis formed associations and conducted regional tournaments during warm-weather months. Loosely organized professional golf organizations were formed in Massachusetts and Illinois. The Eastern Professional Golfers' Association, which included players in New York, Connecticut, Pennsylvania, and New Jersey, was organized in 1906 and held its first championship at Forest Hill Field Club in New Jersey on October 23 and 24 of that year. In 1914, Harry Bowler

was listed as president of a similar organization in Boston. The first president of The PGA of America, Robert White, helped establish a Chicago-based group in the spring of 1907, organizing the first tournament at the Homestead Club, predecessor of Flossmoor Country Club, which hosted the 1920 PGA Championship. Through a variety of tournaments, these organizations promoted professional golf, thus paving the way for a national organization.

Rodman Wanamaker offered the fledgling organization two things necessary to make it successful: money and a working model based on the British PGA. His commitment of cash, trophies, and medals brought prestige to the first Championship and to the profession itself. In the early 20th century, professional golf was a tenuous business. Prize money for the largest events rarely exceeded $200, and purses for small tournaments barely covered travel expenses. Club professionals' salaries averaged $25 a week, and many golfers in these early years made more money gambling than by winning tournaments. Jim Barnes, the first PGA Champion, remembered that tournaments in Florida often gave giant layer cakes as prizes. The promise of a $500 first prize, the same as the U.S. Open, was enough to convince players to take the first PGA Championship seriously.

RODMAN WANAMAKER

Lewis Rodman Wanamaker (1863–1928), son of the department store magnate who established Wanamaker's Department Store in Philadelphia, was born on February 13, 1863, and played baseball and football at Princeton University. Upon graduation, he joined his father's business in 1886. He went to Paris as resident buyer in 1888 and lived abroad for more than 10 years, broadening Wanamaker's European presence. When his father purchased the Alexander T. Stewart Cast Iron Palace in New York in 1896, Rodman helped revolutionize the department store, pioneering creative merchandising techniques, European fashions, and the use of escalators. Similar to his father, John, Rodman had diverse interests and even proposed the idea of a transatlantic flight to Orville Wright, who deemed it "foolhardy." In June 1914, Rodman christened the first hydroplane, named *America*, and promoted commercial transatlantic travel. When his first plane was destroyed in a storm in December 1916, he built a second one and donated it to England for use in World War I. He was a generous patron of the arts and collected musical instruments, including four Stradivarius violins. Rodman did not play golf, and according to his son-in-law Ector Munn, he found it a silly game, "knocking a little ball across a lot of valuable real estate." But Rodman, worth more than $75 million when he died, belonged to several country clubs because it

was good for business, and the Wanamaker family championed physical exercise as a way to improve the employees' lives. John founded the Millrose Athletic Association in New York and the Meadowbrook Athletic Association in Philadelphia. Rodman began to assume responsibility for the New York store in 1908 and continued to host sporting events, including a golf competition. The Wanamaker-Millrose Games remain one of the nation's premier track-and-field events. The founding of The PGA of America was consistent with Rodman's interest in sports and the merchandising opportunities it afforded.

The PGA of America's first headquarters were in New York City.

The charter members of The PGA in 1916.

Drawing inspiration from across the Atlantic, Wanamaker urged The PGA of America to model its new Championship on the *News of the World* tournament, Great Britain's annual professional event. Instead of drawing inspiration from the British Open or U.S. Open, Wanamaker elected to replicate the 36-hole elimination match play tournament that began in October 1903 in Sunningdale, England. Named for a popular British newspaper, the *News of the World* quickly became the second most important event on the professional golfer's calendar in England. In *The Dawn of Professional Golf,* historian Peter Lewis explained that the event's format was relatively simple, which might suggest why it was so appealing to the newly formed PGA of America. The first four rounds consisted of 18 holes each, and the final round consisted of 36 holes. Players qualified for the 32 places in sectional stroke-play tournaments, and each section was limited to a specific allotment. The total purse

for the 1903 tournament was £200—£100 to the winner and the rest divided among the runner-up, the semifinalists, and the quarterfinalists.

It is not clear whether Wanamaker, who began traveling widely throughout Europe in 1889, actually ever attended the British event. But his guests—many of whom were golf professionals from Great Britain—at the January 17, 1916, lunch were familiar with it. James Hepburn, chairman of the organizing committee of The PGA of America, had previously served as a British PGA secretary and had been a semifinalist in both the 1904 and 1909 *News of the World* tournaments. The PGA slightly modified the British format, making all of the matches 36-hole competitions. Originally, the plan was to hold the annual event on a golf course in New York, but the seven regional districts successfully argued that rotating venues would more fairly represent the best courses in the nation.

Jim Barnes with boxing champion Jack Dempsey, two of the most famous sportsmen of the 1920s.

The Oldest Golf Monthly

The official magazine of The PGA of America began publication in 1920, the same year as the *Saturday Evening Post* and two years before *Reader's Digest*. Until 1944, it was called the *Professional Golfer of America*. The name was shortened in April of that year to the *Professional Golfer*. In 1977, the new and current name, *PGA Magazine*, was adopted. Although not the first, it is the nation's oldest continually published golf monthly. When the May 1920 issue was released, The PGA of America and The PGA Championship were barely four years old. P. C. Pulver, the first editor, expressed his desire for the magazine: "We believe this publication . . . supplies the medium whereby we can get into much closer unity on the many problems which confront our profession." The magazine played an important role in building community among PGA members throughout the United States and continues in that tradition.

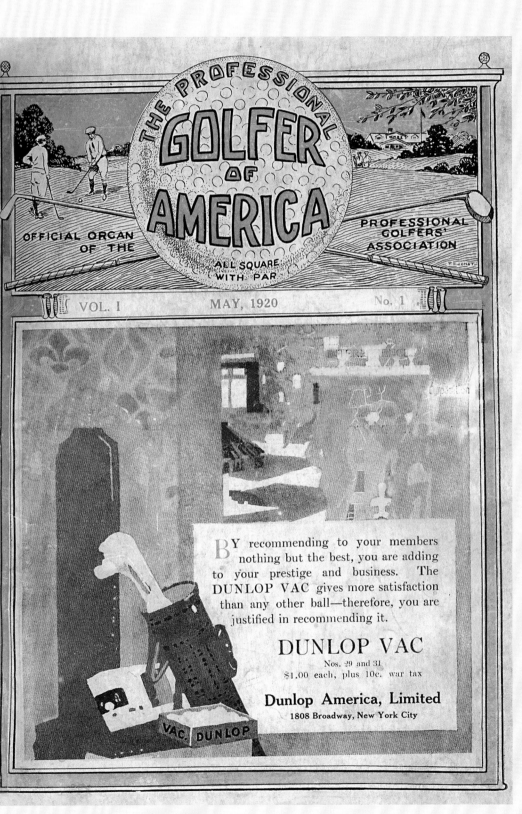

Tom McNamara, a salesman for Rodman Wanamaker, is credited with helping to organize The PGA of America.

Wanamaker sought to capture a larger share of the golf equipment business by selling brands—Silver King golf balls and Taplow golf balls and clubs—that competed directly with A. G. Spalding and Brothers. Two of the more established manufacturers in the early part of the century—Burke Golf Company and Crawford, MacGregor, and Canby (CMC)—focused on amateur golfers, while two of the newer companies, Wilson and Spalding, marketed directly to professionals. In *The PGA: The Official History of the Professional Golfers' Association of America*, Herb Graffis explained, "Spalding remained well ahead of the field because it had been quick to set up retailing connections with the professionals, then continued as practically the only employment agency for professionals during the first decade of American golf."

Wanamaker saw an annual professional tournament, attracting the best players of the day, as a way to promote the brands for which Wanamaker's was the sole distributor in the United States. In 1915, Sumner Hollander, the store's sports buyer, hired Tom McNamara to sell equipment and John G. Anderson to handle sportswear in the same department. They were very successful, and customers flocked to Wanamaker's to buy golf merchandise, many inspired by Francis Ouimet's surprise victory at the U.S. Open at The Country Club in Brookline, Massachusetts, in 1913.

It was McNamara who first introduced Rodman Wanamaker to the idea of establishing a national professional golf association. Like many professional golfers of this era, McNamara began his career as a caddie, first at Warren's Farm Golf Club, then at The Country Club. He took his first job as golf professional in Vermont and then returned to the Boston area. An accomplished player, he placed second in the U.S. Open in 1909, 1912, and 1915. McNamara left the professional circuit for a more stable sales position at Wanamaker's. Herb Graffis pointed out that "his wide acquaintance among professionals, his playing ability, and the high regard in which he was held by British-born and home-bred professionals" brought him in constant contact with players who were clamoring for a national association. McNamara's sales route for Wanamaker's included New York and New England, and he saw a professional association as a way to increase the competition between Spalding and the department store. He hoped to encourage members of this new association to purchase equipment for resale in their individual shops. McNamara introduced the idea to Wanamaker, who immediately recognized the merchandising and promotional opportunities and helped launch The PGA of America, now the world's largest working sports organization.

Jim Barnes kept the trophy that bears Rodman Wanamaker's name for four years, although he only won the event twice. In 1917 and 1918, the Championship was canceled because of World War I, so The PGA of America refocused its energy on supporting the war effort by raising money to purchase and maintain an ambulance for the Red Cross. To assist the Allies, The PGA also sent $1,000 to its British counterpart for war relief. Many professional golfers on both sides of the Atlantic served in the war. Scotsman Tommy Armour, who went on to become the 1930 PGA Champion, began his service as a machine gunner with the Black Watch Highland Regiment. As an officer in the Tank Corps, he lost sight in his left eye at a gas attack during the Battle of Ypres in Belgium. In a later battle, he was further injured by an explosion, which required that metal plates be inserted into his head and left arm.

Because The PGA Championship, U.S. Amateur, and U.S. Open were all canceled for these two years, the best American golfers had few opportunities to play in national competitions. Instead, dozens of relief matches became an informal circuit. From July 25 to 28, 1917, The PGA of America hosted a series of international team matches at Baltusrol Golf Club, Siwanoy, and Garden City that drew the best amateur and professional players of the period, including Bobby Jones, Jim Barnes, and Walter Hagen. The 1918 National Red Cross Tournament, which raised $15,000 and contributed to The PGA's ambulance fund, was held at Inwood Country Club and became the most important tournament held in the United States that year. Tom McNamara, who urged Rodman Wanamaker to sponsor the first PGA Championship in 1916, established the course record of 71. Wilfred Reid, who played in the inaugural PGA Championship, won the tournament with a 36-hole score of 150.

In 1919, The PGA Championship resumed at Engineers Country Club, a club opened in 1918 and designed by Herbert Strong. Barnes successfully defended his title, this time triumphing over 108–pound Fred McLeod, 6 and 5. Thirty-two players convened in Roslyn, New York—with one notable exception. Hagen had failed to qualify. The *New York Times* declared that his absence robbed "the event of its lustre." Hagen was supposed to compete in a qualifying tournament in Chicago on August 25 but did not appear, prompting PGA secretary Alex Pirie to declare him ineligible. The epic battle that would decide whether Hagen, the 1919 U.S. Open Champion, or Barnes, the 1919 Western Open Champion, was the superior golfer would have to come another day.

As the event's favorite, Barnes did not disappoint the galleries on the 6,363-yard course. In the first round he defeated Carl Anderson, 8 and 6, without much effort, while Jock Hutchison and George McLean faced stiffer competition in their struggles to survive. Otto Hackbarth, a virtual unknown from Cincinnati, Ohio, nearly sent Barnes back home to Sunset Hills in the second round in a match that was a close shave for the 1916 PGA Champion. Barnes, who played bareheaded and without his usual piece of clover in his mouth, ended the morning match 3-down. In the afternoon, he donned a woolen golf cap and his signature charm and played exceptional golf for the first eight holes. By the fifth hole, he was 1-up. He went on to win, 3 and 2.

"THE BEST SHOT I EVER PLAYED"
BY JOCK HUTCHISON

"The best shot that I ever played beyond any doubt was in my match against Jim Barnes in the Professional Golfers' Championship at Siwanoy. . . . We came to the fifth hole all square as I recall it. This hole is about 460 yards in length with the green on a plateau. About 70 or 80 yards from the green there is a deep, narrow ditch with water and rocks at the bottom. I missed my second shot and went into this ditch. Barnes had carried it but was still short of the green by several yards with a possible four and a sure five. When I reached the ball it seemed that all I could do was to drop out and take the usual stroke penalty. But this would leave me playing four where I had little chance of beating a six. To get the ball out seemed impossible as it was lying badly and almost directly up against the sheer wall of the ditch about four feet high. But I decided to take a chance. I could hardly swing the club back on account of the narrowness of the ditch but lifting the club head almost straight up from the ball, I tore into it. The ball had to rise at an almost perpendicular lift but not only come safely out—it went out 50 feet in the air and then lopped over the green within three feet of the hole, which I won with a four, beating par a stroke. And after getting away with an effort of this sort I finally lost the Championship. . . . But that is golf."

In the third round the *New York Times* reported that Barnes "shook off another climber for this golfing pinnacle" by defeating Emmett French, 3 and 2. On the way to his victory, he overcame a broken driver on the 11th hole, a series of difficult stymies, and a few errant drives, one of which landed in a pile of granite building stones. In the other memorable match of the day, billed "The Strife of Scots" by the press, Jock Hutchison lost to Bob MacDonald, 3 and 2. In the semifinals, Fred McLeod managed to one-putt five greens in a row on his way to defeating George McLean, 3 and 2. Barnes won his semifinal match, 5 and 4, although MacDonald repeatedly outdrove him an average of 50 yards.

The newspapers cast the final on September 20, 1919, as an epic battle between David and Goliath, with the smallest man in the field facing the tallest. The *American Golfer* reported, "It was six feet three versus five foot three on Saturday, but one would never have guessed this when drives were compared, for McLeod was well up with his bigger opponent." McLeod, a native of North Berwick, Scotland, and the 1908 U.S. Open Champion, held his own on the front nine. On the 11th hole, "his approach was a bit too strong," and he missed a short putt and began to falter. McLeod ended the first 18 holes 5-down, having lost six of the last seven holes. Barnes, declared "cool as a proverbial cucumber" by one sports writer, holed a 40-foot birdie putt on the 31st hole for the victory in front of 700 fans. Although he would never win The PGA Championship again, Barnes enjoyed a distinguished career, adding the 1921 U.S. Open and 1925 British Open to his record.

Hutchison's victory in the 1920 PGA Championship represented the end of the era. Never again would foreign-born professionals dominate the event. A review of the nationalities of the 31 players who teed off in the inaugural PGA Championship in 1916 reveals that the early history of golf in America was dominated by Scottish and English players who immigrated to the United States. The first American-born Champion was Walter Hagen in 1921.

Facing page: Jim Barnes and Samuel Ryder at the 1919 PGA Championship.

Bill Mehlhorn played in 12 PGA Championships, starting in 1919.

The 1920 PGA Championship, held at Flossmoor Country Club, attracted 32 of the best players, yet it received little attention from the media in Chicago that summer. An exhibition match at Skokie Country Club, pitting British players Ted Ray and Harry Vardon against Chick Evans and local professional Phil Gaudin, drew far more coverage. The 1920 PGA resembled the 1991 Championship, won by John Daly. In both cases the eventual Champions failed to qualify and were allowed to compete only when other players failed to appear. The first round in 1920 saw no major upsets, but the second round felled Barnes, the week's clear favorite, who was eliminated by Clarence Hackney, 5 and 4. Hackney dominated the match from the outset, winning the first three holes. By noon, he was 4-up. Barnes, who had won 11 consecutive matches in The PGA Championship, never found his rhythm.

> "DOUGLAS EDGAR, THE PROFESSIONAL AT DRUID HILLS, ATLANTA, GEORGIA, IS A GOLFER WHO IS FITTED IN EVERY WAY, EXCEPT IN TEMPERAMENT, FOR CHAMPIONSHIP LAURELS."
> —GRANTLAND RICE, 1920

Hutchison, who ultimately won the event, entered the third PGA Championship at the last minute only because George Fotheringham and Arthur Clarkson, two of the qualifiers ahead of him, were unable to compete. As with Daly years later, Hutchison was not even supposed to be in the field. Once in, he played brilliantly. Hutchison easily defeated Eddie Loos, Laurie Atyon, and Louis Tellier in the first three rounds. In the semifinals, a few lucky stymies gave him a 4-and-3 victory over Atlanta golfer Harry Hampton. *Golfers Magazine* declared, "Had it not been for a brilliant start and the providential aid of a couple of stymies it is likely that the Atlanta player would have carried the battle to the home green. He made a game fight the rest of the way, and with a few breaks in the afternoon would have put Jock on the anxious seat." In the other half of the semifinals, J. Douglas Edgar defeated George McLean, 8 and 7.

Born in England, J. Douglas Edgar was considered by his contemporaries to be the father of the modern golf swing.

A CAREER CUT SHORT

J. Douglas Edgar's death on August 8, 1921, remains shrouded in mystery. Born in England in 1884, he is considered by many to be the father of the modern golf swing. He gave Tommy Armour lessons, and Harry Vardon is reported to have said, "This is the man who will one day be the greatest of us all." Bobby Jones declared that Edgar invented the outside-in

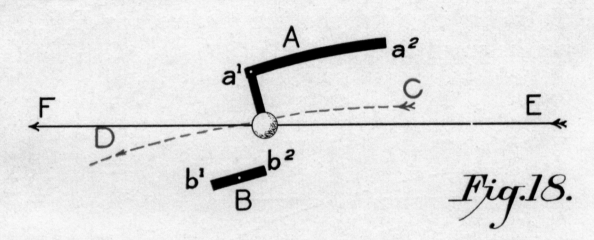

C. D. Line to be taken by the club-head.
E. F. Line of direction.

swing, which Edgar meticulously analyzed in his book, *The Gate to Golf*. His invention of a device he called "Swinging through the Gate" helped players control the club head as they swung. Edgar won the French Open in 1914 and the Canadian Open in 1919 and 1920. A first alternate in the 1920 PGA Championship, he secured a spot when one of the qualifiers withdrew and went on to lose to Jock Hutchison, 1-down, in the final. Edgar was the golf professional at Druid Hills Golf Club in Atlanta, Georgia, from 1919 until he died mysteriously when a speeding car hit him in front of his boarding house at Fifth and West Peachtree Streets. The case, first assumed to be a hit-and-run accident, was eventually investigated as a homicide because of a knife wound found on Edgar's left leg that severed his femoral artery and the "brutal manner in which the driver left the dying man." In his book, *Druid Hills Golf Club in Atlanta: The Story and the People*, James Bryant speculates that Edgar, who was popular among the women of Atlanta, was murdered by a jealous rival. The case was never solved.

Diagrams from Edgar's book, The Gate to Golf.

In the final, Hutchison beat Edgar, the winner of the 1919 Canadian Open, 1-up, in what proved to be a difficult match. The *New York Times* declared that Hutchison showed "beyond all question that he has the shots in his repertoire that rank with the best in the country." Trailing early in the match, on the 16th hole, Hutchison's drive landed in the rough, an inch from the lip of a bunker. After debating which club to play, he selected a spoon (3-wood), and hit the ball 200 yards onto the green in what proved to be the best shot of the match. Edgar, distracted by the crowd's enthusiastic response to Hutchison's shot, missed his approach and three-putted the green. He never fully recovered, and finally lost to Hutchison on the 36th hole.

Barnes, who had been eliminated in the second round, remembered Hutchison's inability to contain his excitement over winning the event: "He tore his cap off his tousled blond head, tossing it violently to the ground and kicking it all the way to the locker room." Although Barnes and Hutchison continued to play in The PGA Championship throughout the 1920s, they never won again, mainly because of a blacksmith's son from Rochester, New York, who first introduced himself to the golf world as W. C. Hagen.

Hutchison, who won in 1920, was the last foreign-born Champion for a decade.

MATCH PLAY

From 1916 to 1957, The PGA Championship was a match-play event, a format by which a golfer wins or loses by holes rather than by strokes. For example, if Louis Tellier took four strokes on the first hole and Cyril Walker took three strokes, Walker won that hole and would be 1-up. If Walker won the match, 5 and 4, he was leading by five holes with only four holes remaining to play. The match ended there because Tellier's four remaining holes could not overcome Walker's five-hole lead. When both golfers had an equal number of strokes on a hole, the hole was halved and neither golfer won that hole. If the score was even at the end of the match, the match was declared all square. The first golfer who won an additional hole won the match. Harry Robert, writing in 1947, explained that match play was "golfer vs. golfer, not golfer vs. field." In the early years, the match-play format of The PGA Championship, which typically included five rounds of 36 holes each, was one of the most grueling in all of professional golf. In August 1923, the *Professional Golfer of America* declared that "to survive a week of match play such as this, one has to be able to produce golf of a super brand at all times." While the format varied from year to year, one thing remained consistent—the winner certainly earned his title. For example, in 1934, Paul Runyan shot a 140 in the 36-hole stroke-play qualifying round on the Tuesday before the Championship. He then competed in five matches with a 36-hole format, which one golf writer declared was "no child's play," ultimately defeating Craig Wood in the final. In sum, Runyan played 209 holes to claim his first PGA Championship title.

Tom Kerrigan, Jock Hutchison, and Bobby Jones, ca. 1920. As an amateur, Jones could not play in The PGA Championship.

A CHAMPION'S RECORD

The PGA Championship's first victor, James M. Barnes (ca. 1887–1966), had a distinguished professional golfing career that included victories in four major championships: the 1916 and 1919 PGA Championship, the 1921 U.S. Open, and the 1925 British Open. He also won the 1914, 1917, and 1919 Western Opens. Upon completing the eighth grade, he became a caddie and apprentice clubmaker at West Cornwall Golf Club in England and later served in the Queen's Guard. He immigrated to America in 1906, first settling in Spokane, Washington. Two years after becoming a United States citizen, he tied for fourth in the 1913 U.S. Open. In 1921, he won the U.S. Open, nine strokes ahead of Fred McLeod and Walter Hagen at Columbia Country Club in Chevy Chase, Maryland, with 69-75-73-72 for 289. On the 18th hole of the third round, Barnes was serenaded by a marine band and became the only Champion ever to receive the trophy from a United States president, who was Warren G. Harding. Several days later, Harding invited Barnes and Fred McLeod, the runner-up in the 1919 PGA Championship, to the White House for lunch. Prior to the founding of the Masters in 1934, Barnes was one of only five men to win all three professional major championships. His *Picture Analysis of Golf Strokes* (1919), a best-selling golf instruction manual, was the first such book to use still photographs on flip pages to give the illusion of movement. After retiring from tournament play, Barnes served as a professional at Huntington Crescent Club in Huntington, New York, and later Essex Country Club in West Orange, New Jersey. Barnes, one of the original 12 inductees into The PGA Hall of Fame in 1940, died on March 25, 1966.

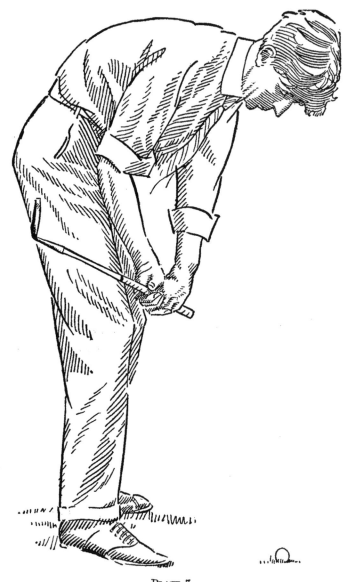

PLATE 7

Top of back swing for short mashie shot. Note that, although the club is taken back only a short way, the wrists are bent or "cocked" to snap the clubhead forward in striking the ball. However, do not permit the forward swing of the hands to stop, and so try to flick or scoop the ball up. Make the hands swing on through.

CHAPTER TWO

THE MAKING OF A MAJOR

The PGA Championship came into its own in 1921 and continued to rise in stature throughout the decade, largely because of the personalities and skill of Walter Hagen and Gene Sarazen, known to golf fans as The Haig and The Squire. In the first 16 PGA Championships, they won or finished second 10 times. Hagen dominated the Championship in the 1920s and became the first player to win it five times (1921, 1924, 1925, 1926, and 1927). In compiling this record, he played in the final six times, winning 22 consecutive matches before losing to Leo Diegel in the quarterfinals in 1928.

Hagen's triumphs and charisma helped professional golfers on both sides of the Atlantic. He was the first player to challenge the assumption that professional golfers were a disreputable bunch. Prior to World War II, tournament organizers made clear distinctions between "gentlemen" (amateurs) and "players" (professionals). In 1930, the United States Golf Association bestowed amateurs with the title of *Mr.* in the U.S. Open program but denied it to the professional competitors. This treatment was largely because

Always elegantly dressed, Walter Hagen, on right, was a showman on and off the course.

of the professional players' working-class backgrounds. Sarazen was the son of Italian immigrants, and Hagen was the son of a German blacksmith. Only a handful of professional players gained national recognition in these early years, and they did not become respected competitors until the 1930s.

> "I'LL WIN. I ALWAYS DO."
> —WALTER HAGEN

Hagen was the first to overcome these prejudices. Sarazen once said: "All the professionals who have a chance to go after the big money today should say a silent thanks to Walter each time they stretch a check between their fingers. It was Walter who made professional golf what it is." A former caddie, Hagen successfully challenged the exclusion of professional players from country clubhouses and brought about a social revolution in American golf. He was also the first golfer to make a career out of playing full time. In 1921, Hagen became the first American-born golfer to win The PGA Championship. That next year, he became the first American to win the British Open.

Many of Hagen's golf clubs are on display at The PGA Historical Center.

More than any other tournament, The PGA Championship played to Hagen's strength. He was a brilliant match-play competitor, who could quickly shatter his opponent's confidence. Hagen was known to arrive at a tournament, walk to the first tee, and ask loudly enough for all his fellow competitors to hear, "I wonder who's going to take second?" After being told that his opponent, Leo Diegel, was in bed on the night before the final of the 1926 PGA Championship, Hagen is reported to have said, "Yes, but he isn't sleeping." Regrettably for Diegel, Hagen was right. He defeated Diegel, 5 and 3, for his fourth PGA title.

Hagen's dominance of The PGA began in 1921 at Inwood Country Club in Far Rockaway, New York. Jock Hutchison was the favorite, but his surprise defeat in the second round by the 19-year-old son of an immigrant Italian carpenter was the story of the week. Sarazen, who, like Hagen, was a former caddie, defeated the defending Champion, 8 and 6, thanks in part to a morning round that included seven birdies. Unfortunately, in

Walter Hagen says

"Every wide awake Professional I have talked to is cashing in on the matched club idea. It's the biggest thing that ever hit the Pro shop because the majority of the members of every club are using old sets consisting of mismated odds and ends. These members are all real live prospects for a set of high grade matched clubs.

"The Pros who are doing the biggest business are the Pros who demonstrate to their members that matched clubs are the proper thing by using a matched set themselves. Unless you are using a matched set yourself, you are doing your sales an injustice.

"I use a set of my matched models and know that it has helped us sell thousands of matched sets. Why not start using a set of Hagen matched irons and woods and boost your sales. I'm sure you'll like them."

Walter Hagen
GOLF EQUIPMENT
Made by **The L.A. YOUNG COMPANY**
DETROIT · · MICHIGAN

Hagen actively promoted equipment that bore his name.

HAGEN'S WILLOW TREE

Throughout the week of the 1921 PGA Championship at Inwood Country Club, Walter Hagen played the 17th hole by driving down the parallel 18th fairway to give himself an advantageous second shot. In his autobiography he described the strategy: "The green on the seventeenth was trapped on the short and left side, and almost at right angles to the line of play from the seventeenth fairway. If I played over onto the parallel eighteenth, I could open up the hole and come in from the right-hand side with my second shot." On the evening of the first day of the Championship, while the golfers were gathered in the men's grill, one of the officials argued that a tree should be planted there to thwart such an approach. After hearing this, Jack Mackie, the golf professional, and Morton Wild, a landscaper, uprooted a 15-foot weeping willow that they found in the woods next to the 16th fairway. They planted it to divide the two fairways. When he arrived on the tee the next day, Hagen quipped, "I never saw such fast-growing trees in my life." At that moment, the wind caught the wires that were holding the tree into place and the willow fell, opening up the 18th fairway to Hagen's drive. Fifty-eight years later, Lon Hinkle discovered a similar addition to the course after the first round of the 1979 U.S. Open at Inverness.

the quarterfinals, Sarazen lost his momentum and composure and fell to Cyril Walker, 5 and 4, largely because of what the *New York Times* described as a "corpulent" round of 80 in the morning. For Hagen, the quarterfinals against John Golden was a "terrific battle," mostly because Hagen was a little wild off the tee. But his "miraculous recoveries to the green" gave him the 8-and-7 victory.

The semifinals between Jim Barnes, who had won the U.S. Open by nine strokes over Hagen and Fred McLeod earlier that season, and Emmett French was halted in the afternoon because of a storm that delayed play. Greens that were "once covered with a velvet of grass" became, as the *New York Times* reported, "lakes and rivulets, seas and oceans." This interruption meant that many of the players had to complete 12 holes early the next morning before beginning the 36-hole final match. When Hagen offered Walker the option of postponing their match, Walker refused—to his detriment. Hagen won, 5 and 4.

In the 1921 final, Hagen closed the match on the 34th hole to win his first PGA title.

Gene Sarazen, posing with H. C. Fownes of The PGA of America, capitalized on Hagen's absence from the field to win his first PGA in 1922.

In the final, Barnes, who shot four rounds under 70 in his previous matches, was unable to best Hagen, who putted brilliantly. Hagen ended the match on the 34th hole, winning 3 and 2. The October issue of the *Professional Golfer of America* declared that "Walter Hagen won the 1921 PGA title because he played well-nigh unbeatable golf, not only once, but in practically every round. His golf was the kind which not only left few openings, but of such a deadly nature as to take advantage of nearly every slip on the part of his opponents."

Hagen could have defended his title the next year were it not for his previous commitments to play in a series of exhibition matches with Australian trick-shot artist Joe Kirkwood. Hagen's decision to bypass the 1922 PGA Championship illustrated the tenuous nature of professional golf in the early years. Players frequently made more money in exhibitions and from

product endorsements than from winning tournaments. Without Hagen, the 1922 PGA at Oakmont Country Club did not have a clear favorite, but it proved to be an exciting chase.

To accommodate the expansion of the field to 64 players, an extra round was added. The gallery paid $1 a day or $5 for the week for the privilege of watching Sarazen become the first player to capture the U.S. Open and PGA titles in the same year— a feat that has since only been matched by Ben Hogan in 1948, Jack Nicklaus in 1980, and Tiger Woods in 2000. The 6,707-yard course was a perfect venue for Sarazen because he knew the layout well. When he arrived, however, he reported a "definite anti-Sarazen" sentiment from the older British players because of his "unblushing remarks" to the press extolling his abilities. His reputation was not helped by the fact that he was several hours late for his first match.

It was a miracle that he made it at all. In *Golf Anecdotes,* author Robert Sommers details Sarazen's near miss. After playing in an exhibition match in Columbus, Ohio, on August 11, 1922, he settled into the hotel restaurant for a quiet dinner. A man who saw him through the window rushed in and demanded to know what Sarazen was doing in Columbus when he was supposed to be in Pittsburgh the next morning for the start of The PGA Championship. Sarazen had mixed up the dates. According to Sommers, Sarazen "raced to his room, piled his clothes in his bag, and sped to the station. He arrived as the train was pulling out, but he managed to leap onto one of the cars just in time." Because he was the reigning U.S. Open Champion, PGA officials allowed him to play even though he arrived late.

> "I DON'T CARE WHAT YOU SAY ABOUT ME. JUST SPELL THE NAME RIGHT."
> —GENE SARAZEN, 1922

In a rare head-to-head duel with Hagen in 1923, Sarazen triumphed in one of the Championship's most exciting final matches.

Sarazen, whom Grantland Rice nicknamed The Squire, spent most of the week proving that he was not full of hot air and was indeed the skilled shotmaker that he boasted to be. In his first two matches, he defeated Tom Mahan and Willie Ogg, but he faced a more formidable opponent in Memphis professional Frank Sprogell. Several of the other players, as Sarazen reported in his autobiography, who thought Sarazen too much the prima donna, "swarmed around Sprogell in the interval between rounds.

They watched over Frank's diet at lunch and limited him to one drink. They saw to it that Frank received a sprucing rubdown, and peppered him with tips and fight talks." All the preparation was for naught; Sprogell dropped nine holes in a row and handed Sarazen a 9-and-7 victory. In the quarterfinals, in front of a gallery estimated at 2,000, Sarazen barely nosed Jock Hutchison out with a 3-and-1 victory on the 35th hole. In the semifinals, he faced Bobby Cruickshank, whose unusual streak of wildness gave Sarazen a 3-and-2 victory. The biggest surprise of the week came in the second round when Johnny Farrell defeated Jim Barnes, the 1916 and 1919 PGA Champion, 1-up. But Farrell's celebrations were short-lived. He fell to Tom Kerrigan, 4 and 3, in the third round.

In the final, Sarazen faced Emmett French, a professional from Youngstown Country Club and his roommate during the tournament. Without particularly

Hagen, far left, shown here with officials, players, and club members, won his first of four in a row at French Lick Springs in 1924.

spectacular play from either golfer, Sarazen defeated French with his putter. He remembered in his autobiography that his 4-and-3 victory was the result of "one of those days when the line to the hole stood out as clearly as if it had been chalked onto the grass." Sarazen one-putted 13 greens; he putted more than twice on only one hole. After winning the match on the 33rd hole, the fans lifted Sarazen on their shoulders and carried him to the clubhouse. Upon receiving the $500 first-place check, Sarazen presented his caddie, Harry Mellon, with a crisp $100 bill.

> "IT SEEMS THAT IT NEVER WILL BE SAFE TO COUNT HAGEN OUT WHEN HE IS PLAYING FOR MONEY, MARBLES, OR GLORY."
> —GOULD B. MARTIN, 1925

Born Eugenio Saraceni in 1902, the same year as Bobby Jones, Sarazen's boldness on the course served him well. He learned to play golf only by pure happenstance. In 1916, he worked briefly at the Remington factory in Bridgeport, Connecticut, until he was diagnosed with pneumonia and had surgery to drain fluid from his lungs. His physicians told him to avoid factory work and find a job that allowed him to spend time outdoors; golf was the perfect alternative. At the 1922 PGA Championship he proved that he could defeat some of the best players in the game, but he remained eager to best Hagen. Sarazen idolized Hagen, but he also resented that Hagen called him "kid" and treated him as a young upstart. In his autobiography, Sarazen said he came to the 1923 PGA Championship wanting "Hagen to respect me as a champion and his equal."

In 1923, Sarazen finally had the opportunity to face Hagen at Pelham Golf Club in New York in what proved to be one of The PGA Championship's most exciting finals, made more so by Hagen's uncharacteristic show of nerves. Arriving at Pelham determined to reclaim his golfing crown, Hagen had been humbled by his loss to Sarazen in the Unofficial World's Championship in 1922. Sarazen came, having been labeled by sports writer Grantland Rice as a

INTO THE CLUBHOUSE

In *Thirty Years of Championship Golf,* Gene Sarazen described how Walter Hagen transformed professional golf: "Before Hagen broke down the walls of prejudice, a professional golfer had no standing whatsoever. In England, which set the example for our country-club conduct, professionals were not allowed to enter the clubhouse by the front door. Walter believed that he was just as good as anybody else, and defied the snobs to pigeonhole him as a lower-caste nuisance. He made his point on his first trip across in 1920. He traveled in high style with a secretary-manager. He made the Ritz his London headquarters. When he was not allowed to enter the dining room of the clubs where he was playing, he had a picnic lunch served to him with conspicuous ceremony by the footman who rode in his rented Rolls Royce. When such unheard-of deportment came to the attention of Lord Northcliffe, the owner of *The Times,* he sent a reporter to interview Hagen, with instructions to put that American in his place. Hagen met the reporter in his suite at the Ritz, glowing like a maharajah in his expensive purple dressing gown. He made sense, and he was charming. The interviewer reported back to Northcliffe that any story he wrote about Hagen would have to be a complimentary one. That was the opening wedge in the new respect Hagen compelled the public to have for the men in his profession."

"flash-in-the-pan whose luck had run out." He had failed to qualify for the British Open, and he lost both the Southern Open and U.S. Open titles earlier that year. So frustrated was he by his inglorious performances that he confessed, "I wouldn't have entered the PGA, the way I was playing, had I not been the defending champion."

Despite his misgivings, Sarazen arrived at Pelham with popular support, ready to "carve his way to the final bracket." After winning his first two matches, 8 and 7 against Lloyd Gullickson and 11 and 10 over D. K. White, Sarazen battled against Alec Campbell in the tough third-round match, which he won, 3 and 2. He then faced the 1916 and 1919 PGA Champion in the quarterfinals. Jim Barnes had a chance to win until the afternoon round, when a police officer stepped on his ball. But the former Champion was sympathetic about the error in an interview afterwards: "The poor guy couldn't help it. He was helping to marshal the gallery. I was told about it too late." After a grueling 35 holes the match was all square. Sarazen's birdie on the 36th gave him a 1-up victory.

Jim Barnes studying his putt in 1923 with an unidentified spectator and Walter Hagen looking on.

With the confidence that came from beating Barnes on his home course, Sarazen defeated Bobby Cruickshank, 7 and 5, in the semifinals. The week before the Championship, a hitchhiker had broken Cruickshank's nose, and Sidoine Jourdan of *Golfers Magazine* declared that "he could not sink his putts in a manner anything like his deadly green work at Inwood, where he tied Bobby Jones for the Open title [but lost in the playoff]." Sarazen's victory meant that he would face Hagen in the final.

But the fight put up by Walter was not enough to edge out Sarazen. In *Thirty Years of Championship Golf,* Sarazen wrote that he turned Hagen's old tricks against him. "Early in the final of the PGA, I nettled Walter by letting him have a taste of his own medicine. On one hole where there was little if any distance between our drives, I pulled my mid-iron from my bag. Walter was away, and remarking my selection, played a mid-iron himself. He hit a fine shot on line all the way, and glowered unhappily when it fell a full 20 yards short of the green. I took my brassie, which I knew was the club from the beginning, put my ball on the carpet, and picked up that hole."

Sarazen's deception might explain Hagen's testiness on the afternoon's sixth hole. On his second shot, Sarazen's ball came to rest on a trampled patch of ground between two green-high bunkers, and Hagen's landed on the green, a dozen yards from the hole. A leaf covered Sarazen's ball, and Warren Wood, the rules official, mistakenly declared that Sarazen was permitted to move it. Hagen disputed that decision, barking that Sarazen had "been around long enough to know the rules." Seething over the insinuation that he had cheated, Sarazen chipped onto the green, but lost the hole. At the turn, Sarazen said to sports writer O. B. Keeler, who witnessed the incident, "Walter had no business to show me up in front of the gallery. I'll give him a licking for that."

The players were all square after 36 holes, sending the match into "sudden death" extra holes for the first time in The PGA

Hagen helped make professional golfers respected competitors.

Hagen married Edna Crosby Strauss on April 30, 1923.

Championship's short history. The 37th hole was halved, and the match almost ended on the tee shots at the 38th when the official declared Sarazen's drive out of bounds. After Sarazen hit a provisional ball, his first one was found just inside the fence. In his autobiography, Hagen remarked, "I never to this day doubted that such luck *could* happen, but having Gene's ball jump back through the fence and be found teed up could have resulted only from the hand of the good Lord or one of the red-sweatered caddies roaming the course." Surrounded by the gallery, Sarazen was heard saying: "I'll put this one up so close to the hole that it will break Walter's heart." When his second shot came to rest two feet from the hole, he knew he had made a certain birdie and one of the best shots of his career. Hagen's pitch from the bunker failed to hole out by a few inches, and he lost the hole and the match.

Although Sarazen would never equal Hagen's record in The PGA Championship, he certainly stymied Hagen's complete dominance of the event in the 1920s.

Hagen returned to The PGA in 1924 at French Lick Springs in Indiana, having recently won his second British Open title over Ernest Whitcombe at Hoylake. In what proved to be an exciting series of upsets, many of the favorites were defeated in the first or second rounds, meaning that another hoped-for formidable duel between Hagen and Sarazen never materialized. Sarazen was eliminated in the second round, 2 and 1, on the 35th green by Larry Nabholtz, who played some of the best golf of his career. In that same round, Ray Derr, in what one sports writer called "a bolt from the blue sky," defeated Bobby Cruickshank, 2 and 1.

Hagen easily defeated Tom Harmon, Al Watrous, Johnny Farrell, and Derr, only to face his old rival, Jim Barnes, in the final. Barnes was defeated by his own putting, a problem that had nearly lost him the semifinals against Nabholtz the day before. The 33rd hole proved to be Barnes' undoing. His tee shot was 30 yards behind Hagen's, and he was 20 yards short of the green on the second shot, taking a five on the hole. On the 36th hole, Barnes pulled his drive behind an oak tree and

> "BEYOND A DOUBT WALTER IS THE MASTER OF THE MAN-TO-MAN STRUGGLE FORM OF COMPETITION IN THE REALM OF GOLF."
> —INNIS BROWN, 1926

At French Lick Springs Golf Club in 1924, Hagen defeated Barnes with a red-hot putter.

Olympia Fields near Chicago hosted the PGA Championship in 1925 and 1961.

shanked his mashie niblick into the rough. Hagen took an easy four, and won, 2-up. Hagen's victory suggested, at least for the time being, that, as P. C. Pulver of the *Professional Golfer of America* remarked, "the seasoned golfer is more dangerous in the long run than the flashy youngster."

Hagen entered the 1925 PGA Championship with a dismal year behind him: he had not won a single event. But he came to Olympia Fields Country Club, near Chicago, to prove that he was still the one to watch. Although exempt from the regional qualifying rounds, Hagen still had to qualify on-site. After shooting a mediocre 75-76, it became clear that he was off to a shaky start. So was Sarazen, who was eliminated, 8 and 7, in the first match by Jack Burke Sr.

Hagen faced Al Watrous, the week's low qualifier, in the first round and beat him on the 39th hole. In the afternoon, he played what Gould B. Martin in the *Metropolitan Golfer* called the "greatest golf shot ever executed." After hitting his drive into the woods on the fifth hole, Hagen used his mashie (the equivalent of a 5-iron) and hooked around a tree "within a hair's-breadth of the thick trunk and complete disaster." The ball cleared the trees and landed on the green, 40 feet from the hole. He made the putt for birdie. Locked in a close match, Hagen used his old bag of tricks to win. On the 34th hole, he gently hit the ball off the neck of his mashie to confuse the Grand Rapids professional. Watrous, who keenly observed his club selection, gave the same club a full swing, overshot the green, and lost the hole by a stroke.

Hagen went on to defeat Mike Brady, 7 and 6, in the shortest match of the day and then Leo Diegel, 1-up, in the quarterfinals in one of the longest. After playing 40 holes to win, Hagen declared that he had never been so near defeat in a championship that finally resulted in victory. Toward the end of the final hole, Diegel reportedly said to fellow competitor "Wild Bill" Mehlhorn, "I never want to play him again; he's killing me." In the semifinals, Hagen defeated Harry Cooper, 3 and 1.

For the final, Hagen played his usual trick of keeping his opponent waiting on the tee. But Mehlhorn was prepared and joked that he had not expected Hagen "for another hour." Stung by the remark, the Haig stepped up to the first tee on the No. 4 course and, without a practice swing, eagled the 515-yard first hole and birdied the second. Jim Barnes declared it "one of the most outrageous (that's the only word for it) extravaganzas of miss and click ever wreaked upon an unsuspecting enemy." Hagen won the match and the Championship, 6 and 5, on the 31st hole.

Margaret Seaton Heck, co-author of *The Walter Hagen Story*, recalled that Hagen's antics were not just reserved for the golf course that year. When the evening's celebrations finally ended around three o'clock in the morning, Hagen mistakenly entered the wrong guest cottage and terrified an elderly woman in her bathrobe. After hurriedly apologizing and explaining how the libations had clouded his judgment, the woman responded: "You've had a hard day. I followed you during the entire Championship."

Hagen beat Leo Diegel in the 1926 final, 5 and 3.

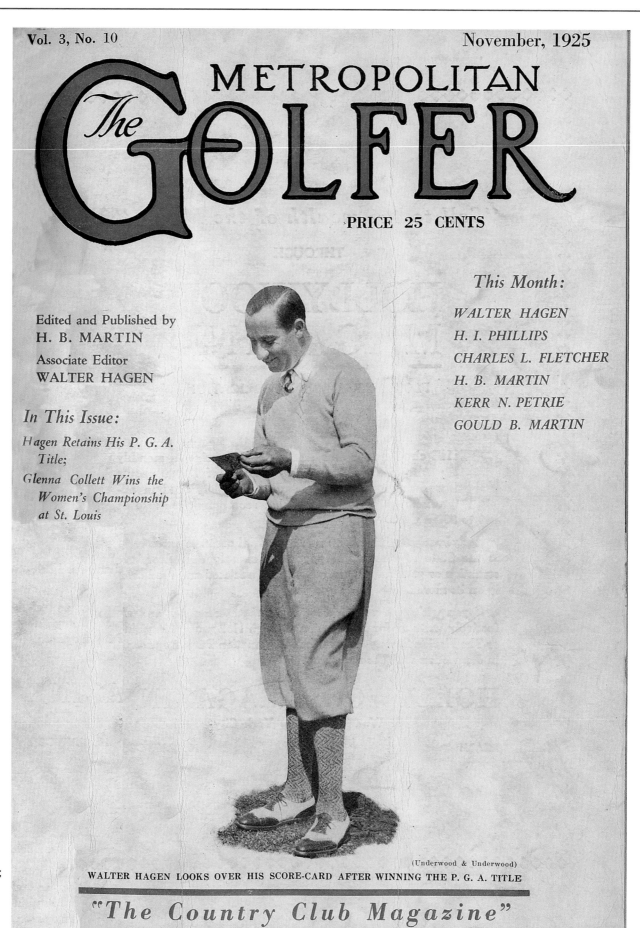

Vol. 3, No. 10   November, 1925

METROPOLITAN
The GOLFER

PRICE 25 CENTS

Edited and Published by
H. B. MARTIN

Associate Editor
WALTER HAGEN

In This Issue:

Hagen Retains His P. G. A. Title;

Glenna Collett Wins the Women's Championship at St. Louis

This Month:

WALTER HAGEN

H. I. PHILLIPS

CHARLES L. FLETCHER

H. B. MARTIN

KERR N. PETRIE

GOULD B. MARTIN

(Underwood & Underwood)

WALTER HAGEN LOOKS OVER HIS SCORE-CARD AFTER WINNING THE P. G. A. TITLE

"The Country Club Magazine"

Hagen, always a tough match-play competitor, began the 1925 final with an eagle on the opening hole.

After settling him on the couch she declared: "Now what you need is a good stiff nightcap. Then we'll sit here and talk over some of those fine shots you played today." They did, and Hagen left early the next morning.

On the No. 4 course at Salisbury Golf Links on Long Island, New York, in 1926, Hagen became the first golfer in the history of The PGA Championship to reach the final for four consecutive years. Sarazen, the one player who had defeated Hagen in The PGA Championship finals, never had the opportunity to face him. In the first round, Sarazen beat Jim Barnes, 5 and 4, after playing an "unbeatable brand of golf." After advancing to the second round, Sarazen was defeated by

> "HAGEN IS A GREAT BELIEVER IN HAGEN."
> —*NEW YORK TIMES,* 1927

New Jersey professional John Golden, 4 and 3, making it the third year in a row that he lost a match in the first or second round. Hagen easily defeated Joe Turnesa in the first round, Dick Grout in the second, and Pat Doyle in the third. He won the semifinals against Johnny Farrell, 6 and 5.

Although Diegel's play was impressive in his first four matches, he was less confident when he faced Hagen in the final. Clearly suffering from exhaustion, Diegel played an uneven match. On the 16th hole, Hagen's 35-foot putt stopped on the edge of the cup. When Diegel bent over the ball, it fell in. Regrettably, he did not have the same luck with his own ball as he missed his putt. He regained his composure on the final hole of the morning round, but was 2-down to Hagen at lunch. The first hole of the afternoon, though, proved to be Diegel's undoing when his second shot with a brassie skipped over the green and his ball stopped on the road, landing under a car. The car was removed, only to reveal Diegel's ball embedded in a deep wheel rut. He conceded the hole after trying to hit the ball three times. After 27 holes, he was still 2-down. On the 33rd hole, Diegel carded a six, handing Hagen a 5-and-3 victory.

Hagen defended his title in 1927 at The PGA Championship's first visit to the South, but his preparation for the tournament had been hampered by his business and personal ventures. In *Sir Walter and Mr. Jones: Walter Hagen, Bobby Jones, and the Rise of American Golf,* Stephen Lowe claimed that Hagen's purchase of a minor league baseball club, the Rochester Tribe, and his love of bass fishing distracted him from practicing much that summer. Out of shape and aware of the odds against him, he decided to "rest his oars." At the last minute, though, he changed his mind, bought a new set of clubs, and arrived in Dallas by train in time to play one practice round. Hagen explained his change of heart: "All of a sudden it dawned on me that unless I defended my title whoever won would not get the credit he would have coming to him. Many would say: 'Well, if Hagen had been there, it would

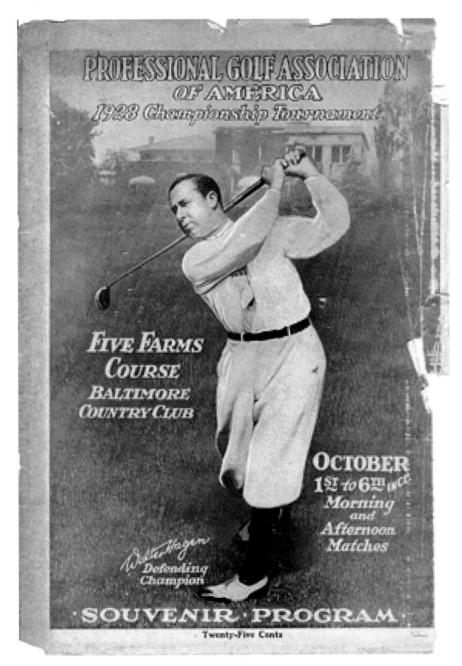

PROFESSIONAL GOLF ASSOCIATION OF AMERICA
1928 Championship Tournament

FIVE FARMS COURSE
BALTIMORE COUNTRY CLUB

OCTOBER 1ST to 6TH INCL.
Morning and Afternoon Matches

Walter Hagen
Defending Champion

SOUVENIR · PROGRAM
Twenty-Five Cents

On two consecutive holes during the 1929 final, Johnny Farrell, left, knocked Diegel's ball into the hole trying to overcome stymies.

have been different.' I knew my chances of winning a fourth straight PGA were slight, considering my lack of practice, but once I got that idea into my head I knew I'd have to go."

In the first round of the 1927 PGA Championship at Cedar Crest Country Club in Dallas, Tommy Armour defeated Johnny Farrell, 4 and 3. Sarazen was forced to play one extra hole to beat J. G. Curley, a New England professional who had barely qualified. Hagen's match against Jack Farrell, the most thrilling of the day, was reported as a "narrow escape." The defending Champion was 4-down in the morning in what appeared to be certain defeat. In the afternoon, Hagen turned things around by shooting under par, ultimately winning, 3 and 2. Hagen's flawless second-round match gave him an 11-and-10 victory over Tony Manero. In the other second-round matches, Sarazen defeated Ed Dudley, 4 and 3, and Joe Turnesa bested Willie Klein,

1-up, leaving the sons of Italian immigrants matched together the next day. In the third round, Joe Turnesa putted his way to a 3-and-2 victory over Sarazen. In front of huge crowds, Hagen battled Armour for his 4-and-3 win. In his autobiography, Hagen recounted an unusual coincidence. Squinting into the sunshine, he remarked loudly that "this is one time I wish I had a cap." A 15-year-old boy stepped forward and offered "a baseball type, peanut-sized cap with his school insigne on the bill." After playing the hole, Hagen walked over to thank the young boy, who introduced himself as Byron Nelson.

> "WHEN A MAN HAS TO MEET ON SUCCESSIVE DAYS HAGEN, SARAZEN, AND ESPINOSA, AS DIEGEL HAD TO DO, HE EARNS WHATEVER HE GETS."
> —WILLIAM D. RICHARDSON, 1928

Facing page: Leo Diegel, putting, beat Hagen in the quarterfinals in 1928, making it Hagen's first loss in five years at The PGA.

In the semifinals, Turnesa handily defeated John Golden, 7 and 6. Hagen, though, did not enjoy an easy ride to the final bracket. After a close round, he found himself 1-down on the final hole of the afternoon, having just overshot the green. Al Espinosa's second shot put his ball 25 feet from the cup, leaving the crowd to assume that the defending Champion would have to concede the title. After hitting a perfect chip shot, Hagen took a four on the hole, leaving Espinosa two putts for victory. Throughout the round, Hagen had conceded all of Espinosa's putts within three feet. After Espinosa's birdie attempt left him three feet short, he turned to Hagen for the signal. But Hagen smiled, turned his back, and began talking with the gallery. Clearly shaken by the rebuff, Espinosa missed, forcing the match into extra holes. On the 37th hole, Espinosa three-putted and Hagen won the match. Walking off the green, he remarked, "You give these boys a chance, and they don't take it."

In the final, Hagen was 2-down at the end of the morning round. After lunch, Joe Turnesa's margin of victory disappeared, and on the 29th hole Hagen birdied to tie the match. On the last six holes Turnesa missed a series of short, easy putts and handed Hagen the match, 1-up. With the win, Hagen

Leo Diegel blasting out of a bunker during the 1928 Championship.

had played in six PGA Championships and lost only one match out of thirty. But his antics off the golf course periodically crept onto the course. In a 1986 article for *Golf Digest*, Ross Goodner recounted this story from the 1927 awards ceremony. Hagen apparently asked PGA President Alex Pirie to give him the first-place check in the basement of Cedar Crest so he "could dodge a couple of gentlemen who were upstairs waiting to attach his winnings for alimony payments."

Hagen's 1927 victory at Cedar Crest gave him his fifth PGA Championship title—his fourth straight win in the same major, to match Tom Morris Jr.'s record in the British Open. Surprised as anyone to have won, Hagen quipped, "I didn't win it. They tossed it to me. What's a guy going to do? A lot of them had me on the ropes."

Leo Diegel's unorthodox putting stroke finally ended Hagen's string of 22 victories in The PGA Championship. Diegel suffered from a severe bout of the yips and, although a frequent contender in major championships, often succumbed to his nerves. To combat his anxiety on the course, he developed his unusual putting style that became known as "diegeling." Diegel was aware of how ridiculous his method appeared, but he always believed it worked. It was successful enough to dethrone Hagen. But Hagen was not anxious to be dethroned or even play. When he failed to appear at the practice rounds, PGA of America officials found him playing exhibition matches in Pennsylvania and sent him a telegram that convinced him to come to Baltimore.

THE 1922 PGA CHAMPIONSHIP, CONTINUED

After Gene Sarazen won the 1922 PGA Championship in which Walter Hagen failed to appear and defend his title, the Unofficial World's Championship was organized to determine who was the better golfer. Both men were interested in the $3,000 prize money, six times the amount Sarazen had won in August at the Championship. Two weeks before the event, Hagen had two pairs of golf hose custom-made with "The Haig" knitted on them. Sarazen, determined not to be outdone by Hagen's antics, ordered two new golf suits and announced that he would discard them after the event. The first

36 holes were played at Oakmont Country Club near Pittsburgh on October 6, and the second 36 were played the next day at the Westchester-Biltmore Country Club in Rye, New York. On the first day, Hagen arrived a half-hour late, and at the end of 36 holes, he was 2-up. Never missing an opportunity to play a joke, Hagen sent Sarazen a package that contained a garish orange and white tie and a note, supposedly from a girl who had been watching the match from the gallery, that read: "Dear Gene, You are my ideal golfer and a clever little fellow. I am sending you this beautiful tie and hope you will wear it when you play Walter Hagen. If you do, you will win." Gene wore the tie the next day, and, unaware of the joke, said to Hagen, "You think you've got all the dames on your side, but you haven't." But Hagen's joke backfired; Sarazen won the match, 3 and 2. Sarazen, however, did not have much time to savor his victory. He was stricken with appendicitis after the round and was rushed to St. Luke's Riverside Hospital in Yonkers for emergency surgery.

At the Five Farms Course at Baltimore Country Club, most of the favorites won in the first round of the 1928 Championship. In the second round, Hagen and Diegel defeated unknowns Julian Blanton and George Christ, 2-up and 6 and 4, respectively. Horton Smith, playing in his first PGA Championship, defeated Willie MacFarlane, 1-up, and Sarazen defeated his old rival, Jim Barnes, 3 and 2. Diegel entered the quarterfinals determined to avenge his winless streak against Hagen. Writing for the *Metropolitan Golfer*, Bob Harlow declared that "Hagen tossed the match away on the first nine holes of the day when he went five down. Diegel's 2-and-1 win ended the longest match play reign in the history of The PGA Championship."

Diegel's victory disappointed spectators and sports writers, who had hoped to see Sarazen and Hagen replay their thrilling finish from the 1923 Championship. It was not to be. In the semifinals, Al Espinosa easily defeated the boyish Horton Smith, 6 and 5, and Sarazen lost to Diegel, 9 and 8. Espinosa began the final match against Diegel by winning the first two holes in the morning, but his three-putt on the third hole made him green-shy for the rest of the match. Diegel did not win, 6 and 5, as much as Espinosa lost when his skill with the putter seemed to desert him. The new Champion was as gracious in victory as he had been in defeat. When The PGA of America offered him the opportunity to captain the Ryder Cup, he responded, "I think Walter is the better man for the job."

Although Diegel won the 1928 PGA Championship, he was not given the Wanamaker Trophy. It appears that after winning the PGA in 1925, Hagen gave the trophy to a cab driver and instructed him to deliver the cup to the hotel. It never arrived. Hagen won the event for the next two years, and in 1928, when asked by The PGA of America about the location of the cup, he replied, "I can't remember. I might have left it in a cab." The PGA thus presented Diegel with a substitute. In 1930, a porter cleaning the cellar of L. A. Young and Company, the firm that manufactured clubs bearing Hagen's name, found the Wanamaker Trophy in an unmarked case. Yet even without the real trophy, the victory was sweet for Diegel. A year later, he would have yet another opportunity to test his newfound approach against Hagen, now the reigning British Open champion.

Hagen came to the 1929 PGA Championship at Hillcrest

> "THE END OF HAGEN'S LONG REIGN AS PROFESSIONAL KING WAS THE BIGGEST PIECE OF DRAMA IN THE TOURNAMENT."
> —BOB HARLOW, 1928

Country Club in Los Angeles in December having recently won the British Open at Muirfield and hoping to gain back the PGA title he had lost in 1928. Most of the favorites won in the first two matches. In the quarterfinals, Diegel defeated Sarazen, 3 and 2, meaning that he faced Hagen in the semifinals. Although Hagen proved a formidable opponent, Diegel was more composed than he had been in previous tournaments. Hagen played around par all day, but could not best Diegel, who defeated him, 3 and 2, on the 34th hole. This loss started a losing streak that would plague Hagen throughout the 1930s. In contrast to his record the decade before, he played in five first-round matches in The PGA Championship in the 1930s and lost them all.

Diegel faced Johnny Farrell in the final, and neither player performed well. Farrell was 1-up following the 18th hole, but Diegel squared the match on the 19th hole and frustrated Farrell for the next eight holes with some well-placed stymies. On the 27th green, Diegel's ball blocked Farrell's five-foot putt. When Farrell tried to negotiate around the stymie, he knocked Diegel's ball into the cup and lost the hole. He repeated the maneuver with the same result on the next hole and found himself 3-down. Diegel ultimately won on the 32nd hole, 6 and 4, becoming only the fourth player to successfully defend his PGA title. At the end of the round, Diegel declared, "I'm just a very lucky boy. Johnny putted for me a couple of times and I guess that was the match."

Tommy Armour, the "Silver Scot," won the 1930 PGA Championship, making him the first foreign-born winner since Jock Hutchison a decade earlier. Armour's first major victory came when he won the 1927 U.S. Open at Oakmont Country Club. In 1926, he played for the U.S. team in a precursor to the Ryder Cup after he had become a naturalized U.S. citizen. After capturing The PGA in 1930, he would go on to win the British Open at Carnoustie the next year.

Armour came to Fresh Meadows Country Club in Flushing, New York, facing 31 players who had secured spots at the 36-hole qualifier. Hagen, Barnes, and Hutchison were not among them because they had all failed to qualify on the Monday before the first match. Diegel, who dominated the previous two PGA Championships, would not play a leading role in the 1930 event either; he was defeated in the second round by Harold Sampson at the 38th hole.

In front of a smaller crowd than anticipated, Armour's spectacular iron play easily defeated Dave Hackney, 11 and 10, and Bob Shave, 7 and 5, in the first two rounds. Armour faced Farrell in the quarterfinals. After losing five of the first six holes, he mounted an incredible comeback and won the match, 2 and 1. In the semifinals, Armour entered into a close contest against a young English professional named Charles Lacey, but won 1-up. Sarazen, the Fresh Meadows professional described as "the most dangerous man in the field," narrowly defeated Charles Schneider in the first round, 1-up, with a great recovery shot out of the rough. He had a much easier time with Bob Crowley, 7 and 6, Al Espinosa, 2 and 1, and Joe Kirkwood, 5 and 4, on his way to the final bracket.

The final, broadcast by CBS for the first time on radio, featured Armour and Sarazen, two of the game's best players battling it out to the final holes. Diegel was asked to referee the match after being defeated in the second round. Neither player could secure much of a lead, and after the morning round Armour was 1-up. After 35 holes, the match was all square. On the 36th, the drama really began. Sarazen hooked his tee shot and put his second shot in a bunker; Armour hit the fairway

Tommy Armour turned professional in 1924 and won three majors, including the 1930 PGA at Fresh Meadows Country Club.

and followed his opponent into the bunker with his second shot. Out of the bunker, Sarazen's ball landed 10 feet past the hole while Armour's was 12 feet away. Distracted by a photographer, Armour backed off his ball, regained his composure, and made his putt. He won, 1-up, and surprised Sarazen because Armour was not known for his skill on the greens. Gracious to the end, Sarazen declared, "I don't know anyone I would rather lose to, if I had to lose, than my friend Thomas Armour." Many years later, Armour would tease Sarazen about the match: "We came to the last hole and both of us topped our tee shots like 24-handicappers. I know Gene would love to forget it, and I always enjoy reminding him of it."

Although they did not win every year, Hagen and Sarazen dominated the 1920s. Sarazen would contend throughout the 1930s and win once more in 1933 at Blue Mound Country Club in Milwaukee. Hagen played in his last PGA Championship in 1940. Five years earlier, in 1935 at Twin Hills Country Club in Oklahoma City, he looked like the Hagen of old. After leading all qualifiers with a 139, at the age of 43, he lost to Johnny Revolta, 1-down, in the first round. Sanguine to the end, he invited Revolta into the clubhouse and offered to buy him a drink, signaling his willingness to pass the torch to the next generation.

CHAPTER THREE

GOLF'S GOLDEN FLEECE

On July 9, 1939, before the first 18-hole qualifying round of The PGA Championship, the players went on strike for the first time in the history of the majors to protest the disqualification of Denny Shute from the year's competition. Apparently Shute's registration card for the Championship arrived at PGA headquarters two days after the May 20 deadline. Tom Walsh, the PGA secretary, explained, "The association is pretty strict about the regulations, so through his own oversight he was out of the PGA meet unless he could win the national open." Not intending to delay the $35 payment, Shute explained that he was unemployed and, without a permanent address, his mail did not reach him promptly. Incensed by The PGA's high-handedness, 51 players sent a petition to PGA President George Jacobus insisting that Shute be permitted to compete. Thus began a controversy that raged on and off golf courses for the next several weeks.

Jacobus submitted an appeal on Shute's behalf and recommended to the executive committee that Shute be allowed to participate. The committee voted by mail against the concession, and Walsh went so far as to declare that Shute's inclusion would make the Championship illegal. The players submitted a second petition, reminding The PGA of the importance of having players of Shute's stature in the field for the benefit of fans and sponsors. Again, the committee refused to make an exception, but it allowed Shute to attempt to qualify, pending further discussion. He calmly shot a 143, placing him in a tie for 23rd place.

Realizing that the bad publicity was jeopardizing the event and alienating the host club, Jacobus boldly declared that he would "take full responsibility for including Denny's name in the draw." Shute was included, and the "revolt at Pomonok" ended.

> "FROM THE BUNKERED FAIRWAYS OF EVERY SECTION OF THE NATION THERE WILL ASSEMBLE . . . THE COUNTRY'S FOREMOST PROFESSIONAL GOLFERS IN QUEST OF WHAT IS TO THEM THE GAME'S GOLDEN FLEECE, THE PGA NATIONAL CHAMPIONSHIP, NOW RECOGNIZED AS THE SUPREME REWARD OF SKILL AND ENDURANCE IN THE ANCIENT GAME."
> —FRED CORCORAN, 1939

Facing page: Tommy Armour defeated Gene Sarazen in the final in 1930 in a match that was refereed by Leo Diegel.

BRINGING THE EVENT TO THE WORLD

Preparations for the 14th PGA Championship in 1931 at Wannamoisett Country Club in Rhode Island exceeded anything the organizers had ever seen. The club's history, published in 1948, offered details. A gigantic pressroom, erected on an indoor tennis court, featured 50 telegraph wires that connected to every major American city and a few abroad. A complete 80-line telephone system, including seven field lines, was installed. A mammoth scoreboard was placed near the tennis courts, and the players' scores were updated every three holes. Tickets, circulars, scorecards, posters, and programs were printed, and the club purchased and cleared surrounding lots to make way for parking. Over 100 caddies were recruited from neighboring clubs, and the top 20 were given the opportunity to select the player they preferred. Twenty thousand people were expected to pay $2 to attend the daily matches. To control crowds, members of the 103rd Artillery roped off the greens, and amateur and professional golfers from Rhode Island, who served as marshals, used bamboo poles to keep the spectators off the fairways.

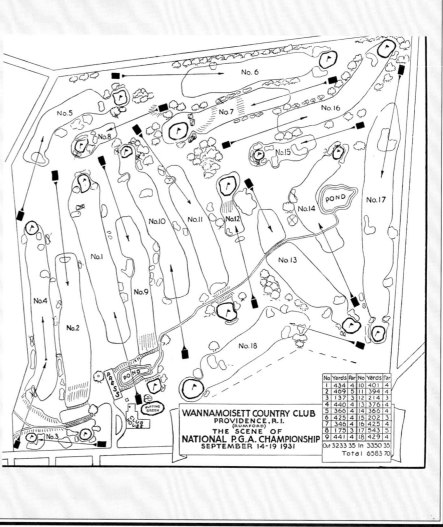

WANNAMOISETT COUNTRY CLUB
PROVIDENCE, R.I.
(RUMFORD)
THE SCENE OF
NATIONAL P.G.A. CHAMPIONSHIP
SEPTEMBER 14-19 1931

No	Yards	Par	No	Yards	Par
1	434	4	10	401	4
2	469	5	11	394	4
3	137	3	12	214	3
4	440	4	13	376	4
5	366	4	14	366	4
6	425	4	15	202	3
7	346	4	16	425	4
8	175	3	17	543	5
9	441	4	18	429	4
Out	3233	35	In	3350	35
			Total	6583	70

The Shute controversy illustrated the problems professional golfers faced during the Depression. The winners of The PGA Championship in the 1930s were journeymen, mainly club professionals who balanced tournament careers with their responsibilities at golf courses. Only a handful of players gained enough prominence to negotiate time off to play in exhibitions and tournaments. Competing in PGA-sponsored events was at best a part-time occupation, and the unemployed Shute faced a very tenuous situation. As Sam Snead quipped in his autobiography, "In the thirties, every poorhouse had its resident golf pro."

The Shute incident was important for a second reason. In the petition to Jacobus, the players declared that The PGA Championship "is a tournament for the members and by the members of the Association." This newly emboldened attitude reflected the players' growing clout and their willingness to assert it when it really mattered. This issue would make headlines again during the 1967, 1968, and 1969 PGA Championships and change golf forever. In 1939, though, the players simply wanted to act in the interest of fair play. But the decade began on a different note.

Six men dominated the first 13 years of The PGA Championship. In the next 13 years, there were 11 different Champions. As a result of the growing financial crisis in the nation, professional golf suffered a decade-long decline, mostly because no charismatic player emerged to replace Walter Hagen. But Hagen was not content to ride off into the sunset yet. On the first day of the 1931 PGA Championship at Wannamoisett Country Club, an impeccably attired Hagen strolled to the first tee, passed his fellow professionals, and asked aloud: "Which of you characters am I going to meet in the finals?" Unable to equal his good-natured boast, Hagen was defeated that September afternoon by Peter O'Hara. Earlier that week, O'Hara drew Hagen's name in a pool and was poised to win a lot of money. He then found himself matched with Hagen, and his 4-and-3 victory cost him the winnings.

The 1931 event was significant for several reasons. It was the first time The PGA Championship was played in New England. It also boasted two notable referees. Francis Ouimet, the first American to win the U.S. Open, in 1913, was asked to oversee the semifinals. PGA President Charles Hall person-

Tom Creavy became the first dark horse Champion in 1931.

ally invited Bobby Jones, who had retired from competitive golf after winning the Grand Slam the year before, to serve as a referee for the final match. Jones accepted and declared the duel between Tom Creavy and Denny Shute as "one of the finest matches ever played." The event was also important because the club announced that it would donate all the profits from the Championship to The PGA's Employment and Relief Fund to help those golfers suffering from the effects of the Depression.

Creavy receiving the Wanamaker Trophy in 1931 with Denny Shute looking on.

The first round became known among sports writers as the "slaughter of the champions," because some of the best-known names in the game—Hagen, Leo Diegel, Johnny Farrell, and Ed Dudley—were defeated. The favorites survived the second round, only to fall over the next two days. In the quarterfinals, defending Champion Tommy Armour lost to Shute, 3 and 1. In the semifinals, Gene Sarazen lost to Creavy, 5 and 3, and U.S. Open Champion Billy Burke lost to Shute, 1-down.

For the final, 5,000 fans came to see Creavy, a former caddie without a proven record, battle for the title against Shute. By the 30th hole, Creavy had Shute 4-down and seemed to have won the match. But Shute won the next three holes. It would not last; on the 35th hole Shute's first two shots landed in the rough, cost-

ing him a bogey and the match. Playing in his first national championship, Creavy, a 20-year-old professional from Tuckahoe, New York, stunned the golf world by defeating the 26-year-old Shute, 2 and 1. Creavy became the second-youngest winner of The PGA Championship, after Sarazen, who was just a few months younger when he won in 1922. Sadly, in 1942, Creavy contracted spinal meningitis and was not able to play golf again until 1949.

In 1932, and for the first time in the event's history, the Championship was played at a public facility. At the 6,686-yard Keller Golf Course in St. Paul, Minnesota, Olin Dutra captured his first major title. Despite the absence of Sarazen and Diegel, who both failed to qualify, the first round—played in 90-degree fleet coupled with a fierce west wind—signaled that it was going to be a difficult week. In the second-longest match in PGA Championship history, Hagen lost to Johnny Golden on the seventh extra hole in the first round. The lead alternated throughout the match until Golden's 10-foot putt on the 43rd hole finally gave him the victory. The Hagen-Golden battle was matched in intensity by the one between Bobby Cruickshank and Al Watrous. Watrous was 9-up on Cruickshank with 13 holes to play when he conceded a tough seven-foot downhill putt. Not one to pass

up an opportunity, Cruickshank won nine of the next 11 holes. On the 41st, he hit his shot from the rough and it landed within five feet of the hole. He made his putt for one of the Championship's greatest come-from-behind victories.

Creavy, the defending Champion, easily won his first three matches before losing to Frank Walsh in the semifinals. Despite being 8-down at lunch, Creavy tied the match on the 36th hole, but he missed a short putt on the 38th green, and Walsh won. Dutra's sub-par rounds throughout the week continued into the semifinals as he overcame Ed Dudley, 3 and 2. In the final, Walsh, who was still recovering from a fractured skull he suffered in an automobile accident the winter before, could not gain momentum on Dutra, who won, 4 and 3, on the 33rd hole. After six days and 196 holes, Dutra was 19 under par, making it one of the most extraordinary performances in the history of the Championship.

Sarazen arrived at the 1933 PGA Championship with just seven golf clubs in his bag and a lot of uncertainty about his game. His 1932 U.S. Open and British Open victories and a string of exhibition matches had nearly exhausted him. He was also frustrated by The PGA of America's last-minute decision to move the event from September to August, giving the members at Blue Mound less than five weeks to plan for the Championship. Sarazen initially planned to follow the lead of three Ryder Cup teammates—Hagen, Craig Wood, and Shute—who refused to attend because of previously scheduled exhibition matches, but he changed his mind and arrived barely in time for the practice rounds. To refresh his game, Sarazen rid his golf bag of those clubs that he felt he could not control. While his fellow competitors started the week with 15 to 20 clubs, according to *Blue Mound Golf and Country Club: Centennial History,*

Olin Dutra played 196 holes to win in 1932.

Eleven years after his first PGA victory, Sarazen defeated Willie Goggin to win in 1933.

1903–2003, Sarazen had only a driver, jigger (similar to a 4-iron), 4-wood, 5-iron, 7-iron, sand wedge, and putter. But Sarazen barely made it in the gate. When he and several other qualifiers forgot their badges, they were stopped by football players from nearby Marquette University who had been hired to work security and were instructed not to allow anyone to enter without the proper identification.

The only surprise in the first round was Leo Diegel's defeat by rookie Willie Goggin, the eventual runner-up, 4 and 3. In the second round, Johnny Farrell knocked Olin Dutra off the Championship throne, 1-up; Sarazen and Paul Runyan also advanced. In the quarterfinals against Ed Dudley, Sarazen showed that he was not the "washed up" golfer Tommy Armour declared him to be earlier in the week. Sarazen led through all 31 holes and would have had a larger margin of victory if Dudley had not placed three stymies in the afternoon. The match generated so much interest that Blue Mound hired additional policemen to keep motorists along Highway 100 from stopping to watch. In the semifinals, Goggin beat Jimmy Hines, 1-up, and Sarazen outplayed his old friend Farrell, 5 and 4. Sarazen and Farrell had known each other since they served as caddies together, but they had never competed against each other in a major championship. They were often partnered in exhibition matches, most notably in 1927 when they played for Benito Mussolini in Italy. In the final, Sarazen easily defeated Goggin, 5 and 4, on the 32nd hole. Armour, who had failed to qualify for the event

and criticized Sarazen earlier in the week, was invited to referee but declined. Upon being awarded $1,000 and the Wanamaker Trophy, Sarazen declared that he was glad to let "Armour eat his words."

The 1934 PGA Championship, played in July, returned to New York for the seventh time, at the Park Club of Buffalo, with Sarazen poised to defend his title. The players were grateful for the return to the Empire State, as one newspaper headline declared, "Nation Burns Up While Lake Erie Breezes Keep Buffalo Cool." The pleasant conditions did not inspire Sarazen, who nearly lost in the first round in a tight match against Herman Barron. Sarazen was 2-down after 27

> "CREAVY PLAYED WITH THE SKILL OF A CHAMPION AND COOL STEADINESS OF A VETERAN BEFORE A BIG CROWD THAT THUNDERED AROUND THE COURSE."
> —JOHN WALTER, 1953

holes, but won five of the next seven holes to take the match, 3 and 2. Hagen, Farrell, Billy Burke, and Diegel did not fare as well; they were all eliminated in the first round. Sarazen ran out of luck in the second round when he bogeyed the 33rd hole and lost the match to Al Watrous, 4 and 3. When Armour fell to Dick Metz, 3 and 2, the field was robbed of the only two former Champions. Denny Shute bested Al Houghton, Woodrow Wilson's former caddie, 6 and 5, in the quarterfinals. Paul Runyan, who weighed a mere 130 pounds, won over Dick Metz, 1-up. In the semifinals, Craig Wood played brilliantly against Shute to win, 2 and 1, avenging his loss to Shute at the 1933 British Open.

Runyan, known as "Little Poison," defeated Gene Kunes, 4 and 2.

The final pitted teacher against student. Four years earlier, Runyan had worked as Wood's assistant at Forest Hill Field Club in Bloomfield, New Jersey. Wood's length off the tee was matched by Runyan's skill on the green. The 38-hole final match, the longest since 1923, was officiated by PGA President George R. Jacobus, who declared the players "sportsmanlike and gentlemanly." The lead shifted back and forth all day. One reporter wrote that "it was one of those jousts in which the match was squared no less than eight times." Runyan dominated the greens with hands that had once been used to milk cows on his father's dairy farm in Hot Springs, Arkansas. On the final green, he made a $1,000 putt with an aluminum-headed putter to the cheers of 4,000 fans.

When the sun set on the 1934 PGA Championship, The PGA of America was still unsure about where it would host the 1935 event. Several months passed before Dorset Carter Sr. of Twin Hills Country Club in Oklahoma City stepped forward and presented The PGA with a $10,000 certified check. Because the Championship was scheduled for October, the club insured the event against thunderstorms, but the policy did not cover the blizzard-like conditions and 43-degree drop in temperature that plagued the final. The Championship would be hard fought, as

Sarazen ultimately captured three PGA titles in two different decades.

GENE HAD A LITTLE LAMB

Spectators were treated to an unusual sight at the 1934 PGA Championship at the Park Club of Buffalo. An avid fan arrived at the gate with two lambs for defending Champion Gene Sarazen. Apparently the giver hoped the pair would eventually end up at Sarazen's Connecticut farm. A bit surprised, Sarazen tied the lambs to a stake outside the first-aid tent, which he had commandeered for his sleeping quarters to escape the heat of his hotel room. After beating Herman Barron in the first round, Sarazen was eliminated in the second by Al Watrous. Historians can only speculate whether Sarazen took the lambs on the train with him to the farm.

the bracket was permanently increased from 32 to 64 players, requiring that the first two rounds of match play be reduced from 36 holes to 18 to accommodate the expanded field. In *The Wonderful World of Professional Golf,* Mark McCormack explained that this change "started the match-play format downhill" because "a lesser player with a hot hand has a much better chance in a shorter match."

Nearly all the favorites turned out to play in 1935, except for Olin Dutra, whose club duties prevented him from traveling from Los Angeles. The only surprise in the first round was Hagen's elimination. In the qualifier, that year's Ryder Cup captain opened with a three-under-par 67 and ended with a 72, leaving him three strokes ahead of his rivals. He did not fare as well in the Championship itself, losing in the first round to 24-year-old Johnny Revolta, 1-down. Defending Champion Paul Runyan,

wearing a brightly colored feather in his green hat, emerged victorious in his second- and third-round matches against Mortie Dutra and Tony Manero. Sarazen, who had come a week early to learn the layout of the course, fell in the second round in a stunning defeat to semiprofessional baseball player Alvin "Butch" Krueger, 2 and 1. Runyan was not far behind. The *New York Times* reported that Al Zimmerman sent Runyan's "crown spinning from his head," winning, 3 and 2, in the quarterfinals on a cold and rainy day in which the wind became the main opponent. Revolta, Armour, and Watrous also advanced. In the first half of the semifinals, Revolta beat Zimmerman, 4 and 3. Despite his 2-and-1 victory over Watrous, Armour's erratic play prompted him to declare, "I could play better golf than this when I was six years old."

Johnny Revolta, left, shown with PGA President George Jacobus, never once relinquished the lead to Tommy Armour in the 1935 final.

As the 1935 PGA Champion, Johnny Revolta won $1,000.

In the final, both Revolta and Armour struggled against a frigid wind. Revolta birdied the first hole and kept control of the morning's match. Armour was more successful in the afternoon, but he could not beat Revolta on the greens. Herb Graffis declared, "The ravioli hangs high, for Revolta's putter was hotter than Latin love." He averaged 1.6 putts per green, good enough for a 5-and-4 victory, a $1,000 check, and his first and only major championship. Bob Harlow, the founder of *Golf World*, wrote, "All year they've been calling Revolta an up and coming player. He's up but not coming. He's here!"

The 1936 PGA Championship was delayed until November to give Pinehurst Country Club in North Carolina a chance to convert the greens from sand to grass. The event was to be held on the venerable No. 2 Course, designed by Donald Ross in 1903. Several big-name players did not qualify out of a field of 117, including Hagen, whose 157 failed to secure him a spot. Diegel,

Sam Parks Jr., and Byron Nelson also missed qualifying. Sarazen, who was on his way to Japan and China after winning the Australian Open, sent a telegram dated November 6 to inform The PGA that he had changed his travel plans and would participate. Regrettably, many of the former Champions who were on hand failed to make their way to the final bracket, prompting Chicago sports writer Charles Bartlett to report, "The captains and the kings departed . . . but the shouting has not died." In the first round, Sarazen, Armour, and Runyan, all former PGA Champions, were defeated. In the second round, Jug McSpaden beat reigning PGA Champion Revolta at the first extra hole.

Many of the favorites advanced in the third round. In the quarterfinals, U.S. Open Champion Tony Manero was defeated by Wood, 5 and 4. The most-advertised match of the day proved to be the dullest when Shute sailed to a 3-and-2 win over two-time Masters Champion Horton Smith. Both Jimmy Thomson and Shute won their semifinal matches, but neither had an easy road to victory. Thomson's first six holes against Craig Wood were disappointing, leaving him 1-down at lunch. But he gained momentum in the afternoon and won, 4 and 3. Bill Mehlhorn's front nine in the afternoon round gave him a 1-up lead over Shute. At one point, Shute was 2-down with four holes left, but Mehlhorn's missed putts on the 33rd and 34th holes eventually cost him the match. On the final hole, Shute won, 1-up, with par.

The final pitted long-hitting Thomson against Shute, nicknamed the "Boston Thin Man" for his 148-pound frame. Thomson consistently outdrove Shute by as much as 60 yards on many holes, but Shute's iron play and putting kept him at bay. At the end of the first half of the match, refereed by golf course architect Donald Ross, Shute had a 1-up lead. In the afternoon, Shute took advantage of Thomson's reduced accuracy off the tee. Known by his peers as the "human icicle" for his calm demeanor on the course, Shute played sure and steady. Two shots helped seal Shute's victory. On the 15th hole in the morning round, he hit a cleek against a head wind, and it stopped eight feet from the hole. On the 34th hole, his brassie shot traveled 230 yards to within four feet, and he made the putt for an eagle and a 3-and-2 victory. The win was particularly sweet for Shute, who had lost in the final of The PGA to Tom Creavy in 1931 and in the semifinals to Wood in 1934.

Shute began playing golf at the age of three; by the time he was five, he was playing matches with members at Westmoreland Club in Huntington, West Virginia, where his father, Herman Shute, was the golf professional. He had won the 1933 British Open in a playoff with Wood, was runner-up to Wood in the 1941 U.S. Open, and was a three-time Ryder Cup team member. Twice runner-up in the U.S. Open, in 1939 and 1941, Shute was elected to The PGA Hall of Fame in 1957.

In May 1937, six months after his first PGA victory at Pinehurst, Shute became the fifth golfer in history to successfully defend his PGA Championship title, joining Barnes, Sarazen, Hagen, and Diegel. The event was held at the Pittsburgh Field Club, a course whose punishing layout prompted *Pittsburgh Sun-Telegraph* sports editor Harry Keck to observe, "Any deviations

In 1934, putting wizard Paul Runyan, left, defeated his former teacher Craig Wood on the 38th hole.

Defending Champion Johnny Revolta putting at the 1936 Championship as Tony Manero, left, watches.

from the beaten path bring plenty of grief." In the pre-tournament press in early May, the club announced that Sam Snead would play in the local qualifier. On the day before the Championship began, Snead easily won the long drive contest with three drives that exceeded 300 yards. The only disappointment came when Hagen declared that he would forego the event for an African safari. Byron Nelson won the 36-hole qualifier with a 139. With the field narrowed to 64, the players began a rain-soaked run for the Wanamaker Trophy.

After the first two rounds, only two of the seven former Champions, Shute and Runyan, were still

> "FROM MANY ANGLES THE PGA CHAMPIONSHIP IS THE MOST DIFFICULT OF ALL TO WIN FOR NOT ONLY IS IT A TEST OF SCORING, BUT OF MAN-TO-MAN COMBATS THAT BRING TOGETHER THE WORLD'S FINEST PRODUCERS OF BIRDIES AND EAGLES."
> —GRANTLAND RICE, 1937

in contention. Sarazen, Olin Dutra, Revolta, Diegel, and Armour were all eliminated. On the fifth hole in the first round, Snead became embroiled in a rules controversy when he picked up his ball, which initially cost him a two-stroke penalty. Upon review, The PGA of America declared that he had not cleaned the ball and reversed the decision. In the third round, Thomson, the 1936 runner-up, could not hold off Ky Laffoon, despite his length off the tee. In the afternoon, Laffoon's two birdies and one par closed the match on the 33rd hole, 4 and 3. Snead lost, 3 and 2, to Jug McSpaden, who had seven threes in his first 18 holes.

Denny Shute was the last repeat Champion in 1937 until Tiger Woods won in 2000.

Shute continued his streak in the quarterfinals and dominated his match against Jimmy Hines, winning, 4 and 3. The other exciting quarterfinal match where Tony Manero rallied to defeat Harry Cooper, 1-up, was reminiscent of the 1936 U.S. Open at Baltusrol. In the locker room after the match, Cooper's frustration was palpable: "I've had many disappointments in my career as a golfer," he said. "But today's pill was the bitterest I've had to swallow." In one semifinal, reigning PGA Champion Shute defeated the reigning U.S. Open Champion Manero on the 34th hole, 3 and 2. In the other semifinal, McSpaden beat Laffoon, 2 and 1.

In the final, Shute faced McSpaden, his neighbor from Winchester, Massachusetts, in what proved to be a difficult match. After five holes, McSpaden had a 3-up lead, but Shute's ruthless consistency kept him in the match. He regained his composure and one-putted nine of the next 13 holes. At the 28th hole, McSpaden's bogey squared the match, but not for long. Shute bogeyed the 31st and 32nd holes, giving McSpaden a two-hole lead. On the 35th hole, McSpaden put his second shot under a pine tree, and he was unable to do more than move it a few feet out of the rough. On the 36th hole, with the match squared, McSpaden's first putt put him three feet from the hole.

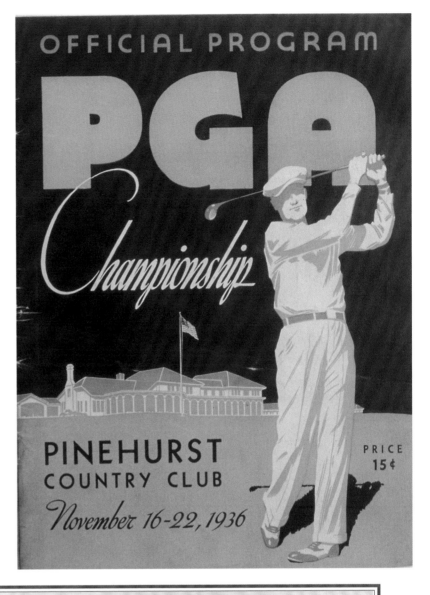

OFFICIAL PROGRAM

PGA

Championship

PINEHURST
COUNTRY CLUB

November 16-22, 1936

PRICE
15¢

Playing By the Rules

The final round of the 1934 PGA Championship was reminiscent of Bobby Jones' experience at the 1925 U.S. Open at Worcester Country Club. Paul Runyan displayed the grace of a good sportsman and nearly lost the match and the Championship. On the seventh hole, his drive landed in the rough. When he addressed the ball, it moved slightly. Although the official scorer and the spectators did not witness it, Runyan called a penalty shot on himself. His honesty cost him the hole, putting Craig Wood 2-up. It also required that Runyan go to the 38th hole to win.

EARLY GOLF EQUIPMENT

The men who played in the early PGA Championships used clubs and balls that bear little resemblance to today's golf equipment. In America, as in Scotland, golf clubs were handcrafted and varied widely. Two important technological advances influenced the game of golf in the early 20th century. Beginning in the 1890s, irons were stamped by a mechanical hammer instead of handforged, which promoted uniformity. Additionally, the wound rubber ball, invented by Coburn Haskell in 1898, gained in popularity because it flew and rolled farther and was easier to control than the gutta percha ball that it came to replace. A. G. Spalding and Brothers, the company with which Rodman Wanamaker sought to compete, was the first company to manufacture and sell clubs in the United States. Although steel shafts were available, they did not receive a warm reception from golf professionals or golf's governing bodies. The USGA and the Royal and Ancient Golf Club of St. Andrews did not legalize them until 1924 and 1929, respectively. Most golfers had developed their swings to account for the flexibility of hickory shafts and were reluctant to retool, despite the promise of greater distance.

Donald Ross' workbench at The PGA Historical Center.

MacGregor golf balls used by players throughout the 1930s.

As he set up for his second putt in front of a gallery estimated at 7,000 fans, McSpaden was distracted by several photographers, forcing him to back away from the putt. After snapping, "Please give me the chance I've been fighting for all week," he missed. Shute made his, putting the match into overtime for the third time in PGA history. The first extra hole proved McSpaden's undoing. He missed a 10-foot putt for par and lost the match.

For both the 1936 and 1937 Championships, Shute received a total of $2,000. His equipment sponsor contributed an additional $750 per year, and, although he did not smoke, a cigarette and a pipe company added a few hundred dollars to use his name. While golfers today expect million-dollar purses upon winning a major, in Shute's era players did not take home much. To defray expenses, Shute remembered that he and the other players would often "travel in car caravans from one tournament to another. The cars were packed with golf bags, clubs, clothes, practically everything we owned. Rather than waste time, the eight of us went into a field beside the road and hit golf balls. Here we were the top professionals in the country practicing in a pasture."

The purse for The PGA Championship, one of the larger ones on the professional circuit in the 1930s, kept the players coming back, evidenced by the 115 men who arrived at Shawnee Country Club in July 1938. The only noticeable absence was Hagen, who had contracted malaria on his world tour through Africa and India. On the first day, the *New York Times* reported that "stars began to fall on Pennsylvania today." Felix Serafin,

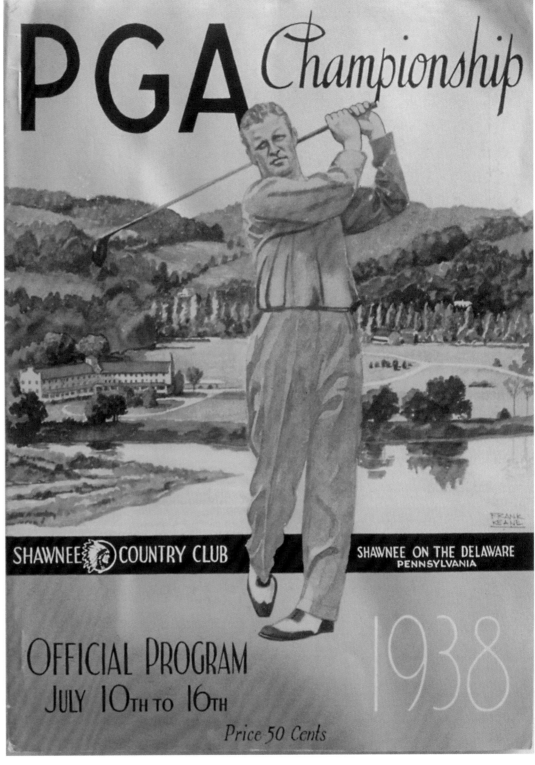

> "GOOD GOLF IS SIMPLY A MATTER OF HITTING GOOD SHOTS CONSISTENTLY. A PLAYER CAN DO THIS FOR MANY YEARS AFTER HE HAS PASSED HIS PHYSICAL PEAK, IF HIS SWING IS FUNDAMENTALLY CORRECT."
> —GENE SARAZEN, 1933

Sam Snead playing out of the water during the qualifying round at Shawnee Country Club in 1938.

"I LOVED MATCH PLAY. I WOULD STUDY A GUY I WAS PLAYING JUST LIKE TED WILLIAMS STUDIED PITCHERS. I'D LOOK FOR A WEAK SPOT OR A CHANGE IN HIS MANNERISMS."
—SAM SNEAD, 1942

a little-known player from Scranton, Pennsylvania, toppled Harry Cooper, 4 and 3, in the first round and Ky Laffoon, 3 and 2, in the second. Also in the second round, Johnny Revolta, Leo Diegel, and Jug McSpaden were sent packing. In the third round, Jimmy Hines thwarted Shute's attempt to match Hagen's record of 22 consecutive match-play victories with a 2-and-1 win. The third round also included a spectacular match by Byron Nelson, who played 26 holes against Harry Bassler without going over par. Nelson shot a 64 in the morning round. In the afternoon, Nelson made eight consecutive pars and won, 11 and 10. Sarazen, also in the third round, narrowly defeated Jimmy Demaret at the 38th hole.

In the quarterfinals, Hines, Snead, Paul Runyan, and Henry Picard advanced, leaving Sarazen out of the race. In the semifinals, Runyan, the 1934 PGA Champion, overcame Picard, 4 and 3. The more exciting match belonged to Snead, who defeated Hines, 1-up after four consecutive threes. Although Hines actually defeated Snead by one stroke, he lost the match.

The four semifinalists, left to right, in the 1938 PGA Championship: Sam Snead, Jimmy Hines, Henry Picard, and Paul Runyan.

On his way to capturing his second PGA victory in 1938, Runyan beat Sam Snead in the final, 8 and 7.

In the final, Snead lost to Runyan, 8 and 7, in the most decisive victory in The PGA Championship's history. Although Snead outdrove Runyan by an average of 40 yards, Runyan's short game more than compensated for his lack of length off the tee. John Walter of the *Detroit News,* reflecting on the afternoon round, declared that "Runyan must have spent the intermission in a Turkish bath and stored his clubs in a fireless cooker, because both came out for the final round smoking hot." Runyan won on the 29th hole on his 30th birthday. He was 24 under par for 196 holes, playing the last 70 holes with only one bogey. Upon losing to Runyan, Snead only murmured, "Lawdy, that man ain't human." At the presentation ceremony, PGA President George Jacobus asked Runyan: "Shall I hand you this check, Paul, or shall I give it to Mrs. Runyan?" With a big smile, he replied: "You might as well allow me to hold it for a minute, George. Mrs. Runyan will get it eventually."

Once the players' strike of 1939 was resolved and Denny Shute was officially entered, The PGA Championship turned into a battle between two golfing giants. Henry Picard, the 1938 Masters Champion, defeated Byron Nelson, the 1939 U.S. Open Champion at the 37th hole. Pomonok Country Club, which had never been considered for a major championship, was selected not for its rigorous layout, but for its proximity to the 1939 World's Fair, which was less than a mile away in Flushing, New York. While Ben Hogan and three other players led the qualifiers with a 138, Sam Snead's 149 failed to make the cut. The first round was a defeat of the old guard, with Gene Sarazen and Walter Hagen falling to Jack Ryan and Tony Manero, respectively. Paul Runyan, the defending Champion, sailed through his first two rounds, beating Mortie Dutra, 3 and 1, and Frank Champ, 3 and 2. Hogan, playing in his first PGA Championship, won two matches, finally losing to Runyan, 3 and 2, in the third round.

Runyan, the 1934 and 1938 PGA Champion, became a well-known teaching professional.

Byron Nelson's mother photographing Byron and his wife, Louise, at the 1939 Championship.

Facing page: Henry Picard, left, giving Ben Hogan advice on his grip during a practice round before the 1939 Championship.

From left to right: Byron Nelson, Jug McSpaden, Ralph Guldahl, Ben Hogan, Paul Runyan, Vic Ghezzi, and Jimmy Hines practicing before the 1939 Championship.

Ky Laffoon, left, and Ben Hogan reviewing their scorecard after the 1939 qualifying round.

Despite the successful campaign that ensured Shute a place on the roster, he did not shine in the 1939 event. The two-time Champion was defeated by Emerick Kocsis, a 45-year-old professional from Michigan, 3 and 2, in the third round. Also in the third round, Nelson overcame Revolta, 6 and 4. Runyan's 2-and-1 defeat by Dick Metz in the quarterfinals prompted William Richardson of the *New York Times* to declare that the 1939 event had become "a championship without a champion." In the semi-finals, Picard beat Metz, 1-up, to advance to the final bracket. In reference to the match between Dutch Harrison and Nelson, one golf writer exclaimed, "There may have been more brilliant golf played than Nelson's on the third nine yesterday, but if so these eyes have never seen it." Nelson won, 9 and 8, and was positioned to become the first golfer since Sarazen in 1922 to hold both the U.S. Open and PGA Championship titles in the same year. He would not succeed.

The final match between Nelson and Picard was decided in overtime for the fourth time in the Championship's history. Fred Corcoran declared that "Henry displayed the outstanding nerve" necessary to win. In contrast, Nelson was as "nervous as a cat" and could not gain his composure until the eighth hole. Picard remembers how Nelson began the round: "The funny part about our match in the final . . . was on the first tee in the morning round. Byron swung and almost missed the ball entirely. . . . The ball went way off to the right into the bushes, so I started the match 1-up." Picard held onto the lead until Nelson, who nearly drove the 330-yard green, birdied the 29th hole. Nelson maintained his lead until a poor shot on the 36th hole squared the match. When Picard's tee shot on the first extra hole rolled under a movie truck, it appeared that he had lost. But after a free drop, his second shot landed within seven feet of the hole, and he made his putt. Nelson missed his, as the *New York Times* quipped, "by the margin of two Japanese beetles" and lost the match. His disappointment, though, only lasted a year. Nelson defeated Snead in 1940 at Hershey Country Club and, in doing so, ushered in a new era.

Byron Nelson sinks a putt for birdie on the 18th hole on his way to eliminating Dutch Harrison in the semifinals of the 1939 Championship.

Henry Picard, the 1938 Masters Champion, was the tour's leading money winner in 1939 when he won The PGA Championship.

CHAPTER FOUR

THE GIANTS OF THE GAME

In the 1940 PGA Championship at Hershey Country Club in Pennsylvania, Byron Nelson and Sam Snead battled for the title, signaling the rise of new giants of the game. Although Tommy Armour, Olin Dutra, Denny Shute, and Paul Runyan won multiple majors in the 1930s, only Gene Sarazen was colorful enough to compete with the likes of Walter Hagen. By the end of the decade, even Sarazen was reaching the twilight of his career as a serious contender.

During each night of the 1945 PGA Championship, Byron Nelson was treated for a sore back.

Milton Hershey, right, with the Wanamaker Trophy in 1940.

The PGA of America waited for the next generation of heroes, and it came in the shape of "Bantam" Ben Hogan, "Slammin" Sammy Snead, and "Lord" Byron Nelson. These three players, who won a combined 21 majors during their careers, ushered in the modern era of American golf. During the 1940s and early 1950s, The PGA Championship was one battlefield upon which they struggled for supremacy.

But the old guard was not quite ready to, as Dylan Thomas wrote, "go gentle into that good night." The story early in the week of the 1940 PGA Championship was the presence of former stars who, as Fred Corcoran declared, made a series of dramatic stands "against the rush of youth." The tournament committee did not know that Hagen, now 48, was planning to play until he arrived the day before the event to practice with Jim Barnes. To beat Gil Sellers in the first match, Hagen played the last five holes in one under par to win on the final hole. His win over Vic Ghezzi, 2 and 1, in the second round was his 40th and last in The PGA Championship. Hagen lost in the third round, 1-down, to Jug McSpaden after missing an eight-foot putt. Sarazen, who had joked with Hagen a few years earlier that they should be

THE FOUNDING OF THE GOLF WRITERS ASSOCIATION OF AMERICA

The Golf Writers Association of America (GWAA) was founded during the 1946 PGA Championship, hosted by Portland Golf Club. A commemorative plaque is located outside the southeast corner of the swimming pool. In 1929, at the U.S. Amateur at Pebble Beach, William D. Richardson of the *New York Times* suggested forming an association, but the idea did not come to fruition for another 20 years. Russ Newland served as the organization's first president in 1946, followed by O. B. Keeler and Grantland Rice. Herb Graffis, the GWAA's president from 1951 to 1952 and author of *The PGA: The Official History of the Professional Golfers' Association of America*, founded four golf magazines, including *Golfdom* in 1927. In 1936, Herb and his brother, Joe, also established the National Golf Foundation to promote the growth of the game.

Byron Nelson, right, retired from competitive golf in 1946 to devote more time to his ranch in Texas.

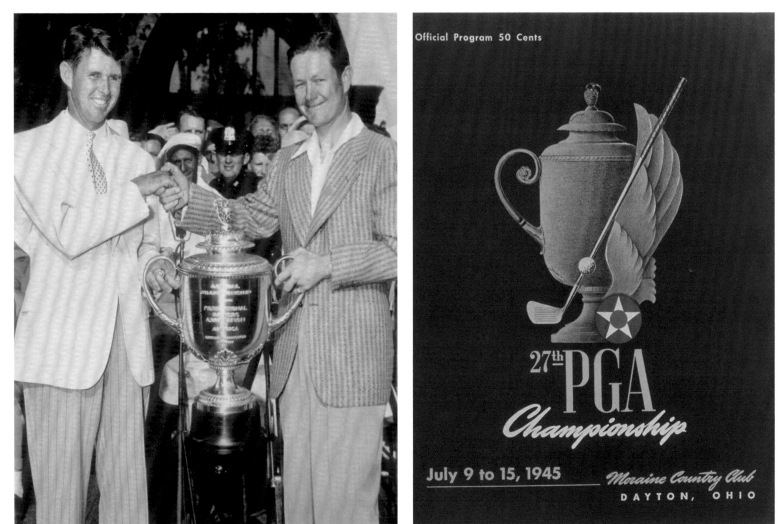

Nelson lost to Henry Picard, left, in 1939, but won in 1940 and 1945.

watching the action from adjacent armchairs, won his first two matches against Stan Stazowski and Ray Mangrum. The Squire's surprise defeat of the defending Champion, Henry Picard, 1-up, in the third round was one of the week's greatest upsets. Sarazen looked like he was on the road to capturing his fourth PGA title until he met Snead in the quarterfinals. In the only close match of the day, Snead did not take the lead until the 34th hole, but his birdie and two halves gave him the 1-up victory on the 36th.

Nelson, then the professional at Inverness Club, easily defeated Dick Shoemaker, 4 and 3, in the first round, but faced a much tougher match against Frank Walsh, which ended on the 20th hole. Snead began the week by winning a difficult match against Nelson Giddens. He faced an easier second and third round against Charles Sheppard and Jimmy Hines. Hogan won his first three matches against Frank Champ, Harry Nettlebladt, and Al Brosch without too much effort, only to fall to Ralph Guldahl, 3 and 2, in the quarterfinals. Because of rain and fog,

the semifinal matches were stretched to two days, the first half played on Saturday and the second on Sunday. Nelson beat Guldahl, 1-up, and remembers that he "had to work at staying calm" and patient because his opponent played so slowly. Snead defeated McSpaden, 5 and 4, which meant that the final bracket pitted the runners-up of the 1938 and 1939 PGA Championships against each other.

With two birdies and a par on the final three holes, Nelson defeated Snead, 1-up, to capture his third major title, after the 1933 Masters and 1939 U.S. Open. Although Nelson had a 2-up lead going into the afternoon, Snead was not prepared to concede and played brilliantly. The final three holes demonstrated the skill, strength, and resolve of both players. On the 34th hole, Nelson's birdie squared the match. At the 35th, Nelson's wedge shot landed within two feet, and Snead missed a six-foot putt, giving Nelson a one-hole advantage. Nelson remembered the final hole in his autobiography, *How I Played*

THE GIANTS OF THE GAME

the Game, "I took my 3-iron, almost hit the flag, and went about 10 feet past the hole; I'd be putting downhill. Sam put his tee shot about 25 feet to the left of the hole and putted up close, so he had three. So all I had to do was make three to win the match, 1-up. I coasted that putt down the hill very gently and made my three to beat Snead and win The PGA Championship." Years after the event,

Nelson received a letter from Charles Fasnacht, a friend of the boy who served as Nelson's caddie that year. The caddie had given Charles the winning ball, and he wanted to return it to Nelson. Moved by the gesture, Nelson wrote back and told him "that if it had meant that much to him to keep it all these years, then I couldn't think of anyone who deserved to have it more."

Golf professionals in the 1940s were usually associated with a country club because they rarely made enough money to support themselves playing on the tour. In his autobiography, Nelson explained that there were two kinds of professionals: "Some pros could go play in tournaments every week, and simply 'played out of' a certain club rather than working there every day, while others worked a full week." Hogan and Snead were associated with Hershey and the Greenbrier, respectively, but never worked full time. Nelson's job at Inverness allowed him to tour for only six weeks out of the year, making it impossible for him to attend every event. While he rarely missed a major championship, he did not have time to perfect his game. Before the 1940 PGA Championship, he was so busy with professional duties that he had not played in a

Sam Snead displays his medalist score in the qualifying round of the 1941 PGA Championship.

Vic Ghezzi coming out of a bunker during the 1941 Championship.

tournament for two-and-a-half months. In retrospect, his game suffered during the first three years he worked at the Ohio club. He was runner-up in 1941 to Vic Ghezzi, lost to Jim Turnesa in the semifinals in 1942, and was runner-up to Bob Hamilton in 1944. That year, Nelson resigned from his position at Inverness and concentrated exclusively on his game. That decision was part of what made his 1945 season possible.

Nelson won his next PGA Championship in what became one of the most extraordinary years in the history of American golf. In 1945, he made 30 starts and won 18 tournaments, 11 in a row, a record that still stands. The next best streak belongs to Hogan and Tiger Woods, tied with six consecutive victories. Writing in *Byron Nelson: The Little Black Book*, 1965 PGA Champion Dave Marr reflected on how times have changed: "In 1945 there wasn't any of the clamor there is today. Nobody bothered Byron. He drove to the next tournament, so he was alone then; he could eat dinner and no one would bother him. . . . With all the buildup there is now, I don't think Byron could do it again."

Nelson entered the 1945 season with the goal of making enough

Left to right: Herman Barron, Ben Hogan, and Jug McSpaden hoping for good luck before the qualifying round in 1942.

money to purchase a ranch in Texas. He wrote in his autobiography, "Each drive, each iron, each chip, each putt was aimed at the goal of getting that ranch." He also wanted to set two records that would endure, the lowest scoring average and the record for the lowest score for a tournament—both of which have since been broken. Not satisfied that his 1944 victories reflected his true talents, Nelson began the 1945 season with a "whole collection of goals." As World War II necessitated the cancellation of three of golf's four majors in 1945, The PGA Championship was his only chance to capture another major title.

> THE PGA IS AS TOUGH A TEST OF GOLF AS THERE IS. TRY PLAYING 36 HOLES EVERY DAY FOR A WEEK AND SEE HOW YOU FEEL ON THE SEVENTH DAY.
> —BYRON NELSON, 1945

THE PGA GOES TO WAR

In 1943, the professional golf tour was almost completely suspended because of World War II. Many of the players served in the war. Vic Ghezzi was stationed at Fort Monmouth, New Jersey, Joe Turnesa and Horton Smith were in the army, Jimmy Demaret and Sam Snead were in the navy, and Ben Hogan served in the army air corps. Lloyd Mangrum, who would win the U.S. Open in 1946, was wounded at the Battle of the Bulge. Byron Nelson was rejected because of a blood condition, Jug McSpaden for asthma, and Craig Wood because of a back injury. To contribute to the war effort, The PGA of America, as it had done during World War I, coordinated exhibition matches and visits to rehabilitation centers. Throughout 1942 and 1943, Nelson and McSpaden participated in more than 100 such events across the United States. Sponsored by equipment companies MacGregor and Wilson, they often traveled with Bob Hope and Bing Crosby and frequently visited camps where their fellow professionals were stationed. In 1942, The PGA of America bought two ambulances for the Red Cross and distributed golf clubs and balls at military bases. By November 1944, The PGA had contributed $550,000 to war charities, service organizations, and rehabilitation projects. As victory seemed imminent, Ed Dudley and Fred Corcoran organized 23 PGA events and reinvigorated the tour.

Nelson, left, instructing convalescing soldiers during World War II, with Jug McSpaden and Jim Turnesa watching.

The PGA of America promoted golf as a form of exercise and rehabilitation during World War II.

The PGA of America donated equipment to help soldiers during the war.

Because of the war and the reduced field, The PGA of America shortened the Championship to five rounds of 36 holes instead of six. Nelson tied Revolta for the qualifying medal at Moraine Country Club in Dayton, Ohio, and began marching toward his ninth victory. In the first round, defending Champion Bob Hamilton fell to Jack Grout, who would later become Jack Nicklaus' teacher. Nelson faced Sarazen, who had asked Fred Corcoran to pair the two because Sarazen "either wanted to get beat early or stay a long time." Despite taking osteopathic treatments for a pulled muscle in his back, Nelson won the match, 4 and 3. In the second round, Nelson nearly lost to Mike Turnesa. Two-down with only four holes to play, Nelson had two birdies, an eagle, and a par to win, which prompted Turnesa to remark, "I don't think anyone can beat him." When Mike's brother, Jim, lost to Claude Harmon, 8 and 7, in the same round, he joked, "We'll have to eat our spaghetti without the meat sauce for dinner tonight." In the quarterfinals, Nelson defeated two-time PGA Champion Denny Shute, 3 and 2, meaning that for the sixth year in a row Nelson had reached the semifinals. Harmon was the last player to stand in his way of the final bracket, and Nelson beat him, 5 and 4.

In the final, Nelson faced Sam Byrd, who was a New York Yankee outfielder from 1929 to 1934, in what Nelson called "the

toughest tournament I ever won." Byrd had a 3-up lead after 21 holes. But the 25th proved to be the turning point, as Byrd bogeyed the hole after a poor approach shot. The lead shifted back and forth, and the brutal conditions played to Nelson's advantage. A native of Texas, he had experience negotiating the 35-mile-per-hour gusts of wind. He defeated Byrd on the 33rd hole. In sum, he played 204 holes that week. The $51,515.26 raised at the event was donated to the Wright and Patterson Air Fields to help rehabilitate soldiers, making it the largest single contribution of its kind from a sporting event during the war years.

To complete his streak, Nelson won the Tam O'Shanter Open and the Canadian Open, only to be defeated at the Memphis Invitational by amateur Fred Haas Jr. In remembering the 1945 season, Nelson explained, "Really, it was a remarkable year. My scoring average was 68.3, I had 18 official wins, 11 in a row, finished second seven times, and had nearly 100 official sub-par rounds, my best being 62. I set new records for most wins a row, most in one year, lowest tournament score, and lowest scoring average."

The 1942 PGA Championship was Sam Snead's first major win.

Jug McSpaden listening in as Byron Nelson is interviewed in 1945 by WBCA announcer Henry Benac during Nelson's incredible streak of 11 victories in a row.

As extraordinary as the 1945 season was, it took a heavy toll on Nelson, just as the 1930 season had on Bobby Jones. The night after defeating Claude Harmon in the semifinals of The PGA Championship, Nelson began discussions with his wife, Louise, about retiring from competitive golf. He elected to play in fewer tournaments, but returned to The PGA Championship in 1946 as defending Champion. Although exempt, Nelson played in the qualifying round, but withdrew after 18 holes to rest his back. He ultimately lost in the quarterfinals to Ed "Porky" Oliver and acted on his plan to retire, declaring, "I had reached all the goals I ever wanted to reach." He finished the season, playing the last event in his own backyard, the Fort Worth Invitational. Although extraordinary, the streak of 1945 did not receive the kind of coverage it would today. Robert Cullen, writing for *Golf Magazine,* pointed out that when Nelson won the first event, the Miami Four-Ball, Allied troops were advancing on Berlin. When it ended in August, the newspapers were more focused on Japan's surrender and the end of the war.

The 1942 PGA Championship was Snead's first of seven major titles and his first of three PGA Championship victories. Having lost to Paul Runyan in the 1938 PGA Championship and to Nelson in 1940, Fred Corcoran declared that Snead "lifted himself by his bootstraps atop as brilliant a field as ever started down the grassy trail" in the 25th anniversary of the Championship. The outbreak of World War II necessitated the cancellation of the other three majors and reduced the match-play field in 1942 at Seaview Country Club in Atlantic City, New Jersey, to 32 players. Although smaller, it still included Jimmy Demaret (1940 Masters Champion); Denny Shute, Runyan, and Nelson (former PGA Champions); Craig Wood (1941 U.S. Open and Masters Champion); Hogan (golf's leading money winner for the past two years); and defending Champion Vic Ghezzi.

When asked years later to recount his most memorable tournament to Al Barkow, author of *Gettin' to the Dance Floor: An Oral History of American Golf,* Snead replied, "Usually your first tournament win is your biggest thrill, but it wasn't necessarily

"Though I won the PGA again in 1949 and 1951, that first win in 1942 was my biggest, and one I enjoyed the most. It happened just so quick."
—Sam Snead, 1986

with me. I think the one I enjoyed the most was in '42, The PGA Championship. I was in Washington, D.C., in line ready to take that one step forward to be sworn in the Navy. There was all these fellows with the scrambled eggs on their bills, and I said to one of them, 'Hey, what's the chance of me skipping this one and doing it next week? They're having The PGA Championship over in New Jersey, just below Atlantic City,' which was not very far away. One of the scrambled eggs said, 'Why don't you go ahead and get inducted, and they'll probably let you go.' I said no, I understood they were really tight about the pros, they wouldn't let us move, and he asked me what it meant to me. I said $2,000 if I win, plus $2,000 from Wilson Sporting Goods, who I represent, and maybe a few testimonials and whatnot. I said I might get $10,000 out of it, and at that time that was a helluva lot of money. Well,

it just so happened that I talked to the right guy. He said to go call the draft board and tell them I'd had my physical and want to go play and I'll be inducted the following Monday. I said, 'Thank you very much.' So I got on the phone and they said it was okay, and I went over and played Jim Turnesa in the final."

The final match of the 1942 Championship on May 31 was billed as a contest between the army and the navy. In the morning round Corporal Turnesa, touted by one sports writer as "one of the Horatio Alger heroes of golf history," was 3-up. After bogeying the 28th hole, he lost the lead and seemed to suddenly lose his game. Snead charged that the crowd, mostly from the nearby army base, kicked Turnesa's ball out of the woods twice. In his autobiography, he quipped, "Well, you would have thought I was a German or a Jap by the way those Fort Dix boys started snarling at me. But I was closing in on Turnesa like a hawk on a delight. I never took my eyes off him, and when he stepped up to play the 29th I saw something that made me want to crow." Snead recognized a change in the number of waggles Turnesa took before he drove and knew his opponent was getting nervous. Snead went on to hole a 60-foot chip shot for a birdie on the 35th hole for a 2-and-1 victory. When Snead finally reported for duty, he asked the recruiter if the navy would have let him play in the tournament. He replied, "Negative, Snead."

GOLFERETTE

PGA NATIONAL CHAMPIONSHIP
May 25-31st

35¢

HERMITAGE COUNTRY CLUB · RICHMOND, VIRGINIA

Sam Snead being interviewed after winning his second PGA title in 1949.

It took Snead seven years to capture another PGA Championship title in 1949, but that was a bittersweet victory because Hogan, the defending Champion, had been seriously injured in an automobile accident in February and could not compete. The third member of the American triumvirate was also absent, as Nelson had retired three years earlier. But the rest of the best professional players in the nation were at Hermitage Country Club in 1949 in Richmond, Virginia, vying for a major title on the 6,677-yard course. Snead, the recent Masters Champion and a native Virginian, was clearly the crowd's favorite, as John Leard of the *Richmond News Leader* reported, "Oohs and aahs could be heard from the distant 14th all the way to the clubhouse."

In *Hermitage Country Club: A History of the First 100 Years*, author Bruce Matson explained that Richmond edged out Columbus, Ohio, for the event. Ben Wahrman, sports editor of the newspaper, and Tom Utterback, an active member of the club, spearheaded the effort. An impassioned speech by fellow member Charles Wilkinson convinced the Sportsmen's Club of Richmond to co-sponsor the event. After two years of course renovations at a cost of $40,000, the players gathered for the qualifying rounds. Ray Wade Hill, an unemployed golf professional from Louisiana, was the medalist with a 136. Snead finished a stroke behind for second. Because of the layout of the course, hitchhikers could pause on their way to Washington, D.C., to watch the action on the first green.

The first round marked the first time a player ever lost his caddie. After taking his driver from the bag on the 14th hole, *Golf World* reported that Jack Burke Jr.'s caddie wandered onto a different fairway with Burke's clubs, delaying the match. He was eventually found by a tournament official sleeping under a tree and raced back to Burke in a jeep. Snead defeated Burke, 3 and 2. In the second round, Snead was allowed to re-tee his drive without penalty on the first hole when his first attempt hit a power line, and he subsequently defeated Henry Ransom, 3 and 1. Jim Ferrier, Jimmy Demaret,

Lloyd Mangrum, and Jim Turnesa also advanced. In the third round, Snead was 3-down with nine to play, coming from behind to best Dave Douglas, 1-up. Ferrier beat Marty Furgol, 8 and 6, after some confusion about marking his ball. In the quarterfinals, Ferrier beat Clayton Heafner, 3 and 2. Heafner reported that Ferrier's wife, who followed Jim throughout the round, was one of the "best instructors in the game." Snead defeated Demaret, 4 and 3. As a bit of good-natured revenge, Demaret removed Snead's straw hat to reveal his bald head to local photographers.

In a semifinal match, Snead was paired against Ferrier, and Snead fell behind in the morning round. When he left a putt short on the 20th hole, Ferrier joked, "Sam, the object of this game is to get the ball to the bottom of the cup." Stung by Ferrier's comment, Snead holed out for an eagle on the 21st. Ferrier was so surprised that his tee shot at the next hole fell 50 yards short, and Snead evened the match. Throughout the afternoon round, Snead one-putted nine times to win, 3 and 2. In disbelief, Ferrier said, "I couldn't do much against . . . that kind of golf, Sam." In the final, Snead came from behind in the afternoon and won, 3 and 2, over Johnny Palmer.

Sam Snead defeated Jimmy Demaret, 3 and 2, in the 1942 semifinals.

Snead struggled in the morning round, but managed to square the match at lunch. In the afternoon, Palmer won only one out of the 16 holes. The PGA Championship purse added $3,500 to his winnings, and Snead was eventually named Professional Golfer of the Year. He won the Vardon Trophy in 1949 for the second of four times with an average of 69.37 for 73 rounds and topped the money list with $31,593.83.

In 1951, Snead won The PGA Championship for the third time in seven attempts and tied Sarazen's record. Only Hagen had surpassed their achievements, with five victories in the 1920s. Oakmont Country Club near Pittsburgh, one of the most challenging courses in the nation, became the first site to host The PGA Championship twice. Chandler Harper came to what Arthur Daley of the *New York Times* called the "impregnable citadel of pasture and pool" to defend his title in a tournament sponsored by the Pittsburgh Dapper Dan Club. The heavy rain that fell in the weeks leading up to The PGA Championship helped soften Oakmont's notoriously fast greens, but it was still a tough test, making Snead's 21 under par for 166 holes in match play even more astonishing.

The first qualifying round ended in a three-way tie, prompting a sudden-death playoff between Lloyd Mangrum, Claude Harmon, and Pete Cooper for the first time since 1939. Harmon won and collected the Alex Smith Memorial Trophy and the $250 prize money set aside for the low qualifier. In the first round, Harper, who earlier in the week took lessons from Bobby Cruickshank to improve his game, lost to Jim Turnesa, 1-down in one of the round's six overtime matches. Snead won his first match against Fred Haas Jr., 1-up, but became embroiled in a rules controversy in his second round against Marty Furgol. On the 14th hole, Snead tried to remove an insect from his ball, which prompted Furgol's accusation that he had cleaned his ball and should be assessed a penalty stroke. While the rules officials were reviewing the alleged violation, Snead and Furgol finished the match all square, requiring a playoff. While waiting for PGA President Joe Novak to announce referee Jimmy Nichols' deci-

The 1945 Championship was Nelson's ninth victory in his streak of 11 in a row.

sion, Snead sat down and ate a sandwich while Furgol went into the clubhouse to hear the proceedings. Furgol ultimately withdrew his protest and allowed the playoff to begin. But he could not regain the lead; Snead's birdie on the 21st hole secured his win. Sarazen won his first match, but lost in the second to Jack Burke Jr., 5 and 3. Twenty-six years earlier, Sarazen had lost to Jack's father, 8 and 7, in the first round of the 1925 PGA Championship.

In the third round, Snead beat Mangrum, 3 and 2, in a violent rainstorm that postponed the match briefly to allow the players to go into the clubhouse to change their clothes. Burke placed two stymies in the quarterfinals, hoping to rattle Snead, but the strategy failed and he lost, 2 and 1. In the semifinals,

Snead defeated Charles Bassler, 9 and 8, and dropped only one of the 28 holes. Walter Burkemo, who was given 100-to-1 odds at the beginning of the week, defeated Ellsworth Vines, a former Wimbledon tennis champion at the 37th hole. Burkemo had been awarded a Purple Heart after spending 18 months in a French hospital during World War II.

In the final, in front of 10,000 spectators, who had paid $2.50 each in admission, Snead dominated Burkemo. Snead won five of the first six holes and kept his lead throughout the morning round. To boost his confidence, Burkemo spent the lunch break calling Tommy Armour and reading telegrams from friends. Snead began the afternoon with a birdie and a 4-up lead and putted beautifully until Burkemo ran out of holes. Snead finally won, 7 and 6, on the 30th hole.

Out of the army for only a year, Ben Hogan, the third mem-

ber of the triumvirate, won his first major championship at age 34 at The PGA at Portland Golf Club in 1946. Don McLeod, executive editor of the *Oregonian*, declared, "123 of the nation's top knights of the niblick were on the scene." The 1946 PGA Championship was brought to the northwest coast by Robert Hudson, the sponsor of the 1944 and 1945 Portland Open. In 1947, Hudson revived the Ryder Cup, going as far as to pay the expenses of the British team.

In the 1946 qualifying round, Jim Ferrier set a PGA Championship record with a 134, shaving two strokes off the previous record set in 1929 by Fred Morrison and tied in 1938 by Frank Moore. The only surprises in the two first rounds were the elimination of U.S. Open winner Lloyd Mangrum and British Open winner Sam Snead. Nelson sailed through his first three rounds against Frank Rodio, Larry Lamberger, and Herman Barron.

Sam Snead, left, with runner-up Walter Burkemo in 1951.

Hogan barely defeated Charles Weisner, 2 and 1, in the first round, but reached his stride in the second against Bill Heinlein. Ferrier's qualifying record did not carry him far; he was defeated by Demaret, 3 and 2, in the third round. In the quarterfinals, Byron Nelson bogeyed the final hole and lost to Porky Oliver, 1-down, in the last match Nelson would ever play in The PGA Championship. In the semifinals, Hogan defeated Demaret, 10 and 9, making it the second-biggest margin of victory in The PGA's match-play history. In the other semifinal match, Oliver won, 6 and 5, on the 31st hole when Jug McSpaden hit his drive into the woods and conceded the match. In the final, the 135-pound Hogan faced the 207-pound Oliver. Hogan was 3-down at the end of the morning round after shooting a 73 to Oliver's

> "ALTHOUGH HOGAN IS BUILT LIKE A BANTAM, HE HAS THE WIRY STRENGTH OF A BULLDOG, AND EVEN SURPASSES THE TENACITY OF HIS CANINE COUNTERPART. HOGAN'S FOREARM MUSCLES ARE LIKE IRON, AND HIS WRISTS ARE LIKE THE BUSINESS END OF A BULLWHIP."
> —*PGA CHAMPIONSHIP JOURNAL*, 1949

70, largely because of Hogan's mediocre performance on the greens. In front of 7,500 fans, Hogan took a 2-up lead after nine holes in the afternoon. He won four of the final five holes and defeated Oliver on the 32nd hole, 6 and 4. The 1946 PGA Championship was the first of Hogan's nine major victories.

Two years later, in 1948, Hogan captured the Championship for a second time at Norwood Hills Country Club's west course in St. Louis, Missouri. A month after this victory, he won the U.S. Open and became the first golfer to hold both titles since Sarazen in 1922. Referring to the hilly topography of the course, defending Champion Jim Ferrier exclaimed, "No old man will win this tournament." Before the event, The PGA of America declared that the players would ad-

Ben Hogan, right, and his wife, Valerie, cutting a cake to celebrate his 1946 victory.

here to USGA rules, particularly the one limiting 14 clubs in a player's bag. It also meant that the stymie, banned from PGA events in 1944, would once again come into play. In February, the association threatened "official punishment" to players who publicly complained about the rules. Finally, The PGA of America declared that African-American golfers would no longer be barred from PGA events, responding to a lawsuit brought by Madison Gunter, Bill Spiller, and Ted Rhodes. The attempt to break down racial barriers, however, would not become complete until 1961, when The PGA removed the "Caucasian Race Clause" from the organization's constitution.

Despite the changes, the 1948 Championship proceeded with the usual thrills and upsets. After qualifying with a 138, Hogan's road to the final bracket was nearly stymied in the first round against Jock Hutchison Jr., son of the 1920 PGA Champion. The match, considered by spectators to be the most exciting of the entire tournament, lasted 23 holes before Hogan made a birdie and won. Hutchison graciously conceded by complimenting Hogan. "I'm glad you won, Ben," he said. "If I had been the winner, I wouldn't go much farther, but you can win this tournament." In the first round, seven of the 32 matches went into overtime.

Ferrier defeated Dutch Harrison in the first round, only to fall to Claude Harmon in the second. The second-round match between Eddie Burke and Chick Harbert went eight extra holes. Also in the second round, Hogan faced Johnny Palmer, who had beaten him at

Louise Nelson, left, and Valerie Hogan passing time in 1948 at Norwood Hills.

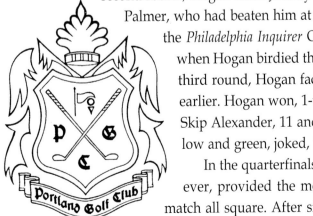

the *Philadelphia Inquirer* Open the week before. Palmer held the lead from the fourth to the 15th hole when Hogan birdied the 16th and 17th and won the match, 1-up, with a three on the final hole. In the third round, Hogan faced 46-year-old Sarazen, who had won his first PGA Championship 26 years earlier. Hogan won, 1-up, on the 36th hole. Harbert's spectacular morning round helped him defeat Skip Alexander, 11 and 10. When Harbert entered the locker room, Demaret, dressed in canary yellow and green, joked, "Now sit down and tell us where you missed some shots."

In the quarterfinals, Hogan beat Harbert, 2 and 1. The match between Snead and Harmon, however, provided the most drama. At the end of 18 holes, Harmon was 5-up, but Snead ended the match all square. After six extra holes, Snead's putt on the 42nd green rimmed the cup and gave the match to Harmon. In the semifinals, Hogan and Demaret battled back and forth, with Hogan winning, 2 and 1.

Ben and Valerie Hogan, left, and Idella and Jimmy Demaret, shown in a private moment.

Porky Oliver, right, congratulates Hogan for his 6 and 4 win in 1946.

Facing page: In his prime, Hogan was one of the best putters on tour.

A New Agency?

During World War II, Gene Sarazen became a representative of the Vinco Corporation of Detroit; during his many trips to Washington, he befriended Robert Hannegan, the postmaster general. Before leaving D.C. for Ohio and the start of the 1945 PGA Championship, Sarazen was invited to the British Embassy for dinner with Lord Halifax. When introduced to the British ambassador to the United States, Sarazen explained that he was on his way to The PGA. According to Robert Sommers in *Golf Anecdotes*, Lord Halifax "frowned for a moment, then said in a puzzled voice, 'PGA, PGA. Well that just goes to show you no matter how closely you keep in touch with what's happening in Washington, the moment you turn your back the government has created a new agency.'"

Mike Turnesa came from behind to beat Harmon, 1-up, and became the third member of this family to reach the final of a PGA Championship. His brother, Joe, lost to Hagen in 1927, and his other brother, Jim, lost to Snead in 1942. Hogan's brilliant iron play helped him defeat Mike Turnesa, 7 and 6.

Hogan's quiet determination did not endear him to the crowds, who were accustomed to the colorful antics of the likes of Demaret. Nor were they impressed by Hogan's vow to never play in the match-play event again because of its rigor. It is hard to know whether he was serious because his nearly fatal car accident in 1949 prevented him from defending his PGA title. But he managed to launch an incredible comeback, winning the U.S. Open in June 1950. Over the next three golf seasons, Hogan won five more majors—the 1951 and 1953 U.S. Opens, the 1951 and 1953 Masters, and the 1953 British Open. He

With nine holes to play, Vic Ghezzi overcame a three-hole deficit to beat Byron Nelson on the 38th hole in 1941.

played in The PGA Championship in 1960 after it had been converted to stroke play, but did not make the cut. In 1964, Hogan tied for ninth; the next year, he tied for 15th.

Four players kept Nelson, Snead, and Hogan from completely dominating the Championship in the 1940s and early 1950s. Although their wins are often footnotes to the giants' victories, they were no less exciting. In *Rubs of the Green: Golf's Triumphs and Tragedies,* Webster Evans points out that "one of the finest finishes occurred during a man-to-man encounter in 1941." Vic Ghezzi, the eventual Champion, came to Cherry Hills Country Club never having made it past the third round in his previous eight attempts.

Two of the big-name players arrived in Denver injured. Prior to the event, Nelson had crushed his finger, requiring the removal of part of the nail, and Snead was suffering from back trouble. But their games did not seem to be affected. Snead led all qualifiers with a 138, and Nelson was

Hiring the Police

Worried that overzealous spectators would disturb his ball during the 1947 PGA Championship at Plum Hollow Country Club, Jim Ferrier hired two policemen to walk on each side of the fairway to monitor his ball while he played against Chick Harbert, a Michigan professional and local favorite, in the 36-hole final. Throughout the week, Ferrier had noticed spectators kicking balls or picking them up, and he did not want to take any chances. He remembered, "I paid them $50 apiece just to stay out in front of me, get to my ball as soon as it stopped rolling and stand guard over it until I got there. It was the best $100 I ever spent."

the runner-up to Ghezzi. After the first day, the *New York Times* reported, "Dark horses roamed the range and upsets tumbled over each other today as the field . . . was whittled down to 16 survivors in two blistering rounds of match play." Paul Runyan, Henry Picard, Jimmy Demaret, Dutch Harrison, and Dick Metz were eliminated in the first round. But former Champions Gene Sarazen, Denny Shute, and Byron Nelson emerged victorious. The third round contained fewer surprises, as most of the favorites advanced. Sarazen's 9-and-7 win over Bruce Coltart was the largest margin of victory. In the quarterfinals, Nelson defeated Hogan, 2-up, in a close contest that went to the final green.

Snead's putting cost him the match against Lloyd Mangrum, who was playing in his first PGA Championship. The *Times* reporter quipped, "On some holes, he would have missed a bucket buried in the green."

The semifinal match between Ghezzi and Mangrum was the most suspenseful of the entire Championship. At the end of 30 holes, Mangrum was 3-down. He won three of the next four holes to square the match. Mangrum's drive on the final hole was the unluckiest shot of the week. It sailed nearly 300 yards over a lake, onto the fairway, and then rolled 25 yards into the deep rough a mere 18 inches from the water. Although

Nelson displaying the clubs that helped him win 11 tournaments in a row.

"BYRON DIDN'T SMOKE, DIDN'T DRINK, DIDN'T PLAY AROUND, DIDN'T DANCE, AND I WONDERED JUST WHAT THE HELL HE DOES DO."
—SAM SNEAD, 1995

he managed to chip back onto the fairway, his final putt missed the hole by an inch. In the other semifinal match, Gene Sarazen lost the lead on the 28th hole against Byron Nelson and never regained control. Nelson, only 10 years old when Sarazen won his first PGA Championship crown, remembers, "One of my most memorable tests of character occurred at the 1941 PGA Championship at Cherry Hills Country Club in Denver. Talk about surviving a gauntlet of great players."

The final between defending Champion Nelson and Ghezzi proved to be an epic 38-hole duel. Ghezzi was 3-down after 27 holes, but he squared the match by winning the first three holes of the last nine. For the next five holes, the lead shifted back and forth until Ghezzi's missed putt on the final hole sent the match into sudden death. The players halved the 37th hole, and at the 38th their balls landed 42 inches from the cup in close proximity. The referee flipped a coin to see who would go first, and Nelson won. When he leaned over his ball to putt, he accidentally tapped Ghezzi's ball. Years later, Ghezzi remembered the moment well, "He was all concentration as he stroked his putt. In fact, he was concentrating so hard that he didn't realize the danger until the head of his putter, on the follow-through, struck my ball and moved it." Ghezzi made it clear that he did not want to win under these circumstances and asked that Nelson not be assessed a penalty stroke. A bit distracted, Nelson missed his putt, giving Ghezzi the win, 1-up, and a reason to say, "I feel like a kid on Christmas morning."

Bob Hamilton was given 10-to-1 odds in 1944.

The 1943 PGA Championship, along with that year's other three majors, was canceled because of World War II. The 1944 event was played at Manito Golf and Country Club, founded in 1922 as one of three private golf clubs in Spokane, Washington. Two years earlier, the 6,400-yard course had played host to the Western Amateur. The field was significantly reduced, as PGA President Ed Dudley explained that "this PGA Championship naturally won't have all the professional entries of the pre-war days. That cannot be expected with over 400 members of our association now in the service." In the 32 months since the Japanese attack on Pearl Harbor, The PGA of America sold $100,000 in war bonds, and the association saw the Championship as another opportunity to contribute to the war effort. The proceeds from the 1944 event, totaling $21,842, were donated to Baxter General Hospital and the Fort George Wright Convalescent Center in Spokane, military facilities that were built during the war. The 1944 *PGA Championship Journal* declared, "It is for the exclusive benefit of the patients in these institutions that this National PGA Championship is being staged."

The day before the event was to begin, The PGA of America announced a dramatic change in the rules—the abolishment of the stymie. This would not be the week's only surprise. Playing in his first PGA Championship, Bob Hamilton

pulled off an amazing upset by defeating Nelson in the 36-hole final, 1-up. Hamilton, one of the best wedge players on the tour, almost missed the tournament because of the travel restrictions imposed during the war. To reach the final bracket, Nelson defeated Mike DeMassey, Mark Fry, Willie Goggin, and Charles Congdon. Hamilton advanced past Gene Kunes, Harry Bassler, McSpaden, and George Schneiter. In the final, both players shot 70 in the morning round, and the match was all square. Hamilton began the afternoon by winning the 19th hole with a birdie and never relinquished the lead again. On the last hole, Hamilton barely missed an eagle, but his 20-inch birdie putt was enough to win the $3,500 purse. Nelson, discouraged by his performance in the Championship, told reporters, "four times in the Championship

final and I've won only one. Maybe I should give up the game."

Jimmy Demaret, the year's leading money winner, set the pace for the 1947 PGA Championship at Plum Hollow Country Club near Detroit, Michigan—a course distinguished by its five par 5's and three par 3's—by scoring a 137 in the 36-hole qualifying round. Demaret had served as head professional at the club in 1943. But this would not be a year for the favorites. Demaret, Hogan, Snead, and South Africa's Bobby Locke were eliminated in the opening two rounds, leaving Australian Jim Ferrier to win the title with a 2-and-1 victory over Chick Harbert. Ferrier immigrated to the United States and turned professional in 1940. He won the Australian Amateur four times and captured the Australian Open in 1938 and 1939.

But the surprise upsets of the big-name players did not dampen the crowd's enthusiasm. In the third round, in front of more than 10,000 spectators, U.S. Open winners Lew Worsham and Lloyd Mangrum advanced. Three-time PGA Champion Sarazen fell to Ky Laffoon. Porky Oliver, the 1946 runner-up of The PGA Championship, lost to Harbert. Ferrier faced a diffi-

Jim Ferrier, right, accidentally hit seven spectators with his ball in the 1947 final.

An aerial view of Plum Hollow Country Club in 1947.

cult match against Claude Harmon, but won on the first play-off hole when Harmon hooked his drive and made a bogey. In the quarterfinals, Lew Worsham was defeated by the 1941 PGA Champion, Vic Ghezzi, 3 and 2. Art Bell beat Ky Laffoon, and Ferrier dominated his match from the second hole to defeat Mangrum, 4 and 3. In the last match of the day, Leland Gibson lost to Harbert. In the semifinals, scheduled on Monday with the hope that it would draw big galleries left over from the weekend, Ferrier beat Art Bell, 10 and 9, the widest margin in the whole Championship. Harbert handily defeated Ghezzi, 6 and 5.

For the first time since 1937, Hogan, Snead, and Nelson did not make it to the final, suggesting that their domination was nearing an end. Herb Graffis remembered the 1947 final as the wildest he had ever seen. Both players sprayed tee shots all over the course; Ferrier managed to hit seven spectators and Harbert one. On the fourth hole in the afternoon round, Ferrier's ball landed on a tarpaulin covering a mower. He recalled his incredible recovery shot as the turning point in the match: "I took a No. 5 iron . . . stood for a wide hook and hit hard. It had to be a crisply hit shot to get anywhere against the wind. That ball travelled as if it had eyes. It got up fast, cleared the trees, sailed out over the barn and then came in towards the green. As it met the full force of the head wind, the ball dropped almost straight, right on to the green and almost dead to the pin."

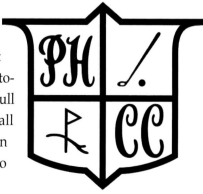

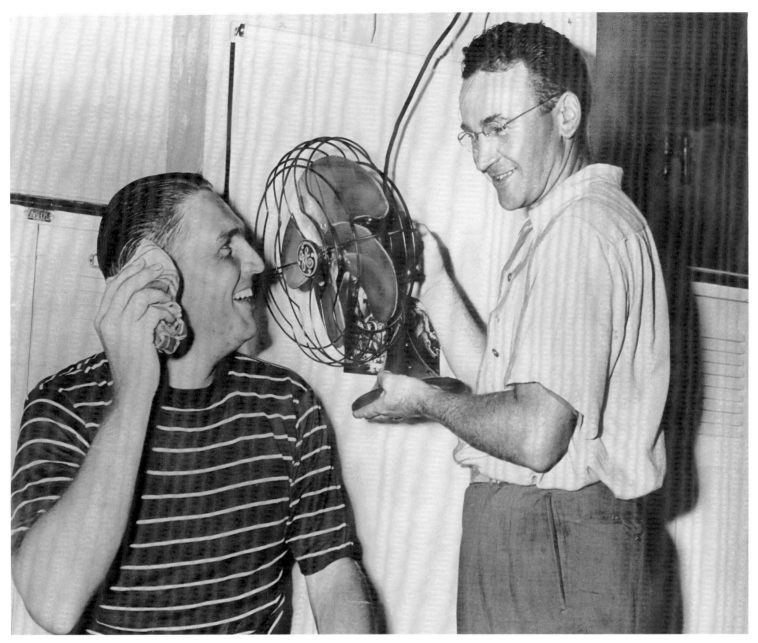

Jim Ferrier, left, trying to beat the heat during the 1947 Championship.

Apart from his extraordinary luck on that hole, Ferrier's putting helped him win the match, 2 and 1. Over the course of 35 holes, he took only 52 putts, extraordinary under the conditions. Sports writers describe the 1947 final as one of the hottest on record, even worse than what Bobby Jones faced at the U.S. Open in Minneapolis in 1930. The thermometer in the press tent reached 112 degrees, and Ferrier is reported to have walked off seven pounds. This would not be the only time in which Ferrier made news. Well past his prime, in the 1960 PGA Championship, he was runner-up to Jay Hebert.

In 1950, Chandler Harper joined Jock Hutchison, who had won the event 30 years earlier, as the oldest PGA Champion at the age of 36. That record stood until Julius Boros, at age 48, won in 1968. Only a professional for two years, Harper was an unlikely victor. Columbus, Ohio's Scioto Country Club, at 7,032 yards, was built for long hitters such as Snead, the week's favorite. Harper did not have the kind of record that made him a contender. He had won the Virginia State Amateur two decades earlier and had won only one PGA Tour event—the 1950 Tucson Open, where he set a record for using only 20 putts in a single round. His best finish in the PGA Championship came in 1946 when he reached the third round.

Chandler Harper on the first hole of the 1950 Championship.

The 1950 Championship was originally scheduled for Richmond, Virginia, but after some problems developed, The PGA of America began looking for another venue, giving James A. Rhodes, Columbus' mayor, a chance to bid for the Championship. With very little notice, Scioto President James Long collaborated with the Zooligans, a sports promotion group established to support the Columbus Zoo, and raised the $50,000 necessary to sponsor the event. The club ultimately donated a portion of the $70,000 in gate receipts to the zoo and the Columbus Boys' Club.

One hundred twenty-nine players gathered to compete for the 64 match-play spots. Snead won the pre-tournament long-drive contest, and, though exempt, he also captured the 36-hole qualifier with a 140. All of the significant players were on hand, with the exception of Hogan, who, despite his recent victory in the 1950 U.S. Open, decided to forego The PGA Championship because the rigorous match-play format was too strenuous for his legs. But Snead, Demaret, Mangrum, Ferrier, and Shute were all contenders.

On the first day, Snead defeated Sam Byrd in the first round, but lost in the second round on the 17th hole to 43-year-old Eddie Burke, a little-known club professional. Burke was elated, revealing that a friend, Henry Wimski, had promised him a Cadillac worth $5,000 if he beat Snead.

Hagen's Humor

Walter Hagen recounted his second-round match in 1940 at Hershey Country Club against Vic Ghezzi in the *Dayton Daily News* in 1957: "I opened up a bottle of Scotch to have a few nips before the match and this young man (Ghezzi) came over and audaciously suggested that I hurry up. He was ready to start the match. I wasn't. It was raining very hard and the course was muddy and I needed a little nip or two for my health's sake." To tease Ghezzi, he suggested that he would spot him the first two holes and meet him on the third. "Of course, I couldn't have done that, but it was an idea. The kid was just mad enough to beat me on the first two holes anyway, in that slush. Then I began to play golf at the third, finally caught up and beat him, 2 and 1."

COUNTRY CLUB OF HERSHEY, PA

Harper won the 1950 PGA Championship with a putter that was over a hundred years old.

Scioto's club historian, Paul Hornung, remembered that Burke's victim was not amused: "Snead took it hard. He truly became the 'slammer' after reaching the Scioto locker room—slamming his golf shoes into a bag, slamming his locker door, slamming the side door of the locker room exit, slamming his clubs and bag in the trunk of his car, slamming the trunk and slamming the car door in the face of the breathless press corps before making the quickest drive of the day, down Scioto's winding blacktop." Snead's hasty departure turned all the attention to Mangrum, who defeated Chick Harbert, 6 and 5, in the third round.

Harper came to The PGA Championship under the press

> "NO OTHER CHAMPIONSHIP IN GOLF
> CALLS FOR SO MUCH COMBINED
> PHYSICAL STAMINA, NERVE CONTROL,
> COURAGE, AND SKILL."
> —HORTON SMITH, 1953

corps' radar. Although he won his first two matches, it was not until he beat Bob Toski in the third round that he began to get any coverage. As one of the shortest drivers on the tour, Harper was overpowered on nearly every drive, but his putting kept him in contention. On the final hole of the quarterfinals, Harper remembered sinking a 12-foot putt to win over Mangrum, 1-up. Mangrum muttered on his way to the locker room, "Good gawdamighty, what a putter!" But later, Mangrum told George May, who ran the Tam O'Shanter tournament, that it was the best match in which he ever competed. After the match, someone brought Harper a bucket of water to cool off, and he asked in jest: "Is that for my putter?"

Ben Hogan's size did not diminish his prowess on the golf course.

In one semifinal match, Henry Williams Jr. defeated the 43-year-old Henry Picard, the 1938 Masters Champion and 1939 PGA Champion, who was suffering from severe arthritis. In the other semifinal, Harper faced Demaret, who came dressed in chartreuse pants and was reported to have sung while walking the fairways. On the 35th green, Harper made a 15-foot putt to the hole that turned out to be an inch smaller than regulation. He defeated Demaret, who had lost in the semifinals for the third time, previously being defeated in 1946 and 1948 by Hogan.

> "I'M NOT PLAYING IN THE PGA.
> I'M GOIN' FISHING."
> —JIMMY DEMARET, 1951

The final between Harper and Williams did not attract much attention; barely 2,000 people showed up for the morning round. The galleries in the afternoon doubled because the start was scheduled for four o'clock to allow spectators time to arrive from Columbus' business district. Harper took an early lead in what one sports writer called "the sloppiest final" ever played. He claimed a 4-and-3 victory on the 33rd hole. At the trophy presentation, Harper confessed, "We didn't play as well as I would have liked, but I think we gave 'em a good show." Then he did something that he declared that "Sam Snead would never do." He took off his hat to the crowd.

HOGAN'S APOLOGY

A few days before the 1950 PGA Championship at Scioto Country Club in Columbus, Ohio, Ben Hogan, the reigning U.S. Open Champion, was criticized for his decision to not play in the event. To explain his absence, he sent the following telegram to PGA President Joe Novak:

Thanks very much for your congratulating wire after my winning the Open. Also thanks for your invitation to be a spectator and referee in the final match of the PGA. I am terribly sorry that circumstances beyond my control prevent me from being there. I want to wish you and Mayor [James A.] Rhodes, the PGA and the city of Columbus the best tournament ever. Please forgive me for not being able to participate. With best wishes and kindest personal regards to all, I am sincerely, Ben Hogan.

CHAPTER FIVE

THE PGA CHAMPIONSHIP
IN THE AGE OF TELEVISION

I n the 1950s and 1960s, professional golf entered into an unprecedented era of prosperity and change. President Dwight D. Eisenhower, one of the game's biggest supporters, helped popularize the sport, and Arnold Palmer's charisma broadened the fan base.

The exposure of golf through the new medium of television led to increased purses for professional tournaments, brought corporate sponsorship into the sport, and made Palmer, Jack Nicklaus, and Gary Player household names. Local television coverage of golf began at the 1947 U.S. Open in St. Louis, but it was not until George S. May's World Championship of Golf at the Tam O'Shanter Golf Club in Chicago was broadcast nationwide in 1953 that the public began to take notice.

Already deemed golf's fourth major—along with the Masters, U.S. Open, and British Open—The PGA Championship was transformed from a match-play to a stroke-play event in 1958 and enjoyed a period of explosive growth. But no single player dominated the Championship in this era; the PGA counted 19 different winners from 1952 to 1970.

As early as 1952, The PGA of America voted on a proposal to modify the Championship's format, partly because stroke play was more predictable to telecast than match play. A proposal was made to have four rounds of stroke play, from which the leading 15 players and the defending Champion would then compete in four rounds of match play spread over three days. On November 13, 1952, the *New York Times* reported that the change was rejected, by a vote of 46-to-7, because the club professionals were worried that the new format "excluded the chance of a lesser light winning."

Walter Burkemo coming out of a bunker on the 16th hole in his quarterfinal match against Dave Douglas in 1953.

Burkemo and Felice Torza using a periscope during the 1953 Championship.

The switch to stroke play was rejected again in 1953, but for the next four years, the Championship's sponsors, players, and organizers kept the debate alive. The 1953 PGA Championship at Birmingham Country Club outside Detroit made it clear that change was inevitable. Ben Hogan, Bobby Locke, and Lloyd Mangrum elected not to participate; Jack Burke Jr., Denny Shute, and Jimmy Demaret withdrew; and Doug Ford, ranked third on the money list that year, was 14 days shy of being eligible to play according to PGA of America regulations.

Eligibility was not the only problem. On the first day of play in the 1953 Championship, called "Black Friday" by the press, six former Champions fell in the first two rounds. The title eventually went to Walter Burkemo, who defeated Felice Torza, a club professional nicknamed the "Toy Tiger," 2 and 1. Historian Howard Johnson, writing in the *Birmingham Country Club History*, declared that the 1953 Championship "may have been the

> ALL MAJOR CHAMPIONSHIPS ARE TOUGH TO WIN. BUT FOR ALL AROUND PHYSICAL AND PLAYING DEMANDS, THE PGA TOPS THEM ALL.
> —SAM SNEAD, 1952

death knell of the major match-play events. That's because the name players all lost in early matches. Sam Snead went out in the second round to Dave Douglas, who earlier defeated Lew Worsham. The great Gene Sarazen lost to former bellhop Torza. Other name golfers to suffer defeat were Jack Fleck, Chandler Harper, Chick Harbert, Dutch Harrison, George Fazio, Vic Ghezzi, Porky Oliver, Jim Turnesa, Cary Middlecoff, Fred Haas, Tommy Bolt, and Claude Harmon. . . . While Burkemo had been runner-up in the 1951 event, he was a local boy and not considered a favorite leading into the tournament. The PGA struggled with this loss of its big-name draws at a major event and the looming presence and economics of television coverage, which was replacing radio and newsreels."

The 1952 PGA Championship the year before told a similar story. At Big Spring Golf Club in Louisville, Kentucky, Snead, who was trying to become the first player since Walter Hagen to win four PGA titles, did not make it past the first round, much to the dismay of the event's sponsors. The Associated Press' Will Grimsley labeled the first two rounds the "Debacle of Big Spring," suggesting that the "list of survivors looked more like 'Who's He' than 'Who's Who.'" In the third round, Cary Middlecoff, playing in his first PGA Championship, defeated Al Smith, 4 and 2, with two well-timed eagles. In the quarterfinals, Middlecoff floundered and lost to Ted Kroll, a player who had received the Purple Heart four times for being wounded during World War II. In front of six thousand spectators, Chick Harbert beat Bob Hamilton, 2 and 1, and Jim Turnesa overcame Kroll, 4 and 2, in the semifinals. In the final, Turnesa reversed a 25-year jinx that had plagued him and his famous brothers, Mike and Joe, from winning the title and defeated Harbert, 1-up.

Turnesa's long struggle to win The PGA Championship in 1952 resembled Harbert's journey two years later at the Keller Golf Course in St. Paul, Minnesota. Harbert, playing in his eighth PGA Championship in 1954, had come close to winning twice. Both times he lost in the finals—to Australian-born Jim Ferrier in 1947 and to Turnesa in 1952. In St. Paul, he "traded his oft won runner-up cap for a winner's crown," as reported by the *Professional Golfer*. Harbert's road to victory left John O'Donnell, Porky Oliver, Jerry Barber, Tommy Bolt, and Walter Burkemo, the defending Champion, in his wake. Upon defeating Burkemo in the final, 4 and 3, the 39-year-old Harbert confessed in the locker room, "It has taken me a lifetime to win this one." His timing was perfect. That morning, he received a telegram from his parents that read: "Congratulations and good luck. A win would be a nice birthday present for your mother. We are praying for you. Mom and Pop."

Doug Ford's victory at the 1955 PGA Championship at Meadowbrook Country Club helped launch his career. Ford was known as one of the most consistent and quickest players on tour. In one semifinal match at Meadowbrook, Ford and Shelley Mayfield played 33 holes in five hours and 10 minutes. Eligible to play in the Championship for the first time, Ford would ultimately capture 19 PGA Tour wins, but one stood out in his mind. He recounted the moment in Nevin H. Gibson's *Great Moments in Golf*: "My 'greatest moment in golf' was the winning of the PGA Championship in 1955. My reason for this feeling is that it was my first major title and was won under grueling circumstances. I won the Qualifying Medal . . . and then played match play, finally winning 4 and 3 on the 33rd hole. We played for seven days in the heat and humidity that set records in Detroit for that time of year."

Jack Burke Jr. putted his way through the largest PGA Championship field in match-play history in 1956.

Chick Harbert swings an iron from a difficult lie on the first hole of the 1954 final.

Cary Middlecoff's response to sinking a long putt on the fourth green during the final match of the 1955 Championship.

Ford was the first player since Tom Creavy in 1931 to win The PGA Championship in his first attempt. He became the fourth player to win both the qualifying medal and the Championship, joining Walter Hagen, Olin Dutra, and Byron Nelson. By defeating Cary Middlecoff in the final, 4 and 3, Ford won $5,250 and an automatic place on the Ryder Cup team. Overwhelmed by emotion, Ford accepted the Wanamaker Trophy in tears: "Nothing like this has ever happened to me before; this is big, real big and when you win it, you are just too filled up inside to say anything except, Thanks." This victory helped him win The PGA Player of the Year Award. But it did not make him famous. That would come two years later, when he holed out from a bunker on the 72nd hole to win the 1957 Masters.

In 1956, at Blue Hill Country Club near Boston, Jack Burke Jr. became the first player since Sam Snead in 1949 to win the Masters and The PGA Championship in the same year. For the first time in the event's history the qualification rounds had been eliminated, so the entire 128-man field competed in the first 18-hole match play round. Burke, whose putting that week made him virtually unbeatable, became the first PGA victor required to win seven matches to claim his title.

It certainly proved to be the Championship of tempers. On the first day, Tommy Bolt accused the spectators of heckling him. On the 16th green, an ice cream vendor refused to stop hawking his wares while Bolt was putting. A marshal finally removed the offender, but Bolt could not regain his composure and lost to Charles Prentice, 1-down. Vic Ghezzi forfeited his first-round match against Al Smith in a rules dispute. On the 22nd hole, Ghezzi's ball landed in a marshy, unmarked portion of the fairway. When PGA President Harry Moffitt declared it a water hazard, *Golf World* reported that Ghezzi refused to accept the decision. After a heated exchange of words, he left the course and began walking toward the clubhouse, leaving his caddie to dig the ball out of the mud.

The third incident involved defending Champion Doug Ford and Mike Dietz. On the 15th hole during the second round, Dietz asked spectators to estimate how far the ball was from the green, violating, at the time, Rule 9-1 of the *Rules of Golf,* which held that competitors can not ask for advice from anyone other than their caddie, their partner, or their partner's caddie. Ford asked referee Ernie Doherty to assess a penalty stroke against Dietz, which he seemed reluctant to do. Exasperated, Ford declared that he would play under protest, although the incident clearly took a toll on his concentration. At the end of 18 holes, with the players all square, PGA officials declared that the match would continue into extra holes. Ford finally won on the fifth extra hole.

In the face of all this controversy, Burke's victory was a welcome respite. In the final, the affable Texan and the son of club professional Jack Burke Sr. defeated Ted Kroll, 3 and 2, declaring, "My chipping and putting won for me today." Burke, who had won the Masters in April, one-putted 15 greens in the 34-hole final. At the end of the morning round, Kroll had a 2-up lead. In the afternoon, Burke produced a string of five birdies in six holes. The only disappointment of the week was that Burke's father, who died in 1942, was not there to celebrate. In addition to Burke, only Sam Snead (1949) and Jack Nicklaus (1963 and 1975) have held The PGA and Masters titles in the same year. Years after the win, in a 1981 article for *Golf Magazine,* Burke explained that his 1956 victory gave him the opportunity to build Champions Golf Club with his close friend Jimmy Demaret in Houston.

In 1955, Doug Ford was the low qualifier and eventually the winner.

CAUCASIAN RACE CLAUSE

Restricted from tournaments sponsored by The PGA of America, African-American golfers resigned themselves to compete in all-black tournaments organized by the United Golfers Association (UGA) and smaller local tours before World War II. This policy barred some of the finest professional golfers of the era—including Ted Rhodes, Bill Spiller, and Charlie Sifford—from competing at the highest level. Spiller fought The PGA's exclusion more militantly than any of his peers and probably had the greatest impact. He turned professional in 1947 and toured on the UGA circuit with Ted Rhodes and boxer Joe Louis. In 1948, Spiller placed in the top 60 of the Los Angeles Open, which qualified him for the next PGA tournament, the Richmond Open outside Oakland. When Spiller, Rhodes, and Madison Gunter, two other black players who qualified, arrived to play, PGA official George Schneiter declared them ineligible under the Caucasian Race Clause, a part of The PGA's constitution since 1933. Instead of leaving quietly, as Pete McDaniel explained in *Uneven Lies: The Heroic Story of African Americans in Golf,* the two men told their story to Ira Blue of ABC Sports. Finally, at a meeting on November 10, 1961, The PGA of America voted to remove the passage from the constitution. By then, Spiller was beyond his playing prime, and Charlie Sifford became the first black member of The PGA of America in 1964. Tiger Woods became the first African-American golfer to win The PGA Championship, 38 years after African-American golfers were declared eligible to play.

Charlie Sifford, one of the first African-American golfers to play on the tour, tied for 33rd with Gary Player and Arnold Palmer and five other players in 1965.

In 1957, Lionel Hebert, the 29-year-old golfer from Lafayette, Louisiana, who studied music at Louisiana State University and occasionally played trumpet in Tommy Dorsey's band, became the last PGA Champion to win the event at match play by defeating Dow Finsterwald, 2 and 1. Before he won, he had earned less than $3,000 on the tour and was given 100-to-1 odds. It was Hebert's first and only major victory. He overcame a great field, led by Jack Burke Jr., the defending Champion, who earlier in the week bruised the tendons in his left wrist. On the injured list, Burke was joined by Ed Furgol, who hurt his right elbow at the Wilmington Open in the spring. Several weeks before The PGA Championship, Furgol fell through a fence in Montreal and injured his thigh. Chick Harbert was recovering from whooping cough, and Sam Snead was battling bursitis.

In the first two rounds that year at Miami Valley Country Club in Dayton, Ohio, many of the big-name players survived, with the exception of Furgol, Jim Turnesa, and Harbert. Gene Littler, in the field by special invitation because The PGA of America finally agreed to relax its

Jay, left, and Lionel Hebert, the only brothers to ever win The PGA Championship.

eligibility requirements, defeated Don Fairfield, 1-up. In the second round, Milon Marusic, who was not well known outside of his home state of Missouri, eliminated Burke, 2 and 1. Walter Burkemo, who defeated Jay Hebert, 3 and 2, in the quarterfinals, lost to Jay's brother, Lionel, in the semifinals, prompting him to quip, "Two brothers are one too many for me." In the other half of the semifinals against Finsterwald, Donald Whitt made a hole in one at the 13th hole, leading one elderly spectator to exclaim, "It was worth the price of admission just to see that." Snead, who had been the week's favorite, was playing a new driver. But it did not help much; he fell to Finsterwald in the fourth round.

When Hebert and Finsterwald reached the final, they became the youngest men since Byron Nelson lost to Vic Ghezzi in 1941 to battle for the Wanamaker Trophy. In the face of intense heat and fierce competition, they proved Walter Burkemo correct. Before the Championship, he observed, "You've got to give some edge to youth in a long tournament like this."

The 27-year-old Finsterwald, who turned professional in 1952, was making his PGA debut. He had been in the money for 56 straight tournaments. Hebert, who had been largely overshadowed by his older brother, was playing in his third Championship.

Hebert recalled the moment that he knew he had won, "On the 16th (34th) hole when Dow hit his second into the creek. I thought that was the turning point of the match. I played a safe shot to the green and just wanted to make four." Hebert's birdies on the first three holes after lunch foreshadowed what was to come. His 18-foot putt on the 31st hole that gave him a 1-up lead also helped. The $8,000 first-place check moved him from 49th to 15th place on the money list. Although Chick Harbert called it "the best run Championship I have ever played in" and Warren Orlick, who would become PGA president in 1971, deemed it "big league," The PGA of America lost money, mostly because of the elimination of the big-name players in the first round, which caused a dramatic drop-off in attendance.

As a result of the financial losses incurred from the 1957 event,

> "THIS TOURNAMENT IS AN ENDURANCE CONTEST. YOU'VE GOT TO BE STRONG TO GET THROUGH IT."
> —CARY MIDDLECOFF, 1954

The PGA began seriously debating a change in the format of the Championship. While such players as Walter Hagen complained that it would "make it just another 72-hole event," Ben Hogan, Sam Snead, Jack Burke Jr., and Cary Middlecoff supported the move. Always willing to change with the times, Gene Sarazen asked, "Why fight it? Medal play has become the thing in these days of television." In *Byron Nelson: The Little Black Book,* Nelson explained why match play was difficult for spectators, "Having a two-man final match on Sunday would be nearly impossible in terms of crowds. There wouldn't be enough room for them on each hole at one time."

So, for the first time, The PGA Championship shifted to a stroke-play format, and the 1958 PGA Championship at Llanerch Country Club in Havertown, Pennsylvania, attracted 45,000 spec-

In the fourth round in 1958, Dow Finsterwald shot a 67 and won by two strokes over Billy Casper.

ALL BETS ON SNEAD

The *Professional Golfer* detailed how caddies were selected for the 1955 PGA Championship. Caddie master Fred McGlone gave 33 of the best caddies, all young boys ranging from 14 to 18 years of age, the opportunity to choose the player they would loop for that week. Their decision mattered, as each boy was paid $5 per 18 holes and $1 an hour to shag balls. In addition, the caddie could expect a $5 tip. The one who caddied for the winner could make as much as $300. Defending Champion Chick Harbert, the home professional at Meadowbrook Country Club, helped draw the numbers out of a hat. The first caddie, Matt Sherock, chose Sam Snead. The second, Larry Williams, selected Walter Burkemo. Jim Sheffield chose Harbert, and Steve Kozar made Tommy Bolt the fourth pick. Cary Middlecoff, selected by Don Robinson, was fifth. These boys were brave, as McGlone observed, "They have learned to think for themselves. . . . They draw their numbers out of Harbert's own cap with him standing right there as their boss, and the defending champion. And they pick two other players." The boys who chose Middlecoff and Bolt made a bit of money. The ones who chose Burkemo, Snead, and Harbert did not fare as well.

tators. Gate receipts totaled $95,000, and program sales brought an additional $50,000. The *Professional Golfer* (The PGA of America's magazine changed its name from the *Professional Golfer of America* in April 1944) reported that "millions all over America watched the action Saturday and Sunday over the coast-to-coast television network of the Columbia Broadcasting Company." The new format eliminated the grueling endurance test and replaced it with the same four-round format used by the Masters, the U.S. Open, and the British Open. The change significantly reduced the possibility that a dark horse player such as Bob Hamilton, Tom Creavy, or Vic Ghezzi could win the Championship. The PGA of America further loosened its eligibility requirements, allowing "approved tournament players" to compete, even though they had not completed the five-year apprenticeship. This put Arnold Palmer, Ken Venturi, Billy Casper Jr., Frank Stranahan, and Billy Maxwell—all among the top 10 money winners—in the field. Fortunately, the thrilling finishes of the stroke-play events that followed the change continued to elevate the stature of The PGA Championship.

The first exciting win came in 1958, when 28-year-old Dow Finsterwald captured The PGA with a score of 67-72-70-67–276. Having failed to qualify for the U.S. Open earlier in the year, Finsterwald finished two strokes ahead of Billy Casper and pocketed the $5,500 first-place check. Lionel Hebert, whom Finsterwald lost to in the final the year before, finished tied for 16th place. Sam Snead, who seemed poised to win his fourth PGA Championship, was leading after 54 holes with a 207. On the last day, he fell apart on the back nine, taking a double bogey on the 13th hole. *Golf World* reported him as saying as he walked down the 18th fairway, "I've given the tournament away. I've missed enough of those six-footers to lose it." He finished third. Colorful Jimmy Demaret, who declared on the first day that "match play was for amateurs," was disqualified after the second round when he signed an incorrect scorecard. He left the course muttering in disbelief, "That's the first time I've ever been disqualified in 30 years of golf." Although he was playing badly, shooting an 83 that day, he joked with a *Golf World* reporter that he was just making his move.

In 1957, Lionel Hebert, right, was the last match-play Champion.

Stanford University graduate Bob Rosburg shot a 66 in the last round to beat Jerry Barber and Doug Sanders in 1959.

The cut, set at 154, eliminated former Champions Gene Sarazen, Chandler Harper, and Jim Turnesa. Tommy Bolt, who had been fined $500 for making "insulting remarks to tournament officials" and put on indefinite probation by The PGA of America for his display of poor sportsmanship at the Pepsi Open at Pine Hollow on Long Island earlier that year, spent most of the week trying to control his temper. Paired with Billy Maxwell in the second round, he missed an easy wedge approach and, without a second thought, tossed his club in the air. Remembering his promise to behave himself, he ran forward, caught it, and grinned at the crowd, who roared with applause.

On the final day, Finsterwald, nicknamed "Mister Conservative" by his peers, shot a 31 on the front nine and was poised to win the tournament over Billy Casper, who was playing in the Championship for the first time, and Snead. Finsterwald claimed that he won with what has been called the "Houdini par" on Llanerch's 12th hole. In *Golf Digest*, he recounted the shot: "It was a fairly short hole (178 yards) and the green was guarded on both sides by trees. I hit some of those trees off the tee and was in some real tough, matted rough. What's more, I had to wedge to a downslope. I got that wedge to within 12 feet of the pin—and made the putt. I scrambled on that one, all right, but it gave me a lift and I was able to finish well." He finished with a 67 and the title, challenging anyone who accused him of never taking a risk on the course.

After the first round in the 1959 PGA Championship, the event seemed almost anybody's to win. Nine players were tied for the lead after opening-round 69s on the par-70, 6,850-yard layout at Minneapolis Golf Club. The 43-year-old Jerry Barber, among the first-round leaders, turned in a 65 on the second day to put him out in front. Although Doug Sanders posted a 66, he was still four strokes behind Barber. Mike Souchak, who followed up his opening-round 69 with a 67, trailed Barber by just two strokes.

On Saturday, Sanders continued in good form, shooting 68 along with Sam Snead, Tommy Jacobs, Tommy Bolt, and Pete Cooper. But it was the sixth player to score 68 on Saturday, Bob Rosburg, who turned out to be the man to beat on Sunday. Rosburg's opening rounds of 71 and 72 left him at three over par, nine strokes behind the leader, and seemingly out of contention. For the final round, Sanders could not keep up the pace, shooting two over par. Barber fared no better, going three over par, with bogeys on the last two holes. Rosburg did not have the tournament handed to him, however. His closing-round 66, which included a first-nine 30, was the lowest round of the last day and won him The PGA Championship by just one stroke over Sanders and Barber, who tied for second.

Golf course architect Robert Trent Jones Sr. renovated Firestone Country Club in Akron, Ohio, for the 1960 PGA Championship by stretching the course from 6,585 to 7,165 yards, relocating 16 of the tees, and adding 28 new bunkers, all without changing the par-70 configuration. Arnold Palmer, in the midst of one of his best years on tour after winning the Masters and the U.S. Open and finishing second in the British Open, opened The PGA Championship with a 67, the day's lowest score. The ageless Sam Snead shot a 68, and Doug Sanders once again put himself into contention with a 70. But the course did not give up much after the first round. While Palmer struggled to a 74 in the second round, Jay Hebert, carved out a 67 and eased into the lead. Sanders shot 69 on Saturday to Hebert's 72, but it was 45-year-old Jim Ferrier's 66 that made headlines. After reaching five over

Jay Hebert, who won in 1960, and his brother, Lionel, were the first American brothers to win the same major.

par for his first two rounds, Ferrier moved to one over par, tied with Hebert. Snead's even-par round on Saturday kept him in contention, with Sanders leading by a stroke.

On Sunday, Hebert, who was awarded a Purple Heart at Iwo Jima in World War II, only needed to shoot a 35 on the front nine to pull ahead of the other three contenders. One hole later, he lost the lead to Ferrier. The Australian later bogeyed both 14 and 15 and birdied 17, and the congestion at the top of the leader board was complicated by Snead's birdie at 16. Sanders, still in contention and playing with Hebert in the final pairing, did not completely end his chances until the end of the tournament.

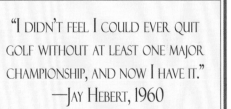

"I DIDN'T FEEL I COULD EVER QUIT GOLF WITHOUT AT LEAST ONE MAJOR CHAMPIONSHIP, AND NOW I HAVE IT."
—JAY HEBERT, 1960

When Hebert came to the 465-yard 18th it appeared that a par might win the event or at least put him in a playoff. Snead bogeyed the hole, and all Ferrier could manage was par for second place. Sanders' bogey would leave him tied for third with Snead. At the 18th hole, Hebert hit his approach shot to 25 feet, and his two-putt made him the winner by a stroke. Lionel and Jay Hebert are the only two brothers to have ever won The PGA Championship.

In 1961, Olympia Fields became the first club to host the Championship in both match- and stroke-play formats. To accommodate CBS' 90-minute television broadcast on Sunday, the layout was altered to end with four par 4s. The 6,722-yard, par-70 course seemed fairly short for tour professionals. But three under par proved to be the winning score, as the North, or No. 4 Course, where Walter Hagen won The PGA in 1925, held up to the best in the game.

> "THE BEST PLAYER DIDN'T WIN TODAY—BUT I'M GLAD I DID."
> —JERRY BARBER, 1961

For the third year in a row, Doug Sanders was in contention after the first two rounds, which took until Saturday to complete because rain washed out Friday's play. Jerry Barber, who had nearly won the 1959 PGA Championship before he bogeyed the final two holes, took the lead after Saturday's play. With a 36-hole finale scheduled for Sunday, it appeared that Don January would be Barber's nemesis this time. January shot a 67 for the morning round. He took a four-stroke lead with only three holes to play in the last round.

Barber did not seem likely to emerge victorious. At age 45, the five-foot-five-inch golfer was reported to be colorblind and suffering from poor depth perception. The diminutive Barber's strength was putting, and he put on a clinic on the last three holes of regulation play. On the 16th hole, he sank a birdie putt from 20 feet.

Jerry Barber being kissed by his wife, Lucille, after winning in 1961 in a playoff against Don January.

The clubhouse at Aronimink Golf Club was designed by Charles Benton King and built in 1927.

Then on the 17th, he made a 40-footer to place himself only one stroke behind January. When his approach shot stopped 60 feet from the flag on the 18th, it appeared that January had won, but Barber sank the putt and forced an 18-hole playoff on Monday. As former PGA President Joe Black described it in *Golf Digest* more than 30 years later, "He putted from the center left of a two-tiered green, and it had to ride a ridge to a hole cut on a little protrusion. The greens would probably have been a nine on the Stimpmeter—they were as fast as we could get them at the time." Lloyd Lambert, former legal counsel of The PGA of America, described the galleries at the moment Barber sank the last putt as "explosive." In the playoff, Barber shot a 67 to January's 68, and his performance helped him earn The PGA's Player of the Year honors. He was also named playing captain of the victorious U.S. Ryder Cup team.

Gary Player came into the 1962 PGA Championship recognized as one of the best golfers in the world, although it had been 15 months since his last win. He had won the 1959 British Open and the 1961 Masters. Earlier in 1962, he finished tied for second with Dow Finsterwald at the Masters. After a disappointing performance at the 1962 British Open at Troon, where he

Gary Player became the fifth international player to win The PGA title in 1962.

Player added the 1962 PGA to his 1959 British Open and 1961 Masters victories.

missed the cut, Player, whose home was still South Africa, became worried that the constant travel was negatively affecting his playing ability. In his book *Grand Slam Golf,* Player discussed how Aronimink Golf Club, the site of the 1962 PGA Championship, transformed him. "A fantastic change came over me," he wrote. "Here was a marvelous course, green and ripe, with lush fairways, dazzling white bunkers, holding greens, lovely trees everywhere. All my life I have loved trees—and there are no trees at Troon. The whole setting was so peaceful and sympathetic to me, after the brutalities of Troon, that I felt happy and relaxed and invigorated."

As relaxed as he was, Player was still two over par on the par-70 course after the first round, trailing the leader, John Barnum, who broke the course record with a 66. Player, using a $50 putter he bought in Japan, shot a 67 on Friday to advance into a tie for second, behind Doug Ford, who shot a 66. With a 69 on Saturday, Player finally took the lead by two over George Bayer. Ford was three strokes back, and Bob Goalby's 71 in the third round put him four strokes behind.

Playing together on Sunday, Goalby still trailed Player by three strokes after 13 holes. Birdies at 14 and 16 brought Goalby within a stroke of Player, and then both golfers parred the 17th hole. Still one stroke ahead, Player had a long putt for birdie on 18 and missed, settling for par. Goalby missed his birdie attempt,

THE TURNESA DYNASTY

With his victory in 1952 at Big Spring Country Club in Louisville, Kentucky, Jim Turnesa finally ended the jinx that had plagued the Turnesa brothers in The PGA Championship. Seven of the Turnesa brothers played golf. Six played professionally, and Willie remained an amateur. He won the U.S. Amateur in 1938 and 1948 and the British Amateur in 1947. Four of the brothers placed second in one of golf's major championships. Joe Turnesa lost to Bobby Jones in the 1926 U.S. Open and then lost in the 1927 PGA Championship final to Walter Hagen. Fifteen years later, Jim, then a corporal in the army,

lost to Sam Snead in the 1942 PGA Championship. In 1948, Mike Turnesa was defeated by Ben Hogan in The PGA Championship. It appeared that the Turnesa family was never destined to hold the Wanamaker Trophy. Jim changed all of that in 1952, and the *New York Times* reported, "Jim's victory this afternoon brought the golfing Turnesas to a unique place in the world of sports. No other family has been able to win both the amateur and professional golfing championships of this country."

Jim Turnesa with the Wanamaker Trophy in 1952.

and Player won The PGA Championship by a stroke. "Obviously you're uptight when you know that you have the possibility of winning a major championship," Player later recalled. "Bob Goalby is right there and we're battling it out together . . . and the shot I hit at the last hole I will never forget. I hit my drive to the right in the trees and then I took a 3-wood and I aimed it 100 yards left of the green and hit the biggest slice around the corner and onto the green. I think that was the shot." Three years later, after capturing the U.S. Open title, Player joined Gene Sarazen (1935) and Ben Hogan (1953) as the only golfers to have won all four professional majors. Jack Nicklaus (1966) and Tiger Woods (2000) would eventually become part of this elite group.

Nicklaus wasted no time in joining Sarazen, Hogan, and Nelson as the only players at that point to win all three majors played in the United States: the Masters, the U.S. Open, and The PGA Championship. To win the 1963 PGA Championship, he endured some of the hottest temperatures recorded at the event. At the Dallas Athletic Club, the thermometer surpassed 100 degrees, and one of the policemen assigned to escort the eventual Champion around the course passed out after Nicklaus completed one of his rounds. With a shot of 341 yards, Nicklaus won the long-drive contest the day before the event began and foreshadowed things to come. Exhausted from the British Open a week before, his first round of 69 put him in a tie for second with Julius Boros, Bob Charles, Mason Rudolph, and Shelley Mayfield. Club professional Dick Hart's 66 set the standard. Nine players eagled the first hole.

On Friday, Nicklaus lost some ground with a two-over-par 73. Hart shot a 72, giving him a three-stroke lead over Tony Lema, Boros, and Mayfield. Saturday's round produced low scores that resulted in significant changes on the leader board. Bruce Crampton shot a 65 to take the lead, followed by Dow Finsterwald, whose 66 left him two strokes behind. Nicklaus hung onto third place with a 69.

Dave Ragan invigorated the crowd early in his round on Sunday by making four birdies in his first seven holes. By the time Ragan bogeyed the 13th hole, Nicklaus birdied 12, leaving Crampton, Nicklaus, and Ragan tied for the lead. Nicklaus managed only one more birdie coming in, at 15 with a 30-foot putt, but it would be enough for a two-stroke margin of victory. Ragan made another birdie, but he also bogeyed two holes. Crampton bogeyed two holes coming in and parred the rest. On the 18th hole, Nicklaus made a par for the win.

At the age of 23, Jack Nicklaus won his first PGA Championship in 1963.

When the presentation of the Wanamaker Trophy was made after the event, no one could touch it because it had been sizzling in the sun the whole day and was literally too hot to handle. Nicklaus managed, though, to hoist the prestigious hardware with the aid of two towels. He was also given an unusual bonus—the first lot in The PGA development at Palm Beach Gardens, the home of the organization's new headquarters. The lot, valued at nearly $5,000, was promised to the winner by developer John D. MacArthur.

Going into The PGA Championship in 1964 at Columbus Country Club, Arnold Palmer was still seeking the one major title that had eluded him. In April of that year, he had won his fourth Masters. He previously won the U.S. Open in 1960 and the British Open in both 1961 and 1962. For the 1964 PGA Championship he put together four extraordinary rounds of 68-68-69-69, but it was only good enough to tie him for second with Nicklaus. The record crowds included evangelist Billy Graham, who was in town for a weeklong rally.

Bobby Nichols opened with a 64 and remained in the lead for the next three rounds. The week before the Championship, he had purchased a used putter for $5 at the golf shop at Owl Creek Country Club near his home in Louisville, Kentucky. Driving to his downtown hotel after the first round, his car broke down, and fortunately a passing fan recognized him and gave him a ride. Nichols shot one over par on Friday and kept a one-stroke advantage over Palmer. Regaining his form on Saturday, Nichols shot 69 and then added a 67 on Sun-

In 1963, Nicklaus posted a 68 in the fourth round to win over Dave Ragan.

day to win by three strokes. His wife was so excited that she nearly gave birth to their son, Ricky, three months early. Nichols' 271 total for The PGA Championship remained the lowest score until Nick Price shot a 269 in 1994 at Southern Hills Country Club. When Price broke the record, Nichols called to congratulate him and reported fondly that Price was "almost apologetic."

As a teenager, in 1952, Nichols was nearly killed in a car ac-

cident when he went through a windshield. He was unconscious for 13 days and suffered from a concussion, broken pelvis, collapsed lung, and injured kidney. During his 96-day stay in the hospital he received two letters of encouragement from Ben Hogan, who also survived a nearly fatal car accident in 1949. In the final round of The PGA in 1964, Nichols, who was paired with the legendary golfer, finally had a chance to thank him.

Although he struggled from tee to green in the final round, Nichols made some amazing saves on the green, which included a 35-foot eagle putt at the 10th hole, a birdie putt from 15 feet at the 15th hole, an 18-footer to save par at the 16th, and a 51-foot putt at the 17th. "He never said anything during that last round when I was making those impossible shots," Nichols recalled of Hogan. "But when I holed that long putt, there was Ben with a great big smile on his face. He looked at me, shook his head, and then had to smile again." Nichols was so grateful for the win that he used part of his first-place prize money to erect a statue of Saint Jude, the patron saint of lost causes, at Columbus Country Club.

Dave Marr received a bit of advice in a note from his cousin, Jack Burke Jr., before the final round of the 1965 PGA Championship at Laurel Valley Golf Club. "We were staying at the same place, the Mountainview Inn, and it just said, 'Fairways and greens, Cuz.' I knew what he meant," said Marr, recalling the event in *Golf Digest* in 1997. "Just hit as many fairways and greens as you can. That's what you have got to think about. Not winning. Don't make up your speech too early." Marr heeded the advice and remained in control.

> "SURE I'M STILL HUNGRY. I'M IN THIS GAME AS A COMPETITOR, AND I WANT TO WIN EVERY TIME I PLAY. I DON'T THINK THE TIME WILL COME VERY SOON WHEN I LOSE MY DESIRE."
> —JACK NICKLAUS, 1963

Bobby Nichols, left, shown with Kentucky Governor Edward T. Breathitt, led every round on his way to victory in 1964.

Bobby Nichols, left, the 1964 Champion, with Ben Hogan, the 1946 and 1948 Champion.

Marr's father had been a club professional in the Houston area and, as a young man, Dave served as a club professional for seven years, including working for Claude Harmon, three summers at Winged Foot and three winters at Seminole Golf Club. In his 12 years on the tour, Marr amassed three victories. The year before his win over Billy Casper and Nicklaus in 1965, he finished 65th in The PGA Championship, the last person in the money.

Fog delayed the start of the 1965 Championship by two hours on the first day, requiring that half of the field begin on the back nine. Tommy Aaron's first-round 66 was the best of the day, but several players also scored well, including Gardner

Dickinson and Mason Rudolph with 67s, Bruce Devlin, Sam Snead, and Raymond Floyd at 68, and Nicklaus with a 69. Marr shot a one-under-par 70 to tie him for eighth. Tommy Aaron's second-round 71 on the 7,090-yard course kept him in the lead, but Marr shot 69, which put him in a tie for second with Nicklaus, the year's Masters Champion.

Ray Kienzl of the *Pittsburgh Press* claimed that the fog never lifted from hometown favorite Arnold Palmer, who lived nine miles from the course. He opened with a 72, then shot 75-74-73 to finish in a tie for 33rd. To complicate matters, he was assessed four penalty strokes during the tournament. On the opening hole of the first round, though he was entitled to a free lift, Palmer

Dave Marr with Harry Pezzullo, a PGA rules official in 1965.

watched several marshals dismantle the railing on a small wooden bridge to allow him a clear shot to the green. Five holes later, he was informed by Jack Tuthill, the tournament director, that the marshals' action violated Rule 17-1 of the *Rules of Golf* and cost him a two-stroke penalty. The next day, while in a bunker on the 11th hole, he hit a stone in his backswing, which gave him another two-stroke penalty for grounding his club in a hazard. This put Palmer 10 strokes behind Tommy Aaron, the leader, after 36 holes. At the trophy ceremony, Dave Marr joked about the honorary membership that Laurel Valley had extended to Palmer, "Now that Arnold's been made a member here, he's starting to play like one."

Pete Brown, left, tied for 33rd at the 1964 PGA Championship.

With an opening-round 68 to tie for the lead at Firestone Country Club in 1966, Sam Snead proved, yet again, that he had one of the most durable swings in golf. Al Geiberger, who made peanut butter sandwiches famous that week, matched his score. *Golf World* reported that while playing at The PGA Championship at Laurel Valley the year before, Geiberger was paired with hometown hero Arnold Palmer and found that he could not fight his way through Arnie's Army to reach a concession stand. Anticipating the same problem in 1966, he borrowed some of his three-year-old daughter's sandwiches. To boost his energy and settle his nervous stomach, he ate one during every round. When asked why, he replied, "Think what your golf bag would smell like if you carried sardine sandwiches." At the interview in the press tent, Bob Gorham, the PGA's press secretary, presented him with a three-pound jar of peanut butter and a loaf of bread.

In the second round, Snead shot a 71 to Geiberger's 72 and, at the age of 54, took the lead after 36 holes. "I lost my lead on the second day but came back on the third with another 68 and led by four shots," Geiberger recalled in Nevin Gibson's *Great Moments in Golf*. "Then in the last round, I bogeyed the first two holes, parred the third and bogeyed the fourth. On the par-3 fifth hole, I dropped a 25-foot putt which really gave me the boost I needed. When you start bad and go three over on the first four holes, how can you get back on the rugged Firestone Course? What a shock! But this long putt came at a crucial time to give me the confidence I needed. After I made my par on the 16th hole, I knew then that I had won the National PGA Championship. My principal objective which I concentrated on was to get through the 16th hole. You can imagine the elations I experienced when I conquered this task. It was a great feeling to know that I could six-putt the final hole and still win the PGA Championship. . . . When I achieved this, I knew that I would never be considered a 'flash' winner. It was indeed a great honor to win this most prestigious championship under the conditions which existed."

By the end of the third round, Marr caught Aaron by shooting a 70 to Aaron's 72. Some formidable players were close to the lead on Sunday. Gardner Dickinson trailed by a stroke. Billy Casper was two strokes behind the leaders, as was Nicklaus. After Aaron double-bogeyed the first hole on Sunday, he never regained the lead and faded with a 78 to finish in a tie for eighth. Casper took the lead on the front nine, but Marr responded well and birdied the 10th and 11th holes. As it had so many years before, everything came down to the last hole. Although Marr had missed an 18-inch putt at the 16th for par, he led Casper and Nicklaus by two coming to 18. On the long par 4, Marr hit his third shot to just under four feet, sank the putt, and won.

Dudley Wysong carded a 66 on Saturday, bringing him into contention. But he could not catch Geiberger on Sunday and settled for second place. Billy Casper, Gene Littler, and Gary Player finished tied for third. Julius Boros, Jacky Cupit, Arnold Palmer, Doug Sanders, and Snead were all tied for sixth. The only sad note of the week came after the trophy ceremony. That evening, on July 24, Tony Lema, one of golf's most colorful figures and the 1964 British Open Champion, and his wife died in a small plane crash en route from Firestone to an appearance in Illinois. The PGA Championship was Lema's last event, and he shot 295 to tie for 34th place.

Columbine Country Club in Denver had originally been scheduled to host the 1966 PGA. But the extensive damage to the golf course from a flood in 1965 required that Firestone switch years with the Denver club. Dave Hill, who had won the 1961 Denver Open, led the 1967 PGA Championship early with a first-round 66, followed by Nicklaus with a 67. Davis Love II, father of 1997 PGA Champion Davis Love III, opened with a 69 and tied with three other players. Despite the high altitude that allows golf balls to fly nearly 10 percent farther, the 7,436-yard layout proved to be a good test. On Friday, Tommy Aaron, who had contended in the event two years earlier, shot a 65 to take the lead. Jack Nicklaus shot a 75, but his 69 on Saturday put him back in the hunt. Arnold Palmer, once again seeking the one title that eluded him, was four behind leader Dan Sikes on Saturday, only to shoot a 74 on the last day to finish tied for 14th place.

With scores of 71-72-70, Don January did not show any heroics in the first three rounds. Tied for fifth, though, he was in reach of the lead on Sunday. Don Massengale, who was six strokes from the lead, did not seem to be a threat until he posted the lowest round on Sunday, a 66, and marched to the top of the leader board. Nicklaus posted a respectable 71 on Sunday,

Dave Marr, who later became a successful golf commentator on television, won over Jack Nicklaus and Billy Casper in 1965.

Added security during the 1966 PGA Championship helped escort Al Geiberger, center, and his wife to the trophy ceremony.

which left him only one shot behind the eventual leaders, January and Massengale. January made four birdies between the 12th and the 17th holes to shoot a 68 for a tie at the end of regulation play. The next day, he won the 18-hole playoff with a 69 to Massengale's 71.

Throughout the 1960s, off-course debates between tour players and The PGA of America threatened the future of the Championship. As early as the end of World War II, it became clear to the PGA that it had two businesses that served two distinct constituencies. In *The Wonderful World of Professional Golf,* Mark McCormack explained the dichotomy: "The first, included a large group of teaching professionals, focused on how the game is taught, merchandised, and organized at the local level. The second included a small but visible group of touring professionals, focused on conducting tournament golf for a national

audience." The tension between these two factions, which had been simmering for nearly two decades, boiled over at the 1966, 1967, and 1968 PGA Championships.

High-profile players, led by Palmer and Nicklaus, began clamoring for control over the television rights while The PGA of America argued that the revenues should benefit all the members. On the eve of the 1966 event at Firestone, the players made a demand for autonomy, but to no avail. The next year, at the 1967 event at Columbine, they raised the issue again with a bigger threat. Two weeks before the event was to begin in Denver, they declared that they would boycott the Championship unless a deal could be made. The PGA rejected their pleas, saying that the event would continue even if the field consisted only of local professionals. The host club became involved and raised the stakes, declaring that they would not sponsor an

Bill Gannon, left, the brother of Geiberger's caddie, Mickey, led the cheering section at Firestone.

event without the big-name players. With both sides threatening lawsuits, the PGA was played under less-than-ideal circumstances.

In 1968, the battle was resumed at Pecan Valley in San Antonio, Texas. Once again the players threatened to boycott the Championship. And once again the players and The PGA of America reached an uneasy stalemate. But this time the players held the cards. In late August, after The PGA Championship, the players announced the formation of the American Professional Golfers (APG) and began soliciting sponsors for a separate tour. Over the next three months, most of the high-profile players signed on with the APG. On December 1, 1968, they announced a 28-event tour that included $3.5 million in prize money. ABC threatened to cancel the contract to televise the 1969 PGA Championship at the National Cash Register (NCR) Country Club in Dayton, Ohio, if the best players were not in the field. The Dayton Chamber of Commerce threatened to pull its sponsorship for the same reason.

PGA President Max Elbin made his position clear in a report to the membership in November: "A philosophical difference of long standing between the men elected to guide your Association and the few privileged to enjoy the benefits of the tour program has reached a flash point." The deadlock lasted until Leo Fraser became president in 1969, and the Tournament Players' Division was established. The tour players got their own organization, led by Joe Dey, who served as the first commissioner. The PGA of America retained control of The PGA Championship and the Ryder Cup matches.

Despite the distractions, the 1968 PGA Championship had an exciting finish because Arnold Palmer was once again in contention. Played in mid-July, the usual Texas heat was oppressive throughout the tournament. That made it all the more remarkable that the Champion that year not only was the oldest winner, at the age of 48, in PGA Championship history, but also in the history of all the majors. Two of the game's best golfers were not a factor in San Antonio. Nicklaus missed the cut after shooting 71-79, and Player, worried about the high temperatures, did not enter the event. It was so hot that Will Grimsley of the Associated Press listed his byline for one story as Wilt Grimsley.

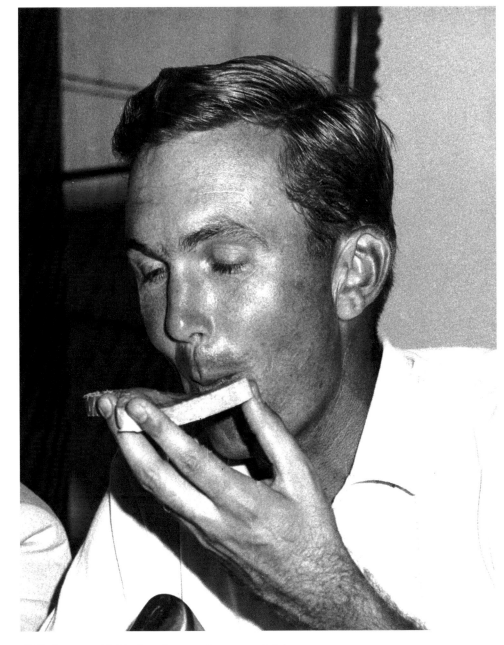

Al Geiberger with his famed peanut butter sandwich.

Marty Fleckman was among only five players to break par on the course in the first round. His first-round 66 gave Fleckman the lead; Palmer and Julius Boros were five strokes back. Lee Trevino, the U.S. Open Champion, opened with a 69. He followed with a 71 on Friday to be within two strokes of Fleckman and Frank Beard, who were tied for the lead. No one dominated the course on Saturday, but Boros moved up to tie for third after shooting even par. Fleckman and Beard both posted 72s to stay tied for the lead; Palmer's 72 put him two strokes back.

On Sunday, Palmer, Boros, Bob Charles, and Fleckman were tied after the first nine holes. Defying his age, Boros continued to press on in the heat, and he sank a birdie putt at the 11th hole, bogeyed the 14th, then came back with a birdie at 16. Another bogey at 17 cut his lead to one stroke ahead of Palmer, Fleckman, and Charles. Palmer struggled the whole day with his putter; only one of his nine birdie putts from less than 15 feet found the hole.

Palmer, playing in the group ahead of Boros, knew that he probably needed a birdie on the final hole to catch him. His drive found the thick rough, but Palmer's determination shone through. He hit a 3-wood that curved around a tree and found the green, hitting the flagstick and coming to rest eight feet above the hole. For a moment it appeared that he had made the putt, but it slipped past. Boros, who was nearly 30 years old when he gave up a career in accounting to pursue golf, parred the hole and won the 1968 PGA Championship by one shot. He refused, however, to smile for the cameras, later confessing that he had chipped a tooth.

In 1969, The PGA of America, finally heeding requests of players who complained about its proximity on the calendar to the British Open, moved the Championship to August. Except for the 1971 Championship, which was played in February, it has remained there ever since, building its reputation as "the season's final major."

Nine players shot 69 on the opening day at the National Cash Register's South Course to tie for first, among them Raymond Floyd, who followed with rounds of 66 and 67 to stay in the lead, despite impressive 64s shot by Don Bies on Friday and Miller Barber on Saturday. Palmer withdrew before the second round after having problems with his hip, and Floyd became the center of a controversy on Friday when he accused his playing partner, Jim Ferrier, the 1947 PGA Champion, of slow play. Floyd said, "He's getting old and his nerves are gone, but I don't really feel sorry for him because he shouldn't be out here." On Saturday morning, Ferrier demanded and Floyd delivered a formal apology.

Player had put himself into contention by shooting a 65 on Friday to go with his first round of 71. But events beyond his control conspired against him. Prior to the event, civil rights activists led by Melvin J. Jackson met with the Dayton Chamber of Commerce and issued 23 demands that ranged from a request for 3,000 tickets for the poor to a boycott of California grapes. Their main concern, though, seemed to be the city's willingness to spend money on a professional sporting event rather than helping the needy. When the demands were rejected, they threatened to disrupt The PGA Championship. The protestors tried to involve Lee Elder and other African-American golfers in the protest, but they refused and claimed that this was their livelihood and that they intended to play. Most of the protests were directed against Player, who was from South Africa. Ignoring Player's open opposition to the apartheid government, the protesters began harassing him during Saturday's third round. Even with a police force that swelled to 400, the players were repeatedly disrupted and threatened. Nicklaus, who was playing with Player, also bore the brunt of the attacks.

Don January, left, won in a playoff against Don Massengale in 1967.

January's first-place check was $25,000.

Al Geiberger shot two rounds of 68 on his way to winning in 1966 at Firestone.

On the fourth hole, a spectator threw a program onto the tee as Player began his swing. Trying to make light of the situation, Nicklaus ducked behind his golf bag acting as if he was taking cover. On the ninth green, several protesters shouted while Nicklaus was putting. Player had a cup of ice thrown in his face as he and Nicklaus walked to the 10th tee. An astonished Player asked, "What have I ever done to you?" to which the man replied, "You're a damned racist." Then, as Ray Kienzl of the *Pittsburgh Press* wrote, "all hell broke loose." Roy Porter, currently a volunteer at The PGA Historical Center in Port St. Lucie, Florida, was standing nearby and saw four protesters rush Player and Nicklaus on the 10th green. To defend himself, Nicklaus brandished his putter until a security guard tackled one of the men and knocked him into the bunker. Eventually, 11 demonstrators were arrested, and the only other incident came on the 13th hole when a young woman rolled a plastic golf ball onto the green while Player putted. Despite the difficulties he endured, Player

"dusted himself off and went on with his game." He managed to shoot a 71 and stay in contention, but Floyd's 67 gave him a five-stroke lead.

After dominating the South Course for three days Floyd lost his touch on Sunday. By the back nine Player had pulled to within three strokes of Floyd. A bogey by Floyd at the 13th while Player parred cut another stroke off the lead, and it appeared that Player had the momentum. Floyd had just enough determination to persevere, making a birdie at 16 to get back to a two-stroke lead, which he needed, because a bogey at 18 by Floyd left him just a stroke ahead of Player. But it was enough for Floyd to win it.

Years after the event, Player still felt disappointment at the outcome: "How would you feel if you had your life threatened every single day?" asked Player. "During the PGA, they threw ice in my eyes, they threw a golf ball between my legs. All these things happened at vital stages of play. They threw telephone books at my back at the top of the backswing; they charged me

In 1968, at the age of 48, Julius Boros became and remains the oldest player to win the Championship.

Despite a 74 in the fourth round, Ray Floyd captured his first major victory at the 1969 PGA Championship.

on the greens; they shouted at a one-foot putt on number nine and they screamed while standing on the edge of the green. I missed the one-foot putt by five inches because I was so frightened, and I lost the tournament by one stroke. I will go to my grave knowing that I won that tournament. I will go to my grave knowing that I won 10 majors and not nine because that has never happened to any golfer in the history of the game."

To combat the 100-degree heat at the 1970 PGA Championship at Southern Hills Country Club in Tulsa, Oklahoma, the organizers did everything they could to keep the players comfortable. They blasted the air conditioners in the clubhouse, sprayed artificial snow on the windows, and hung icicles from the rafters. But not all the entertainment was planned by the hosts. Prior to the Championship, Mark McCormack reported later in his 1971 *Golf Annual* that a local restaurateur called to tell the Tulsa police that a small group of hippies was planning to sabotage the greens. He explained, "Five nude girls were to appear on the course in a pre-tournament night and lure guards away from the greens. While the guards were engrossed, other members of the group, using grass killing spray, would paint the word 'peace' on the greens." Fortunately, the scheme never materialized.

Arnold Palmer, the favorite at the 1960 PGA Championship, on the practice range before the start of the event.

ELIGIBILITY AND THE CHAMPIONSHIP

The PGA of America's eligibility rules plagued The PGA Championship in the late 1940s and early 1950s, often excluding some of the game's best players. This rule became the main story of the 1953 PGA Championship at Birmingham Country Club when Julius Boros, the recently crowned U.S. Open victor, was issued a special invitation to play by The PGA of America. He would not have otherwise been eligible, as he had only served half of the five-year apprenticeship necessary for PGA membership. An hour before the qualifying round was to begin, he withdrew from the field and issued the following statement: "I sincerely appreciate the PGA making an exception in its rule to invite me to play here. However, after thinking it over, I have decided that I'd rather wait my turn for PGA membership like Cary Middlecoff and the others have done ahead of me. I plan to be a PGA member for many years to come and I want all the PGA members to be my friends. As a result, I have decided to decline the invitation to compete here and go home and visit my folks." Boros was not the only player to suffer under this rule. In 1957, Arnold Palmer was fifth on the money list but could not compete in The PGA Championship because he was not yet eligible. Until 1958, The PGA was a closed Championship, in which only PGA members who qualified in their sections could compete. One PGA official explained the need for change, "We either had to go forward and make it a championship that will rival the U.S. Open, or play it every year at Dunedin as a member's tournament."

*Palmer blasting out of the
rough on the 17th hole in 1968.*

In 1968, Lee Trevino opened with a 69 and tied for 23rd place.

Dave Stockton won in 1970 despite shooting three over par in the fourth round.

After the opening round, Nicklaus and Johnny Miller, who had turned professional just the year before, topped the leader board. Arnold Palmer opened tied for fifth, along with Dave Stockton and several other players. Palmer took a two-stroke lead after 11 holes on Friday, but the difficult 12th hole stopped his charge. On his second shot, he failed to reach the green from the rough, and his ball landed on a clump of weeds growing out of a creek. Instead of taking a penalty drop and settling for a bogey, he stepped into the water and tried to hit it out. He ended up with a double bogey; by the end of the round, he was two behind the leaders.

> "MAYBE IF I DO WELL IN THIS
> TOURNAMENT JACK BURKE CAN BE
> MY COUSIN FOR A WHILE."
> —DAVE MARR, 1965

By posting another 70 on Friday, Stockton shared the second-round lead with Larry Hinson, prompting a Tulsa newspaper to run the headline, "Unknowns Lead PGA." Stockton remembered: "I was a little hurt by that, but it gave me something to work for." After the third round, Stockton said to a Tulsa reporter, "Make it partially unknown instead of unknown." Nicklaus struggled to a 76 in temperatures that soared to 104 degrees in the second round.

Palmer's respectable 69 on Saturday was not enough to catch Stockton, who shot a 66, needing only 28 putts for the round.

The "transportation" for the 1970 PGA Championship.

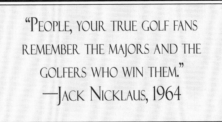

"PEOPLE, YOUR TRUE GOLF FANS REMEMBER THE MAJORS AND THE GOLFERS WHO WIN THEM."
—JACK NICKLAUS, 1964

Defending Champion Raymond Floyd posted a 65, including six birdies, to get within three of the lead. Floyd credited Sam Snead, who earlier in the week gave him a quick lesson on the putting green, for helping him achieve that score. Palmer and Stockton were matched together for the final round, and most observers thought that Palmer might finally break through and capture The PGA Championship. Although Arnie's Army was in full force pulling for him, frequently at Stockton's expense, Palmer could only manage nine straight pars on the front nine on Sunday. Stockton's first nine included an eagle when he holed a 120-yard wedge shot on seven, a double bogey on eight, and a birdie at nine. His lead over Palmer had grown to six strokes.

On the final nine, Stockton built a four-stroke advantage with three holes to play. Although he bogeyed 17 and 18, he had enough of a lead to still win by two over Palmer and Bob Murphy, whose final-round 66 brought him within range of the lead. Two unusual things happened to Stockton during the final holes. While walking up the right side of the 17th fairway, a child reached out to touch him. The mother grabbed his hand and said, "Don't touch that mean man!" Stunned, Dave responded, "Ah, c'mon, lady, a guy's got to have at least one friend out here today." Walking to the 18th green, he remembered, "I started to cry. Here I needed to putt from 10 feet and I was crying. So I had caddie Jed Day bring a towel to me. I tried to talk but I couldn't." Stockton only held the title for six months because the 1971 PGA was played in February at PGA National, making it the event's first visit to the state of Florida. The 1971 Championship would launch an extraordinary series of victories, dominated by Jack Nicklaus, who won his second Wanamaker Trophy in his own backyard.

Warren Cantrell presents a gold money clip and a check for $100 to Jack Nicklaus for winning the 1964 PGA Driving Contest.

CHAPTER SIX

THE MARCH OF THE GOLDEN BEAR

Although Jack Nicklaus was considered one of the best golfers during the 1960s, he won 11 of his 18 professional majors after 1969, including four PGA Championships. When he won at Oak Hill Country Club in 1980, he tied the record of five victories in The PGA Championship set by Walter Hagen over half a century earlier. His 1973 win over Bruce Crampton in The PGA Championship at Canterbury Golf Club gave him 14 major championship titles, including two U.S. Amateurs, surpassing Bobby Jones' record set in 1930.

Two years earlier, when he won at PGA National Golf Club in February 1971, Nicklaus had set yet another record. He spoke of what this meant to him in *Jack Nicklaus: My Story*, written with Ken Bowden: "This victory made me the first golfer to win each of the major championships at least twice. The possibility of that had been in my mind from the time I began preparing for the event in December, and there had been a lot of press hoopla about it all week. I had tried to downplay it as much as possible, but, now that it had happened, it was wonderfully satisfying. I had long ago recognized that setting records must one day become my primary goal and motivation if I hoped to go on being truly competitive. This was a record to savor and be proud of."

Jack Nicklaus' dominance of The PGA Championship equaled Walter Hagen's in the 1920s.

At PGA National in 1971, Nicklaus became the first golfer to win each major at least twice.

The 1971 PGA Championship was played in February instead of August because of a commitment made to John D. MacArthur, who had financed The PGA of America's new headquarters in Palm Beach Gardens, just five miles from Nicklaus' Florida home. The overall development created by MacArthur included two golf courses, and the East Course, designed by Dick Wilson, was to be the host site for the 1971 event. As part of a settlement that The PGA of America reached with MacArthur eight years earlier, they agreed to his stipulation that the event must be held in Florida. They chose February to avoid the extreme summer heat.

The PGA of America had trouble recruiting caddies for the week, so then-PGA Secretary William Clarke sent letters to PGA members and apprentices, asking them to consider serving in that capacity. He reported a "roaring acceptance" to his request, and the 1971 event had some of the best caddies of any Championship. Lou Strong, the managing director and head professional at PGA National and former PGA president, predicted that no player would shoot better than 280 for four rounds. He

was right; Nicklaus won with a 281. Nicklaus also became the first wire-to-wire winner since Bobby Nichols in 1964.

Despite some tee-to-green difficulties in an opening round that Nicklaus called "good, bad, beautiful, terrible," he scored 69 and ended the day in first place. He credited his friend Deane Beman, who won the 1959 British Amateur and the 1960 and 1963 U.S. Amateurs, with his performance on the greens. On Monday night, before the Championship began, the Bemans and the Nicklauses were playing bridge at Nicklaus' house. In *Golf World*, Dick Taylor reported that, while playing cards, Beman made a suggestion to Nicklaus about how to improve his putting stroke. Later, Jack and Deane went outside to practice on the astroturf that surrounded the swimming pool. Nicklaus was impressed and remarked later, "I have done my best putting in a tournament in my life this week." Nicklaus one-putted eight of the last 10 greens in the first round and followed with another 69 on Friday. During the third round, after giving up two bogeys against one birdie through 10 holes, he finished with a 70 to keep the lead.

> YOU CAN'T BEAT THE RATES AT JACK'S
> HOUSE, AND IT'S BEGINNING TO LOOK
> LIKE YOU CAN'T BEAT THE HOST.
> —GARY PLAYER, 1971

Dave Hill and Jack Nicklaus during the 1971 Championship at PGA National.

Gary Player, a houseguest of Jack and Barbara Nicklaus for the week, was four strokes behind going into the fourth round. Player had joked that the two players came to the Championship in separate cars because "Jack was afraid I'd slash his tires or something." At breakfast each morning, Player teased Barbara Nicklaus, saying that he'd let "Jack taste everything first. When he sipped his milk I switched glasses. When he took some grapefruit, I switched them. When he wasn't looking, I switched plates." But his chances to contend ended on the 15th hole, when his drive hit the cart path, bounced out of bounds, and gave him a double bogey. *Golf World* reported that Player, who finished in a tie for fourth place, was approached in the airport the next morning by a fan who gallantly said, "On behalf of fat, middle-aged men everywhere who insist upon riding golf carts, causing golf cart paths, I apologize."

Even with Nicklaus' domination of the event, there were some surprising stories throughout the week. Anticipating a winter freeze, course superintendent Carl McKinney had fertilized and overseeded the greens. When the cold weather failed to materialize, the grass grew too fast and the greens played too slow. After his practice round on Monday, Arnold Palmer asked Lou Strong, "When are they going to cut the grass? I hit 18 greens and lost two balls on 'em today." Tom Shaw, one of the year's leading money winners, did not make the cut. At the age of 52, Tommy Bolt followed his opening rounds of 72-74 with a 69-69 on Saturday and Sunday, finishing third. Although he did not make it to the weekend, Gene Sarazen, who first won The PGA Championship in 1922, shot 81-79 in his 50th start in the event.

Billy Casper put some pressure on Nicklaus coming down the stretch on the final day, with birdies on the last two holes to

Nicklaus won his second PGA Championship in February 1971, making it the first major of the year instead of the last.

Jack and Barbara Nicklaus celebrating with the Wanamaker Trophy in 1973 after Nicklaus defeated Bruce Crampton by four strokes.

finish with a 68. Nicklaus, though, was undisturbed by his competitor and birdied the 17th hole for a two-stroke cushion going into 18. He made par and ended with a two-stroke victory over Casper. The 1971 win gave Nicklaus nine majors—three in the Masters (1963, 1965, and 1966), two in the U.S. Open (1962 and 1967), two in the British Open (1966 and 1970), and two in The PGA Championship (1963 and 1971). He became the first player to win the Championship at stroke play twice. Until Nicklaus' victory that year, the Championship had had a different winner each year since 1952.

While an opening-round 72 at Canterbury Golf Club in Cleveland in 1973 did not suggest a record-breaking performance, Nicklaus quickly reasserted himself. The next two days he forged ahead with back-to-back 68s that put him in the lead after three rounds. Bruce Crampton was three strokes behind after a 67 on Saturday, and first-round leader Don Iverson was just one stroke off the lead. One of the most poignant moments in the Championship came after Nicklaus holed out on the 18th hole on Friday. His four-year-old son, Gary, slipped under the ropes and jumped into his father's arms. During the press interview that followed, Gary chatted with the writers. Although memorable, Nicklaus reported that he "got grounded the last two days" because "he got too frisky out here."

On Sunday, it was not a question of whether Nicklaus would win, but rather which hole would determine the outcome. In his own assessment it was the 14th, where he hit a cut 4-iron to the green from 215 yards. "My best shot of the tournament," he said later. He finished with a 69 and a four-stroke advantage over Crampton, who came in second. One of Nicklaus' staunchest competitors was noticeably absent on the weekend. Shooting 76-74 for the first two days, Arnold Palmer missed the cut at The PGA Championship for the first time in 15 years. In contrast, Nicklaus scored 72-68-68-69–277, seven under par. Awed by Nicklaus' accomplishment, Crampton sounded more like a fan than a competitor: "It was an honor to be an eyewitness to history being made. It is bordering on the unbelievable that he has won so many major events and still is so young, and did it with such ease."

Nicklaus won his fourth PGA title and 16th major in 1975.

Although he had broken Bobby Jones' record of 13 major victories, including the U.S. Amateur, Nicklaus displayed some modesty over his win at Canterbury. "Jones won his in a much shorter time," said Nicklaus. "How many more would he have won had he not retired? After all, 14 is just a number, and I don't know which is the better feat, Jones' or mine."

The 1975 PGA Championship site, Firestone Country Club's South Course in Akron, Ohio, was a venue whose difficulty Nicklaus respected. "Firestone is hard for me to play for 72 holes," he said after the event that was held in his native state. "You have to swing so hard all the time that you get to swinging too hard and you always play one bad round. But I played solid golf all week." But he also joked, "You can fall asleep on it because you're always hitting the same kind of shots—woods or long irons."

In 1975, four months before the PGA came to Ohio for the ninth time, Nicklaus became the first golfer to capture five Masters titles. In the previous four PGA Championships, he had won twice and finished second once (to Lee Trevino in 1974). Although Nicklaus was favored to win, Trevino came to Ohio as the defending Champion. Two months earlier, he shot a 66 on Firestone as part of National Golf Day and was prepared to do it again. But this would not be his week; he tied for 60th place with a 297.

Ed Dougherty, who learned to play golf while serving in the army and had placed 12th in The PGA Club Professional Championship in 1974, shot a 69 in the first round. His second and third rounds of 70 and 72, respectively, meant that he would be in the final threesome with Nicklaus. He was so awestruck on the first tee that he confessed, "I wanted to ask him for his autograph, but I didn't want to bother him while he was playing." Dougherty ended up with a 77, which put him in a tie for 22nd place.

Bruce Crampton, who finished in second place, four strokes behind Nicklaus in the 1973 PGA Championship, set a record for low score in the 1975 Championship with his second-round 63. "Quite honestly, I didn't realize 63 was the course record until somebody told me after I finished my round," Crampton said. "I wasn't thinking totals. . . . I was playing each shot as it came along." A month shy of his 46th birthday, Arnold Palmer was not ready to concede to the next generation: "I don't care if I'm the sentimental favorite; I just want to win myself a golf tournament." Although he made the cut, his 73-72-73-73–291 was one of the worst scores he ever carded at Firestone. Frustrated afterward, he explained, "My irons were simply terrible."

A spectator at the 1974 Championship in North Carolina.

Jack, Barbara, and Michael Nicklaus hoisting the Wanamaker Trophy for the fifth time in 1980.

After rounds of 70 and 68, Nicklaus was four shots behind the leaders. His 67 in the third round, though, catapulted him into first place. With a 75, Crampton was now trailing Nicklaus by four strokes. By this point Tom Weiskopf was six behind Nicklaus, Casper was eight strokes out of first place, and Hale Irwin was five out.

By the time Nicklaus reached the 625-yard, par-5 16th hole in the third round, he had a five-stroke lead. When he walked to the tee box, he realized that the markers had been moved 30 yards forward and that his driver was the wrong club. Without

time to get a 3-wood from his caddie, Angelo Argea, whom he had sent ahead, Nicklaus decided to make do with his driver. Instead of an easy shot, he hit it hard and the ball landed in a lateral water hazard on the left. After taking a penalty drop, he hit a 6-iron 230 yards into the right rough, behind a tree. With 137 yards to the green, his next shot went down in history as one of the greatest in The PGA Championship. Nicklaus opened the face of his 9-iron, hit a shot that cleared the tree by a few inches and a pond by a few feet, and put the ball 30 feet from the hole. Expecting at least a bogey, he holed for par. "It was a trick shot," said Nicklaus of the 9-iron to the green. "It was a shot I would take any time, but it was a gamble. And for some reason when I got up to the ball, I thought I'd make the putt, and I did." A bogey on 18 gave him a 67 and a four-stroke lead going into Sunday. After that, his 71 on the last day seemed anticlimactic.

After winning at Firestone, Nicklaus made a surprising confession. He began the 1975 golf season poised to win the Grand Slam. He made a good start by winning the Masters, and as Ron Coffman reported in *Golf World,* "but for a couple of swings at Medinah and a single shot at Carnoustie, he might have won all four." After winning The PGA Championship, he explained that had he met his goal, he "probably would have gotten out of the game." Instead, he seemed more determined than ever to win, declaring, "I have probably played my best golf this year."

As if to put an exclamation mark after his name for tying Walter Hagen's five PGA Championship victories, Nicklaus won the 1980 PGA Championship at Oak Hill by seven strokes, the largest margin since The PGA's change to stroke play in 1958. On Hagen's former stomping ground, Nicklaus trailed Gil Morgan by one stroke after two rounds. In the third round, Nicklaus shot a 66 to move into first. "After the first 14 holes I was ready to come in," Nicklaus joked to the press. "But they made me play the last four." Andy Bean, who finished second, was six strokes behind after three rounds. Hometown favorite Terry Diehl's 68 on Saturday put him in the next to last group. He finished on Sunday with a 76 and a tie for tenth place. Tom Watson, not really in contention on Sunday, had the day's low round of 67.

Nicklaus' four rounds, totaling 274 on the course that George and Tom Fazio were hired to make "more competitive," were

> "ANOTHER WEEKEND WITH NOTHING TO DO."
> —ARNOLD PALMER, 1978

The 18th green at Oak Hill Country Club in Rochester in 1980.

flawless. But it was a long road that involved a lot of practice and assistance from friends and family. Phil Rodgers helped Nicklaus with his short irons, and longtime teacher Jack Grout tried to flatten his swing plane. On the Monday before the Championship began, Nicklaus' son, Jack Jr., observed that his father was stopping his putter just past the ball and pulling it left. After making some adjustments, Nicklaus declared, "I could hardly wait to get to Rochester."

> "IT'S BEEN A TOUGH THREE YEARS IN WHICH I
> PUT IN A LOT OF HARD WORK. . . . BUT I
> GUESS IT KIND OF PAID OFF TODAY."
> —LANNY WADKINS, 1977

Despite making eight bogeys in four days, he was the only player to break par. The field averaged 74.8 strokes per round,

while Nicklaus averaged 68.5 on the East Course. This performance came from a golfer who finished 71st on the money list in 1979, and for the first time in 18 years as a professional, had not won an event. Jim Warters in *PGA Magazine* declared it "the most heroic return since MacArthur in WWII." With his victory, Nicklaus became only the third golfer to have won The PGA Championship and the U.S. Open in the same year, joining Gene Sarazen (1922) and Ben Hogan (1948). Tiger Woods matched the feat in 2000.

For an 18-year stretch, from 1952 through 1970, The PGA

SUDDEN-DEATH PLAYOFFS

The Masters and The PGA Championship pioneered the change to sudden-death playoffs in the majors. Although most players preferred an 18-hole contest to resolve a tie because luck is minimized over the round, it became impractical. Jack Nicklaus explained the dilemma, "As a player I prefer 18 holes, but I understand how things are today. The public wants a winner on Sunday. I can live with that." Television networks and spectators wanted the contest resolved, "and this pressure, more than anything else, became the rationale for the change." In 1976, Clifford Roberts decreed that the Masters would adopt a "sudden victory" format, one that Bobby Jones approved before his death in 1971. The rain delays at the 1976 PGA Championship encouraged The PGA of America to alter its format, even though it would not need to implement it for another year.

Cathy and Dave Stockton, who narrowly avoided a playoff in 1976.

Championship had no repeat winners. This trend changed over the next 10 years. Jack Nicklaus won in 1971, 1973, 1975, and 1980. Gary Player, who won in 1962, captured the title again exactly a decade later. Dave Stockton added the 1976 Championship to his roster of victories, six years after he defeated Arnold Palmer and Bob Murphy at Southern Hills. Although Nicklaus dominated the 1970s with his four victories, his challengers—with names like Player, Trevino, and Wadkins—were never far behind.

The normally impregnable Oakland Hills, where Walter Hagen served as the club's first professional, gave up seven rounds under par on the first day of the 1972 PGA Championship. This was largely because two inches of rain, which resulted in a cancellation of the final practice round, softened the course. But nothing dampened the crowd's enthusiasm. They wanted to see Jack Nicklaus win his third major of the year. He had won the Masters and U.S. Open and barely lost the British Open to Lee Trevino. And, he was poised to become the first back-to-back PGA Champion since Denny

At the 1976 PGA Championship, Ben Crenshaw tied for eighth place.

Shute. Tickets for the weekend sold out a month before the event began. Club professional Stan Thirsk and Brian "Buddy" Allin shot 68s to lead after the first round. Most of the fans, though, focused on Arnold Palmer, who, after opening with a 69, finally seemed poised to win the one major that eluded him. Thirsk finished his round at 7:25 P.M., after some sports writers had already filed their stories. The Kansas City Country Club professional apologized to the press for causing them to miss their dinner. Later that evening, he received dozens of congratulatory telegrams. But his 82 on Friday prompted one of the members at Thirsk's home club to joke: "What in the hell are you doing teaching me to play golf?"

Jerry Heard had opening rounds of 69-70 to take the lead at the halfway point, and he was the only golfer by Friday night under par. Lanny Wadkins' 68 was the low round on day two, putting him three strokes behind Heard. Gary Player opened with 71-71 to put himself within three of the lead, along with Tommy Aaron. Nicklaus, recovering from an operation on his finger, seemed to lose momentum after his second round of 75. For Palmer, a 75 on the second day put him too far behind to make much of a challenge to the leaders. He left the course Friday muttering, "I'm just sick and tired of my golf." Palmer would end the 1972 season without a single win for the first time since 1955.

On Saturday, Player, who had wearied of reporters asking him if he would "ever win another big one," posted a 67. Billy Casper also shot a 67 after opening rounds of 73-70 and moved into second place, a stroke behind Player. Raymond Floyd, who had been a stroke behind Heard after two rounds, struggled to a 74 in the third round and was four off the lead. A front-nine score of 31 seemed to bring Nicklaus back in the hunt, but a back nine of 37 left him at 215, along with Trevino and Hale Irwin. Nicklaus was six behind Player, and he later admitted that his 68 came too late. Palmer, Sam Snead, and Sam's nephew, J. C. Snead, were at 216.

At the age of 60, the elder Snead found himself playing the same course that had witnessed his defeat in the U.S. Open 35 years earlier. He shot a 66 during Tuesday's practice round and stayed in contention throughout the week. In the fourth round, Snead was paired with his nephew, who confessed that he was so enthralled with his uncle's fourth-place finish that he could not concentrate on his own game. J. C. ended with a 75, his worst round of the week, and a tie for 20th place. After accepting the fourth-place check for $9,275, Sam was asked if he really thought he had a chance to win. He replied, "Sure I did. I can beat these young so-and-sos. I thought if I could get in at 65 or so, I

> "I'M SORRY THAT THIS IS THE LAST MAJOR EVENT. MONEY DOESN'T MEAN A DAMN THING TO ME. IT'S WINNING THAT COUNTS, ALL THAT COUNTS."
> —TOM WEISKOPF, 1973

could do it. But these are the toughest greens we play all year."

After the course allowed several low rounds during the first three days, the scoring tightened on Sunday. Player's statement—"this tournament doesn't start until the 10th hole on Sunday"—proved true. At one point in the fourth round, seven golfers were tied for the lead. Player bogeyed three of his first four holes and lost the lead when Jim Jamieson birdied 12. Throughout the week, the press, which had been promised $1,700 worth of champagne if he won, cheered Jamieson wildly. After bogeys at 14 and 15, it appeared that Player had no chance. But he was not about to give up.

Gary Player's blind 9-iron shot helped him win the 1972 PGA title at Oakland Hills.

Earlier that morning, his father, Henry, called from South Africa asking him to "win the tournament for me." This meant a lot from a man who, Player later explained, had worked 31 years in the gold mines and had bounced a check to send his son on his first golf trip abroad. Player was even cheered on by his fellow competitors. Chi Chi Rodriguez left a note in his locker on Sunday morning that read, "Take it all. I want you to win."

The most memorable moment of the 1972 Championship was Player's extraordinary 9-iron shot on the 16th hole on Sunday. Afterward, he called it "one of the best shots of my career." He pushed his tee shot into the right rough, and the ball landed behind a row of large willow trees. Needing as much loft as he could get, Player selected a 9-iron, which would not typically be enough club to cover the 150 yards he needed to reach the green. Later he described what was riding on that single shot: "If I don't hit it perfectly, I'm in the water. . . . The only ones who care if you finish second are yourself and your dog." It cleared the willow and landed four feet from the hole. He sank the putt for a birdie. He parred the last two holes and ended one over for the Championship, two strokes better than Jamieson, who bogeyed the last three holes, and Tommy Aaron.

The win at Tanglewood in 1974 gave Lee Trevino his fifth major.

"This is the best and toughest American course I've ever played," Player later said of Oakland Hills. "It is certainly quite humbling." No one disagreed. At the four U.S. Opens held at the club, no player had ever bested par, not even Ben Hogan.

The *Toronto Star* reported that Lee Trevino came to the 1974 PGA Championship "armed with a new putter and his old confidence." Throughout the late 1960s and early 1970s, he foiled Nicklaus' dominance of the majors by taking the 1968 and 1971 U.S. Opens and the 1972 British Open from the Golden Bear. Once again he was able to hold off a challenge from Nicklaus and win another major title at Tanglewood Golf Club outside of Winston-Salem, North Carolina. Trevino captured his fifth major during the same week that Richard Nixon resigned the presidency. PGA Secretary Henry Poe reported that few golf fans let this news dampen their enthusiasm for the event. One spectator even tried to make light of the situation, suggesting that The PGA of America should place the president's name on the leader board with a "withdrawal" beside his name.

Robert Trent Jones Sr., who designed both courses at Tanglewood, renovated the West Course of the 36-hole public facility that was part of a thousand-acre park established by the estate of tobacco magnate W. N. Reynolds. After The

Forsyth County
Tanglewood
Park

PGA of America agreed on the site, Tanglewood agreed to spend $2 million to build a new clubhouse and give the course a face-lift. The course featured 111 bunkers and played to a par 70. Additionally, Jones reduced the total size of the greens by nearly 40 percent. A week of rain before the event began meant that while the greens could hold approach shots, the rough was difficult to negotiate. Sam Snead, who at age 62 finished tied for third 23 years after his last PGA Championship victory, said of the conditions, "I've won more tournaments in sloppy weather than anything else." His opening-round 69 was a testament to

his enduring skill. Nicklaus matched Snead's round on the first day and was already marching toward another major.

On Friday, play was suspended for nearly an hour right after lunch because of rain. Gary Player overcame the saturated greens and shot a six-under-par 64 to complement his opening 73. He had warmed up in the rain and then waited in wet clothes in the locker room for the weather to pass. This put him two strokes behind the leader, John Schlee, and one behind Hubert Green. Nicklaus posted another 69, three off the lead. In the second round, Tom Weiskopf, who opened with a 75, mysteriously quit after 16 holes, which prompted a $1,000 fine by The PGA of America.

After his practice round on Tuesday, Trevino discovered a new putter that played a key role in his win. The widow from whom he was renting a house that week asked him to look at a set of her late husband's clubs to see if they were valuable. They were—to Trevino. He found the putter he had been looking for.

Left to right: John Mahaffey, Leonard Thompson, Tom Watson, and Lee Trevino at the 1976 PGA Championship.

Left to right: Gene Sarazen, Ben Hogan, Gary Player, and Jack Nicklaus won all of the professional majors, an accomplishment later achieved by Tiger Woods.

"It's the same type of putter I've always putted with, a paddle grip, but it has paper under the leather grip, not rubber like most of them are today. They quit making them that way 15 years ago," he said of his find. He opened without any fanfare with a 73 on Thursday, but in the second round he shot a 66, which put him one stroke behind Nicklaus. On Saturday, he sustained his momentum with a 68, one stroke ahead of Nicklaus and Bobby Cole. During his third round, Trevino sank five birdie putts ranging from four to 20 feet.

Sunday's leader board featured the big-name players, including Trevino, Nicklaus, Player, and Snead. But it also included some new names—Bobby Cole, Frank Beard, and John Schlee. Cole looked up to the challenge when he eagled the first hole with a 78-yard wedge shot, and he and Trevino were tied for first after eight holes, with Nicklaus one stroke behind. On the 17th hole, a double bogey took Cole out of contention, and his 71 for the day left him three short of the victor. Nicklaus, playing with Trevino, thought he might have a chance coming to the 18th hole after his fellow competitor three-putted the 17th. Both golfers were on the green in regulation at the final hole. Nicklaus missed his birdie attempt. Trevino, eager to finish after his lag putt, asked to putt out and sank his 18-inch putt for the victory. He ended up with a 276, four under par, and a $45,000 check. After the trophy ceremony, he explained his sudden breach of etiquette, "I was so nervous, I couldn't wait around." PGA President William Clarke described Trevino as a great Champion; he was so good at entertaining the crowds that it was like "the Barnum and Bailey Circus."

Congressional Country Club proved to be a strong test for the 1976 PGA Championship during the nation's bicentennial celebration. It was, as the *Professional Golfer* reported, "a long knocker's playground, a driving range for the guys who can keep the ball airborne a little longer." Located in Bethesda, Maryland, just 10 miles from downtown Washington, D.C., Congressional was incorporated in 1921 with a membership list that included Calvin Coolidge, Woodrow Wilson, William Taft, and Warren G. Harding. The club opened in 1924 on land that General Washington's troops reportedly once trod. During World War II, it was the site of the Office of Strategic Services, where espionage agents were trained. Tommy Armour was the professional at Congressional when he won the U.S. Open at Oakmont in 1927. Prior to The PGA Championship, the club hosted the 1949 Junior Amateur Championship, the 1959 U.S. Women's Amateur Championship, and the 1964 U.S. Open.

The most amusing event of the week involved Gary Player. After his practice round on Wednesday, enthusiastic fans seeking autographs accidentally pushed him into the lake behind the 18th hole. He dried out by Thursday, and opened with a 70. Tom Weiskopf scored five strokes better than Player in a round that included an eagle on the sixth hole. But then he fell back with a 74 on the par-70 layout on Friday and ultimately ended the event tied for eighth. Lee Elder, whose practice round with President Gerald Ford generated a lot of pre-Championship publicity, began with a 68. Gil Morgan was the leader after two

More than 143,000 spectators passed through the gates at Congressional Country Club in 1976.

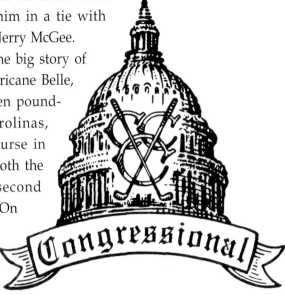

days, but his two 75s on the weekend finished him in a tie with Weiskopf and Jerry McGee.

Rain was the big story of the week. Hurricane Belle, which had been pounding the Carolinas, bathed the course in water. It cut both the first and second rounds short. On Friday, a storm rolled in just minutes before television coverage was to begin. In the middle of the afternoon on Sunday the rain came again, postponing the fourth round until Monday. To avoid having to spend another day on the course in the event of a playoff, PGA officials elected to use a sudden-death format in the event of a tie. Dave Stockton was determined to avoid that scenario.

In the fourth round, on a rain-soaked course, Stockton hit only nine greens in regulation and used his 3-wood instead of his driver off the tee. But his confidence never wavered. On the way to the 10th fairway, he told his wife, Cathy, that he was preparing his acceptance speech. His putter saved him, especially on the 18th hole, where he needed to make a difficult 10-foot putt for par to win and avoid a playoff with Raymond Floyd and Don January. He made it, later saying, "And it was a helluva feeling when it went in."

The first sudden-death playoff in the history of The PGA Championship came in 1977 when Lanny Wadkins defeated Gene Littler with a six-foot putt for par at the third extra hole. The players arrived at Pebble Beach Golf Links on the Monterey Peninsula, the first PGA Championship played in California since 1929, to find the state suffering from one of the worst droughts in recent history. It was so dry that "Save a Plant Plan" signs were encouraging visitors to ration water by placing a bucket under the shower while waiting for the water to reach the desired temperature as a conservation measure. No surprise, then, that the course was not in its best condition. The grass was brown, the greens were hard, and cracks had formed in the fairways. But PGA President Don Padgett declared, "Pebble Beach is a particularly sturdy course . . . a challenging and adaptable course that is always a thrill to play under any conditions."

Gene Littler, who had overcome cancer five years earlier, shot a 67 and led the field on the first day. After two rounds, only 13 players were under par. Seventy-one golfers made the cut, including the 65-year-old Sam Snead and six club professionals. Littler went into Saturday with a two-stroke lead over Jerry McGee. Nicklaus started the third round with an eagle on the second hole and a birdie on the sixth. Littler, at age 47, birdied four of the first seven holes, and, by the eighth hole, he had a five-stroke lead over Nicklaus. Both he and Nicklaus finished with 70s, giving Littler a four-stroke lead. Charles Coody was third, and five players tied for fourth. Despite his lead, Littler left the course saying, "I don't feel real comfortable right now. I might feel a little better if the guy in second wasn't Jack."

"SUDDEN DEATH IS AN EXPEDIENCY, BUT IN TODAY'S FAST PACE IT IS LEGITIMATE."
—JOE DEY, 1967

Living in San Diego, Littler, nicknamed "Gene the Machine," had played Pebble Beach often and faced similar conditions in the 1947 California State Amateur Championship. However, he was not in top form. Six weeks before The PGA Championship, he stopped playing golf and began seeing a chiropractor to treat what he called a degenerated disc and sacro separation. He confessed, "I didn't hit a golf ball until the weekend before the PGA." Littler, who had the 1961 U.S. Open and 29 tour titles to his credit, led by five strokes with nine holes to play on Sunday, but the back nine sealed his fate. By the 14th hole, his lead had been reduced to one stroke. A bogey on the 15th tied him with Nicklaus. But Nicklaus' bogey on 17 and par on 18 took him out of contention. Wadkins, who was close behind, declared, "I really thought I had a chance to win it outright when Nicklaus bogeyed 17." Littler's par on 18, giving him a 41 on the back nine, tied him with Wadkins, who had finished half an hour earlier with a 70. Littler, whose 76 on Sunday gave him "a bitter taste that gnaws at him," declared that "the three-putt at the 12th seemed to start if off. I made a lot of bad decisions and some bad shots. I must have misclubbed half a dozen times. But that's easy to do at Pebble Beach."

Lanny Wadkins won in 1977 in the first time the Championship was decided in a sudden-death playoff.

Assuming that he would have time to rest before the 18-hole playoff on Monday, Littler began making preparations to leave the course. When a PGA official told him that he was expected on the first tee, he was astonished and a bit annoyed that the new sudden-death format, adopted at the March 1977 PGA executive committee meeting, had not been clearly communicated to the players. On the first playoff hole, Wadkins hit his second shot out of the deep rough and made a difficult 15-foot putt to tie Littler's par. When asked about Wadkins' putt later, Littler declared with disbelief, "He couldn't have done that again in 50 tries." Both players birdied the second hole. On the third hole, Littler missed the green with his second shot, while Wadkins chipped to within six feet. Littler bogeyed the hole. Wadkins made par to win the $45,000 first-place check and his first event in four years.

Wadkins first broke 80 when he was 10; by age 15, he was competing in the U.S. Amateur. He played on Wake Forest's golf team on a scholarship that was established by Arnold Palmer. In 1970, Wadkins won the Southern, Western, and U.S. Amateur Championships. He turned professional in 1972, won $116,616 in his first year and entered the 1973 season as the tour's next golden boy. That year, he netted $200,455. But in 1975, he had gallbladder surgery and, anxious to get back on

the course, refused to wait for a full recovery. His hasty decision affected his swing and his game. In 1974, he only won $51,124. For the next two years, he failed to make the top 60 on the money list. But his slump did not last long; in 1977, he made his comeback with two second-place finishes in advance of The PGA Championship.

After winning at Pebble Beach, Wadkins reflected on his revived career, "I guess I did have some doubts about my career at one time. I was working hard, and sometimes it seemed that I was getting nothing out of it. It's been a tough three years, but I guess it all kind of paid off today." But he did not want to win at the expense of Littler. He said he "felt like a villain" because "Gene's been through a lot more than I have and more than I ever hope to." He confessed that he did not expect to win, explaining that he was simply hoping to finish in the top eight so he could get an invitation to the Masters. He did more than that. He left California with a big check, 10 years' worth of exemptions, a place on the Ryder Cup and World Cup teams, and some newfound confidence.

In 1978, at Oakmont, John Mahaffey, trailing Tom Watson by seven strokes heading into the fourth round, made one of the most exciting come-from-behind charges in the history of The PGA Championship. This was no small feat on a course that the

Oakmont Country Club hosted the 1922, 1951, and 1978 PGA Championships.

members vowed would never again see the 63 that Johnny Miller shot in the final round of the 1973 U.S. Open. They hired Arnold Palmer and architect Ed Seay to lengthen and tighten up the course. Prior to the Championship, *Golf Magazine* reported that the tee at the fourth hole was pushed back 18 yards, while the seventh hole was 35 yards longer. They also added a bunker to the fairway on the first hole and enlarged the bunker on the ninth. Twenty other bunkers were reshaped or contoured. Oakmont's greens were tough, but Jim Warters pointed out in *PGA Magazine* that the rain "took some of the sting out of those devilish putting carpets."

The final group in 1978—Mahaffey won, while Watson tied for second and Weiskopf for fourth.

Tom Watson dominated the week, prompting one newspaper headline to declare on Sunday morning, "Watson Running Away with the PGA." After 54 holes, he held a commanding five-stroke lead. On Thursday, rain necessitated nearly two hours of delays. Gary Player four-putted the first hole and ended with a 76, followed by a 72 on Friday. Many of the favorites, including Jack Nicklaus and Arnold Palmer, failed to make the cut. Palmer, extended a special invitation to play by The PGA of America, shot a 78 on Thursday. Nicklaus shot a 79, and declared, "It just wasn't my day." On Friday, Nicklaus shot a 74 and missed the cut for the first time in a major since the 1968 PGA Championship. Palmer did one better than Jack, a 152, but still did not make it. John Mahaffey began with a 75 on Thursday and bettered his score by eight strokes on Friday.

On Saturday, Gil Morgan and Jerry Pate both shot 66s and

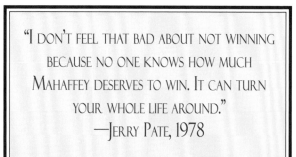

"I DON'T FEEL THAT BAD ABOUT NOT WINNING BECAUSE NO ONE KNOWS HOW MUCH MAHAFFEY DESERVES TO WIN. IT CAN TURN YOUR WHOLE LIFE AROUND."
—JERRY PATE, 1978

began to gain on Watson. Mahaffey shot 68 on Saturday and told the press, "This is the closest I've been in a long time to swinging a club the way I want to swing it." But he was still seven strokes behind Watson, who had 67-69-67–203 going into the fourth round. Pate had a 208, and Tom Weiskopf and Joe Inman Jr. were tied at 209. Georgia's DeWitt Weaver led the club professionals with a 216. Rex Caldwell was disqualified when he signed an incorrect scorecard on Saturday. But he did not realize his error until he came to the tee box on the first hole on Sunday. He disqualified himself, explaining "I couldn't go out there and play knowing that I'd cheated. It's like stealing. "

The collapse of Tom Watson on Sunday, who had the lead going into the back nine, was a tragedy of epic proportions. Watson was one under par for the day at the turn, followed closely by Pate at two under and Mahaffey at three under. Mahaffey was playing well, but did not make his move until the 10th hole. Watson carded a double bogey, while

THE GROOVES CONTROVERSY

The 1977 PGA Championship featured a controversy regarding equipment. A week before the Championship, on the second tee at the Greater Hartford Open, Jerry Heard casually mentioned to George Burns that his irons were illegal because the grooves were too large. Deputy PGA Commissioner Clyde Mangrum proved Heard correct, declaring that Burns' Ram clubs were not regulation. In 1941, the USGA stated that the grooves in the face of the irons "shall not exceed 35/1000 of an inch in width and shall not be any closer together than three times that width." When the players arrived at Pebble Beach for the Championship, those who also played custom-made Rams were affected. Raymond Floyd brought an extra set of his old Hogan clubs just in case. Only Gene Littler's Ram clubs passed the test. Gary Player found that half of the clubs in his bag did not meet the specifications, so he spent one of the practice days modifying another set. Tom Watson, though, had the most problems. He was unable to use his set of Rams that he had only had for 14 months and had used to win the Masters and British Open earlier in the year, prompting one newspaper to run the following headline: "Watson Wins Need an Asterisk." When he had a backup set shipped in, they were also deemed illegal. Left without any equipment, he went to the practice tee on Thursday morning to ask, "Anybody got a set of clubs I can use?" He ended up using a set of Tommy Armour Silver Scots borrowed from Roger Maltbie and started off on the first hole with a birdie.

Though he lost his clubs in the grooves controversy in 1977, Watson came back in 1978 to place second.

John Mahaffey's fourth round 66 in 1978 forced the event into a sudden-death playoff.

Mahaffey's 45-foot putt gave him a much-needed birdie and put him only two strokes behind Watson. After that shot, he said, "I had a feeling right there that I was in the game." On the 14th hole, Mahaffey captured the lead; by the 16th Watson had fallen to third place. Pate, who was playing in the group ahead of Watson and Mahaffey, birdied the 17th and took the lead. Pate only needed to par the 18th hole for the win. He left his 18-foot birdie putt four feet short of the hole, and his next putt missed, giving Pate a bogey. Mahaffey and Watson made par, leaving a three-way tie, which forced a sudden-death play-off for the second year in a row.

At 7:15 P.M., all three men assembled on the first tee and parred the first extra hole. On the second, a par 4 that measured 343 yards, Pate's sec-

> "HE'S UNBELIEVABLE. HE'S GOT TO BE THE GOLFER OF THE YEAR. HE'S GOT MY VOTE. TOM WATSON HAD A FANTASTIC YEAR, BUT THE BEAR IS HUNGRY."
> —LEE TREVINO, 1980

ond shot landed in the rough; Watson's second landed on the green, 35 feet from the flag; and Mahaffey's 9-iron shot put the ball 12 feet from the hole. He made his putt to win the $50,000 first-place check and The PGA Championship.

A glance at Mahaffey's record made him an unlikely contender at Oakmont. Like Lanny Wadkins before him, he had had a string of bad luck in the years preceding his PGA victory. In both 1975 and 1976, he lost in the U.S. Open, once in a playoff with Lou Graham at Medinah and once on the Atlanta Athletic Club's final hole to Jerry Pate, whose incredible 5-iron shot over water contributed to his win. At age 30, Mahaffey's career seemed in a downward spiral. In 1976, he hyperextended his elbow. In 1977, clearly the low point, he only earned $9,847, got divorced, fell off a ladder and broke his thumb, and barely qualified for the 1978 Championship. At that time, eligible players were determined by a point system in any given year. The top 70 were invited; Mahaffey was 65. At the trophy ceremony, he seemed to put the past behind him, saying, "It's been a long road back but this makes up for all of that. I had a lot of personal problems and injuries. But that's behind me now. I'm healthy and I have more than a healthy marriage. Susie's helping me. She makes me work. In fact, she won't let me come in from practice until dark." Mahaffey capitalized on his victory at Oakmont and went on to win the World Series of Golf with a 267 at Firestone Country Club and a $100,000 first-place check.

David Graham, who dropped out of school and left home at the age of 14 to pursue a career in golf, defeated Ben Crenshaw in 1979 with a birdie on the third extra hole to become the second Australian to win The PGA Championship. It was the third straight year the Championship was decided in a sudden-death playoff. Oakland Hills was born the same year as the Championship, 1916, and was known as one of the nation's toughest courses. Once called "the Monster" by Ben Hogan, it had hosted four U.S. Opens, a Western Open, a Carling World Open, and the 1972 PGA Championship. Robert Trent Jones made some important changes to the course in advance of the 1979 Championship. He moved the green on the seventh hole farther back and to the right and reshaped it to resemble the original Donald Ross design. On the eighth hole, he placed a bunker where an elm tree had once been. On the 12th, a four-bunker cluster was added, and on the 14th hole he planted some new trees. But the course was softened by the rains and deemed only "as scary as a Japanese horror flick," by Jim Moriarty of *Golf World*. Jack Nicklaus, who tied for 65th place, said, "Oakland Hills was as much of a piece of cake today as it will ever get."

David Graham celebrating his 1979 victory with his son on the course that Ben Hogan once called "the Monster."

Tom Watson opened the week with a 66 and seemed poised to reverse the slump that had plagued him all year. On Friday, Crenshaw surged ahead with the 36-hole lead, with Jay Haas, Rex Caldwell, and Graham trailing by a stroke. The cut was set at six-over-par 146, and it proved to be the best Championship for club professionals since 1973, as 10 of them made it to the weekend. Saturday brought torrential rains, 45-mile-per-hour winds, and a 45-minute delay. Caldwell shot a 66 and took a two-stroke lead over Ben Crenshaw. In the interview room after the round, Caldwell was brimming with confidence, "Sure I'm going to win this golf tournament. I know that's a brash statement for a guy who's never won a golf tournament. But that's the way I feel. I've got to play bad to lose." Jerry Pate predicted that he would need to shoot under 71 to win. He shot a 71 and landed in a tie for fifth.

Graham had won three tour events and 11 international events, but The PGA Championship would be his first major. Playing on Sunday with Caldwell and Pate, Graham's best shot of the day came at the 388-yard 15th hole. After his drive landed in front of the bunker in the center of the fairway, his second shot with a 4-iron landed eight inches from the cup. He remembers that his putt on the 17th hole made him feel that he "was in total command of what I was doing on the golf course." But then everything changed. Graham was two strokes ahead of Crenshaw going to the 459-yard 18th hole. He needed a bogey

to win, but then the pressure seemed to overwhelm him. He pushed his drive right, and his approach shot flew over the green. After two chips, he was on the green in four. He missed a four-foot putt and took a double-bogey six to tie with Crenshaw. "When I walked off the 18th green, I felt like I was six inches tall," Graham recalled.

Graham won on the third playoff hole with a birdie after making two impossible downhill putts with a brand-new putter on the first two extra holes. On the third hole, Crenshaw pushed a 4-iron into the right bunker and barely missed his par putt. At the time, he had played in and lost five playoffs, but "the one I remember most was the 1979 PGA at Oakland Hills with David Graham, who double-bogeyed the last hole to get me in. I shouldn't have been in the playoff, but once there I should have won." Then the usually unflappable Crenshaw lamented, "I've been second place four of my last five tournaments and I don't like second worth a damn."

> "WHAT CAN I SAY—I'M ABSOLUTELY DELIGHTED. BUT WHAT I'VE JUST DONE PROBABLY WON'T SINK IN FOR TWO OR THREE DAYS."
> —JACK NICKLAUS, 1973

David Graham beat Ben Crenshaw on the third playoff hole in 1979.

CHAPTER SEVEN

SUNDAY AT THE PGA

The PGA of America made some important changes to The PGA Championship during the 1980s, ushering in a new era. In 1986, Jim Awtrey was hired as manager of tournament operations and given the specific task of taking over active control of the conduct of the event. Prior to that, the host club appointed a chairman and hired their own staff. The PGA of America's vice president served as chairman of the event during Championship week. According to Patrick Rielly, who was PGA president from 1989 to 1990, Awtrey "developed the model we still use today, and Kerry Haigh, managing director of tournaments, perfected it." Awtrey was promoted to executive director in 1987 and named chief executive officer in 1993. Haigh, who still oversees the event, has helped make The PGA Championship one of the best organized tournaments in the history of the game.

The Championship was played in Georgia for the first time at the Atlanta Athletic Club (AAC) in 1981, and hometown favorite Larry Nelson won by four strokes over Fuzzy Zoeller. Nelson, who was given 20-to-1 odds before the Championship, served as a cartographer in a light infantry unit in the Vietnam War in the late 1960s and was working as an illustrator at Lockheed-Georgia when a close friend suggested that he learn to play golf. In 1969, at the age of 21, he began hitting balls during his lunch hour at a range across the street from the plant. For comparison, by this age, Jack Nicklaus had already won the U.S. Amateur twice and had been runner-up in the U.S. Open.

Nelson taught himself the game by studying Ben Hogan's *Five Lessons: The Modern Fundamentals of Golf.* Two years later, he left Lockheed to become an assistant golf professional under Bert Seagraves at Pinetree Golf Club. He completed an associate's degree at Kennesaw Junior College, turned professional in 1971, and began playing on the mini-tours in Florida. Nelson was the last player in a 23-man class—which included Ben Crenshaw and Gil Morgan—to qualify for The PGA Tour in 1973. Prior to his 1981 PGA victory in Atlanta, Nelson had four tour wins, including the 1981 Greater Greensboro Open. And he knew something about pressure, although he had a knack for putting things in perspective, "Walking to the first tee is nothing compared to walking through a jungle in combat."

> "HISTORICALLY, IT'S BEEN EASIER TO GAIN RE-ELECTION TO THE U.S. SENATE THAN TO COP THE PGA IN BACK-TO-BACK STRAIGHT ATTEMPTS."
> —AL STUMP, 1983

The Atlanta Athletic Club was host to the U.S. Open in 1976, when Jerry Pate hit his 5-iron out of the rough to within three feet of the flag on the final hole to win. But the club was made famous long before Pate stepped up to the tee. Founded in 1898, the AAC gained stature in the early 1920s as Bobby Jones' home course. Its East Lake facility, near downtown Atlanta, was home to three-time U.S. Women's Amateur Champion Alexa Stirling and 1938 British Amateur Champion Charlie Yates. Former PGA President Harold Sargent served as head professional after his father, George, who had served since 1932, retired. Harold was then followed by his brother, Jack, who worked at the club until his death in 1985. When the Athletic Club sold off its East Lake facility and moved north to suburban Duluth in the 1960s, Robert Trent Jones was hired to build 27 holes. In the early 1970s, Joe Finger added a fourth nine. The Highlands Course was composed of Finger's nine on the front side and Trent Jones' third nine on the back. In advance of the 1976 U.S. Open, George and Tom Fazio modified it. The most difficult hole on the course, the 18th, was untouched and remains one of the most challenging finishing holes in all of golf.

But the course was in terrible shape in the months leading up to the 1981 Championship. Former PGA President Mickey Powell remembered that the Athletic Club had to put down "acres of sod," the last of which were laid on Monday of Championship week, because Atlanta had experienced a colder-than-usual winter. In August, the hot, humid weather and periodic thunderstorms made the greens on the Highlands Course play slow and the rough nearly impossible to navigate.

The first round was suspended twice because of lightning, and 26 players did not have a chance to finish. The interruptions seemed to help Jack Nicklaus, who was four over par when he heard the first siren. Back on the course an hour later, he birdied three holes in a row and finished with a 71. Larry Nelson explained that the extra hour gave him a much-needed advantage as well. "I was putting so badly on the first nine that I went out to the putting green and practiced," he explained. "I'm convinced it helped me win." He opened with a 70. Bob Murphy was the first-round leader with a 66, one stroke better than Bob Eastwood and Mark Lye. Eleven players, including Nelson, were under par.

In the first round, Ken Lindsay, a well-known rules expert who became PGA president in 1997, encountered an unfortunate rules violation. After the first round, Lee Trevino, Tom Weiskopf, and Lanny Wadkins entered the scorers' tent, and Trevino somehow failed to sign his scorecard. William Clarke, the rules chairman, declared it an "innocent mistake," but still had to disqualify Trevino. When the three men realized what had happened, Weiskopf, who had mistakenly signed Trevino's card on the contestant line but was not disqualified, asked rhetorically, "Why can't I get through one year without getting involved in something?"

> "I'D LOVE TO SAY, 'HEY, I WON THE PGA.'"
> —ARNOLD PALMER, 1989

THE MISSING MAJOR

Arnold Palmer is the only player who competed in the first 37 stroke-play PGA Championships. In 1994, after missing the cut with a 153, he announced his retirement: "I'm going to leave the U.S. Open and the PGA to the younger guys." But it was not easy to say goodbye to the only major he had not won. He was runner-up twice. Thirty years earlier, in 1964, Palmer became the first player in PGA's stroke-play history to shoot four rounds in the 60s, but he still lost to Bobby Nichols, the first wire-to-wire winner. In 1968, he lost by one stroke to 48-year-old Julius Boros. Tom Watson has not fared much better. In 1978, Watson had a five-stroke lead after the third round, but lost to John Mahaffey, who came from a seven-stroke deficit to shoot a 66 and force a playoff. Mahaffey beat Watson and Jerry Pate on the second playoff hole. In the fourth round of the 1996 PGA Championship, Watson birdied five of the first nine holes to get within two strokes of the lead. But bogeys on the 12th and 13th holes ended his chances. After finishing in a tie for 17th place he explained, "I've had a few opportunities to win a PGA and I haven't won it. I'll have a few more."

Facing page: Palmer and Trevino in 1976.

With a 69, Murphy kept his lead after the second round. Tom Watson, who shot 75-73, failed to make the cut and explained, "My iron game was not sharp, and I just couldn't make anything happen." Johnny Miller, Ben Crenshaw, and Gene Littler were also packing their bags on Friday night. Nelson shot a 66 and was only one stroke behind Murphy. On Saturday, weather delays required that The PGA divide the field and begin players on both the first and 10th tees. Seve Ballesteros, who had been disqualified earlier that year at the U.S. Open for missing his starting time, almost did so again. Former PGA President Mark Kizziar recalled that a courtesy car driver happened to see him standing outside his hotel and rushed him to the course. Ballesteros made his tee time and shot a 72. Nelson's 66 put him four strokes ahead of Zoeller and five over Andy North and Tom Kite. Nicklaus' 71 and Murphy's 73 put them too far behind to be threats.

On Sunday, Nelson did not miss a fairway until the 14th hole. He was playing with a new driver that "had a certain loft and certain shaft that was perfect for the rain." He used it to win The PGA and never took it out of his bag again. On the 215-yard, par-3 15th hole, both North and Kite hit into the water, ending their chances to win. Zoeller's

Larry Nelson won a $60,000 first-place check in 1981 in front of a hometown crowd in Atlanta.

drive landed within four feet of the hole, and Nelson saved par. After 17, he had a four-stroke lead going into the final hole. As he had throughout most of the week, he hit his drive in the center of the fairway, and Zoeller realized that his chase was over. Walking around the lake toward the green on 18, Nelson remembered, "It was great to win my first PGA Championship in my hometown in front of a hometown crowd. I looked around, and I could call a lot of people by their first name."

The 1982 PGA Championship was played at Southern Hills in Tulsa in what golf writer Al Stump called "a 103-degree frying pan." This was the second time the course, designed by Perry Maxwell, had hosted The PGA Championship. Twelve years earlier, Dave Stockton had beaten Arnold Palmer and Bob Murphy by two strokes. Southern Hills had also previously hosted the 1958 and 1977 U.S. Opens. After the 1977 event, it was placed in the top 10 of the "America's 100 Greatest Courses" list published in *Golf Digest.* Raymond Floyd, who had won the 1969 PGA Championship and the 1976 Masters, was known as a great front-runner and lived up to his reputation. Unlike some players who preferred to come from behind, Floyd claimed, "I'd much rather be in front than trying to catch up. I feel in control, and I like it up there." He showed how much he enjoyed it at the 64th PGA Championship by leading all four rounds. On his way to shooting 63-69-68-72, Floyd did not three-putt a single green. He recorded only one double bogey, on the final hole, on Sunday.

Floyd began by shooting a 63 in the first round, in weather that was so hot that players

Nelson shot back-to-back 66s on his way to winning the 1981 PGA.

consumed salt tablets to prevent dehydration. He used 28 putts in the opening round and was the leader in greens hit in regulation for the week, prompting him to declare, "That's the best I've ever played, any time." Don Padgett II was the only club professional to make the cut, which was set at 144. Several players, including Fred Couples, Calvin Peete, Jay Haas, Lanny Wadkins, and Greg Norman, were in contention all week, but they could not get close enough to mount significant challenges. On Friday, Floyd's cumulative score of 132 set a PGA Championship record for 36 holes. By the end of three rounds, he had a total of 200 and yet another record.

Ray Floyd opened with a 63 in 1982 at Southern Hills.

PGA Magazine reported that Floyd, on his way to the 12th hole, passed his wife, Maria, who told him to "quit messing around and win this thing." Going into the final hole, Floyd seemed to lose his focus. "I looked up 18 and saw all those people and finally let myself realize what was happening," he explained. "And I guess I put some pressure on myself because I knew the guys were saying I couldn't blow it." On his way to his only double-bogey in the entire week, Floyd hit his second shot in the rough and his third in a bunker. But he still had a three-stroke lead over Lanny Wadkins when he finally picked his ball out of the cup. The 39-year-old Floyd said that his PGA win in 1969 and his repeat in 1982 "showed a bit of endurance."

Throughout the 1983 PGA Championship at Riviera Country Club in Pacific Palisades, California, Hal Sutton, the 25-year-old son of a Louisiana executive, was continually compared to Jack Nicklaus. Similar to Nicklaus, Sutton attained All-America honors in college, and he also won the U.S. Amateur, in 1980. But unlike his hero, Sutton became the tour's leading money winner in his second year; it took Nicklaus three seasons to do that. It seemed somehow appropriate that the fourth round would be a battle between the two men. Jim Warters reported in *PGA Magazine* that Sutton was eight strokes ahead of Nicklaus "after one round; seven in front after two rounds; six up after three rounds and still six ahead with seven holes to play" when he "heard the Bear coming." In those final holes, Nicklaus made up five strokes in five holes, but needed one more to catch Sutton. This performance came from a man who was at the risk of missing the cut after his 73 on Thursday.

Floyd had a five-stroke lead going into the fourth round, but he was, as Jay Haas described, "shaky on the first nine." An unusual incident contributed to his unease. While pitching to the sixth hole, a can of freon exploded in a concession tent nearby, startling the players and spectators. But Floyd remained composed and, after a short delay, nearly birdied the hole. He bogeyed the ninth and 10th holes and found Lanny Wadkins and Fred Couples on his tail. Floyd birdied the 11th and 12th, a hole that Ben Hogan called the "toughest par 4 in America."

Sutton opened with a 65, followed by a 66 on Friday, and broke Raymond Floyd's PGA Championship scoring record for 36 holes by one stroke. He did all this on a course that prompted *Los Angeles Times* sports columnist Jim Murray to quip, "You don't master Riviera. You just try to survive it." With 40 club professionals in the field, one of the biggest surprises of the Championship involved Buddy Whitten of Blythefield Country Club in Belmont, Michigan, who was in a tie for second place after 18 holes and fourth place after 36. Whitten, who had never made the cut in a major event, had an unusual injury—a sewing needle had been lodged in the bone of his right heel for years. But Riviera's soft kikuyu grass, feared by everyone else in the field, proved to be a good cushion for Whitten's aching foot.

> "It's doubtful that those 31 golfers who teed it up at Bronxville's Siwanoy Country Club 67 years ago realized what an important piece of history they some day would occupy."
> —Mickey Powell, 1983

The 1979 PGA Club Professional Champion began one stroke off Sutton's lead with a 66 and followed with a 70 on Friday. He could not hold on and ended with 73-77, which put him in a tie for 27th place.

Tom Watson, who had won two Los Angeles Opens at Riviera and loved the course, was one of the week's favorites. But his chances were stymied on Wednesday when he left the practice round because of neck pain after only two holes. He opened with a 75, which included two sevens on his scorecard, and ended in a tie for 47th place. Peter Jacobsen, who finished third, had the best weekend of anyone in the field, a 68-65, but it was not enough to catch Sutton and Nicklaus.

Thunderstorms delayed play for about an hour and a half on Saturday, and Sutton shot a one-over-par 72, managing to keep the lead. Ben Crenshaw found himself within one stroke of Sutton after the first hole, but ended up with bogeys on the second and fourth holes. His 77 on Sunday put him in a tie for ninth place. Walking off the 14th green after his third bogey in a row, with Nicklaus bearing down on him, Sutton turned to his caddie, Freddie Burns, and said, "This is what it's all about." After the round, he confessed, "The crowd isn't the only one that knew the Bear was comin', believe me." The 17th hole was Nicklaus' best chance to take the lead, but his wedge shot landed short of the hole, and he failed to make a birdie.

Named the PGA Tour's "Rookie of the Year" in 1982, Hal Sutton won by one stroke over Nicklaus in 1983.

"I KNOW THESE GUYS CAN PLAY"

A day after Bob Gilder complained that the 40 club professionals in the field of the 1988 PGA Championship at Oak Tree were taking spots away from legitimate players, Jay Overton shot a 66 in the second round and led the tournament until late in the afternoon. Overton opened with a 68-66 and finished the week tied for 17th place with seven other golfers, including Nick Price and Ben Crenshaw. Five years earlier, Buddy Whitten shot a 66 in the first round at Riviera Country Club, only one stroke behind the eventual Champion, Hal Sutton. In 1972, club professional Stan Thirsk shot a 68 for a share of the lead after the first round. Although difficult to determine with certainty, the last true club professional—that is, a club professional who spent the majority of his time at his club and not on the Tour—to win The PGA Championship was Chandler Harper who won in 1950 at Scioto Country Club. Despite occasional protests, many of the touring professionals believe club professionals should be in the field, including Tom Watson, who once said, "I know these guys can play." In 1994, The PGA of America voted to reduce the number of club professionals in the Championship from 40 to 25—the top 25 players in The PGA Club Professional Championship, which began in 1968. The new rule went into effect at the 1995 PGA Championship at Riviera Country Club. Mainly international players have filled the extra 15 slots in recent years.

Club professional Stan Thirsk played in 10 PGA Championships, with his best finish a tie for 37th place in 1966.

Sutton, whose win propelled him to the top of the money list in 1983, joined Bobby Nichols (1964), Raymond Floyd (1969, 1982), and Jack Nicklaus (1971) as the fourth man in the history of The PGA Championship to lead the event for all four rounds. The fans at home had a chance to see most of the weekend play of an event that proved extremely difficult for television producers. Chuck Howard of ABC explained, "Covering the PGA is one of the most challenging projects we undertake during the year. Golf is a tough event to televise. In other sports you can basically focus on one location. Golf switches to and from a dozen different sites with non-stop action. At the same time, we must maintain the continuity and flow of the story for the viewer."

In 1980, prior to the playing of the British Open at Muirfield, Hubert Green and Jerry Pate met with incoming PGA President Joe Black to encourage him to consider Shoal Creek in Birmingham as a possible venue for a future PGA Championship. In Scotland a few weeks later, Black, then–PGA President Frank Cardi, and Mark Kizziar met with Jack Nicklaus, Shoal Creek's designer, to ask him about the possibility of hosting the event. At first Nicklaus was reluctant, explaining that the course was built for members, not championships. Later in the week, though, he changed his mind, suggesting that with some modifications it would be a good choice. When members of The PGA executive committee finally had the opportunity to visit Shoal Creek, Black remembered that Hall Thompson, the owner, said, "If you come to Birmingham, I'll lay the state of Alabama at your feet."

The 1984 PGA Championship drew huge crowds. In *Shoal Creek: The First Twenty Years,* Ian Thompson observed that more than 138,000 fans attended the event, second only to the 1979 Championship at Oakland Hills in Birmingham, Michigan, which attracted 145,000 spectators. Reporters began the week speculating about how Jack Nicklaus would perform on the course of his own design. Regrettably, he shot one under par for the week, placing him in a tie for 25th place.

Although Shoal Creek was not quite seven years old, former

Calvin Peete finished fourth in the 1984 PGA Championship.

PGA President Frank Cardi observed, "It's an absolute masterpiece of a golf course. There's not a weak hole on it." The scores at the 1984 and later at the 1990 PGA Championship, proved how good it could be. The field included the world's best players, including U.S. Open Champion Fuzzy Zoeller, Masters Champion Ben Crenshaw, and British Open Champion Seve Ballesteros. They were joined by Arnold Palmer, Tom Watson, Jack Nicklaus, and Greg Norman. On Thursday, battling four-inch Bermuda

After winning, Lee Trevino kisses the putter he bought in Holland a few weeks before the 1984 PGA Championship.

grass that was considered the hardest rough in a major that year, Lee Trevino shot a 69 and tied with eight other players at three under par, one stroke behind leaders Lanny Wadkins, Mike Reid, and Raymond Floyd. On Friday, Trevino was in the lead with a 137, tied with Lanny Wadkins, the 1977 PGA Champion, and Gary Player, who shot a nine-under-par 63. When asked about Player's score, Hall Thompson responded, "Who does he think he is, shooting 30 on *my* course?" Although the South African golfer made headlines that day, the rest of the week belonged to Trevino.

The 44-year-old Trevino had not won a tour event since the 1981 Tournament of Champions or a major since the 1974 PGA Championship at Tanglewood. After being struck by lightning in 1975, he had two herniated disc surgeries. After Saturday's 67, Trevino said to the media, "There's no doubt in my mind that I can win. I am playing better golf now than I ever have. I'm striking the ball better than I did in the '70s." On the third day, Player and Wadkins joined Trevino and produced some of the Championship's most exciting golf. Trevino carded a 204 after 54 holes. Wadkins was one stroke back with a 205, and Player had a 206. Going into Sunday, 13 players were within seven strokes of the lead.

Wadkins, Player, and Trevino comprised the final threesome. But Trevino was not worried. He remembered, "I slept like a baby the night before the last round. I led Lanny Wadkins by one and Gary Player by two and a lot of people favored Lanny to win . . . But I was confident." Rain threatened throughout the day, and, when it began to fall, the men took shelter in one of the few homes that had been built on the course. Reluctant to go into the air conditioning, the three men sat in the garage of a home that belonged to the Del Morgans and—except for Player who described himself as a "health nut"—drank iced tea and ate popcorn. When the storm subsided and play resumed, all three men played well, but Trevino dominated the back nine.

In 1984, Trevino duplicated his 1968 U.S. Open record of being the first winner to score under 70 for all four rounds.

The 197-yard 16th hole proved to be the turning point. Trevino hit a 4-iron into the bunker, blasted out of the sand, made his putt, and never looked back. Trevino finished four strokes ahead of Wadkins and Player, kissed his putter, and bowed to the crowd. He confessed later, "I felt so confident when I stood over that last putt that I didn't even line it up." His score, a 15-under-par 273, won him $125,000. It also gave him a major championship in three different decades and, as he said later, "a new life." After receiving a standing ovation in the pressroom, he said, "This is great. When you're young you say it's inevitable you'll win. When you're old, you don't know if you'll ever win again." He became the first PGA Champion to win with four straight rounds under 70.

The 1985 PGA Championship was hosted by Cherry Hills Country Club near Denver, making it the second time in three years that the Championship was played

> "THE PGA TITLE IN '84 WILL STICK OUT IN MY MIND MORE THAN ANY OF THEM. THAT ONE JUST MEANT SO MUCH TO ME IN SO MANY WAYS."
> —LEE TREVINO, 1990

west of the Mississippi River. The course, built in 1922, was modified by Arnold Palmer and Ed Seay in advance of the 1978 U.S. Open. It had been the site of Palmer's incredible shot at the first tee in the fourth round of the U.S. Open in 1960, where he drove the green. Hoping to relive that moment, members of Arnie's Army traveled thousands of miles to see him tee it up once again. During one of the practice rounds, they actually booed him when he tried to play an iron on the fabled hole. But the week belonged to Hubert Green, who shot a six-under-par 278.

It was an important win for Green, who had gone so long without a title that he joked that he would "turn pro" if he won the Championship. He did and captured his second major victory. Eight years earlier, he won the 1977 U.S. Open at Southern Hills. Early in his career, Green failed to get his qualifying card in his first attempt and went to work as an assistant at Merion Golf Club. "I sympathize with the club professionals,"

he said. "They rarely get to play, yet they're almost required to play well. You can't combine both."

Doug Tewell's 64 broke Arnold Palmer's record, set on the course in 1960, by one stroke. Tewell's round included six birdies and an eagle. Afterward, he humbly reflected on his feat, "I'm honored to set a record on such a great course with great tradition." But the press and the fans, clearly pulling for Palmer, who shot a 75, were not amused. Jack Nicklaus, Lee Trevino, Peter Jacobsen, and Corey Pavin were two strokes behind Tewell with 66s. Trevino's 68 gave him the lead after 36 holes. Pointing out that he had shot six successive rounds in the 60s in the Championship, including his 69-68-67-69 in 1984, he asked in jest, "If I score eight do they give me the PGA? Or at least make me president?" Fred Couples, who played brilliantly with his irons, was in second place. Nicklaus shot a 75 and sought relief for his back from an acupuncturist. With a 75-72, Palmer made the cut, to the delight of many. Robert Hoyt, a club professional from Dallas, misjudged where the cut would come and left immediately after his round. When PGA officials finally tracked him down later that evening, he had time to drive back to the course, but his clubs had been sent home. Hoyt had them shipped back, and they arrived 10 minutes before his tee time.

Rain delayed the fourth round in 1988.

1977 U.S. Open Champion Hubert Green added The PGA to his major wins in 1985.

Ray Floyd in front of the leader board at Tulsa in 1982.

HOSTING THE CHAMPIONSHIP

Writing for *Golf Digest* in 1982, Jerry Tarde asked, "Why would a private club like Southern Hills in Tulsa, Oklahoma, suffer the labors and inconvenience of hosting one of golf's major events like the PGA Championship?" The answer for many host sites is simply to give back to the game. But this is only part of the story. Hosting such an event generates millions of dollars in revenue from ticket and merchandise sales, program advertising, corporate hospitality, and concessions. Such events also give the club a national and international reputation that is difficult to quantify. Finally, most sites use such events to make major renovations to the course and the clubhouse. For the 1976 U.S. Open, the Atlanta Athletic Club invested $400,000 in redesigning its course. Oak Hill, the 1980 PGA Championship site, spent $50,000 more than the AAC on renovations. The sacrifices, however, are many. A year or two in advance of the event, clubs must solicit volunteers from their membership to coordinate advertising sales, volunteers, ticket sales, concessions, hospitality, and parking. Prior to and during the event, members lose access to the course and clubhouse and the privacy that goes with membership. Even with these issues, Tarde declared that "there are more clubs than there are championships to go around."

Golf World reported that Armen Suny, Cherry Hills' superintendent, double-cut the greens on Saturday and rolled them with a 60-pound roller, to the frustration of the players. Nicklaus responded, "It is a target golf course and it was changed overnight to a run-in course." Trevino also weighed in, "You could have landed a 747 on 'em and never scuffed 'em." In blustery conditions, Green took the lead with a 206, and Trevino was three strokes behind going into the fourth round.

On Sunday, Green revealed why he was playing so well, claiming that it helped to be a good mathematician. "If you are 170 from the green here you deduct 10 percent for altitude," he explained. "Upwind or downwind and another calculation is needed." He shot a 72 to Trevino's 71 and won by two strokes. But Trevino's loss did not dampen his enthusiasm for the event. "This championship carries as much or more weight as any of them," he explained later. "The PGA is definitely the toughest of the majors. It's always the toughest field."

The 1986 PGA Championship at Inverness Club in Toledo, Ohio, set the stage for one of the greatest upsets in the event's history. The original nine-hole course, built by Bernard Nichols in 1903, was expanded to 18 by Donald Ross in 1919. It hosted its first major, the U.S. Open, the next year. At The PGA Championship, Greg Norman, who had led all four of the majors going into the fourth round that year, lost after Bob Tway holed out from a bunker on the final hole to win.

The PGA of America's junior golf programs have introduced thousands of children to the game over the past several decades.

It was an unusual week. On Friday, Larry Nelson was penalized for taking practice swings in a hazard at the 10th hole and missed the cut by two strokes. Hubert Green explained, "He didn't realize that he was in a hazard. He was having a good ol' time . . . and must have taken three or four swings before realizing what he'd done." After Saturday's round, a television viewer complained that Norman should have been penalized for improving his lie during some practice swings. Standing nearby, Peter Jacobsen joked, "I betcha that was my dad."

Norman, who won the British Open three weeks earlier, began the week with a 65, setting a course record and giving himself a two-stroke lead. Tway started with a 72, and Nicklaus, playing in his 100th major as a professional, was three strokes off the lead. So complete was Norman's dominance that week that he did not relinquish the lead until the final hole. With eight holes to play in the fourth round on Monday (rain washed out play on Sunday), Norman had a four-stroke lead. Jim Warters reported in *PGA Magazine* that he "never disclosed the faintest crack in his armor until the 11th hole of the final round." Tway, playing with Norman and Jacobsen, birdied the 13th hole to narrow Norman's lead to one. So intense was the competition that Jacobsen said that he was "mostly kind of a spectator out there trying to get in the door." When Norman bogeyed the 14th, Norman and Tway were tied and would stay that way until the final hole.

At the 17th hole, Tway hit his second shot into the deep rough and seemed poised to lose a stroke. But his sand wedge helped him save par. Although his final shot on 18 would be more memorable, some writers claimed that the shot on 17 to save par was better. At the 18th hole, Tway holed out from the bunker in front of the green for a birdie. It was the very same bunker from which Payne Stewart holed out in the group just ahead of them. So extraordinary was Tway's shot that the press compared it to Gene Sarazen's double eagle at the 1935 Masters, Nicklaus' 1-iron shot on the 17th hole at the 1972 U.S. Open, and Jerry Barber's 60-foot putt that forced a playoff with Don January at the 1961 PGA. Stunned by the

loss, Norman responded with grace, "It's a game in which you must always expect the unexpected."

Apart from Tway's incredible shot and Norman's surprise defeat, the strangest incident of the week involved Ben Crenshaw. On the 18th hole in the third round, Crenshaw was so frustrated with his second shot, a 9-iron to the green, that he tossed the club in the air. When it came down, it hit him on the back of the head, requiring that he go to the hospital to get three stitches. Crenshaw joked, "It was the best shot I hit all day, but I might not have had enough club." Then the press and the players got into the act. They circulated a joke, reported in *PGA Magazine*:

Bob Tway held off "The Shark" to win the 1986 PGA Championship.

Tway's shot from the bunker won in 1986 at Inverness on the final hole.

Question: What's the difference between a professional golfer and an amateur golfer?

Answer: An amateur golfer skulls his wedge. A professional golfer wedges his skull.

On Sunday, the Golf Writers Association of America presented Crenshaw with a Toledo Mud Hens baseball helmet. Former PGA Champion and television analyst Dave Marr showed up in a hard hat, and Lee Trevino covered his head with a wire bucket when Crenshaw arrived on the practice range.

Tway, who had played golf for Oklahoma State University and sported the nickname "Brillo," was second on the money list, behind Norman, in 1986. But it was not an easy road. He played on the mini-tours, the Asian and European tours, and the now-defunct Tournament Players Series. Known for his reserve, Tway's response surprised the crowd, "All I can remem-

ber is standing there and jumping up and down." He should have. In 1986, Dan Jenkins reported in *Golf Digest* that Tway and Norman won more money in that year than Byron Nelson, Sam Snead, and Ben Hogan won in their combined careers.

In 1987, at PGA National Golf Club, Larry Nelson became the 15th player in the history of The PGA Championship to win the event twice or more. It also gave him his third major title. His win was even more extraordinary considering the conditions on the Tom Fazio–designed course. The bentgrass greens, described by Nelson later as "dirt

Spectators at PGA National trying to get a better view in 1987.

A spectator rooting for Greg Norman.

Larry Nelson, shown with his sons, won the 1987 PGA Championship with the highest winning score, 287, in the event's history.

with a few pieces of grass," became infested with pythium blight, a deadly fungus. Jim Awtrey, The PGA of America's executive director at the time, explained that a "series of unfortunate incidents" left the greens nearly bare. But the conditions actually helped Nelson. "I felt I had an advantage because it meant that it would not be a putting contest. It was more of a ball-striking contest, and that was my strength." But not everyone agreed. Dan Jenkins quipped, "You needed more loft on your putter than you had on your 7-iron."

Nelson, who used two different sets of irons on Thursday and Friday, opened with a 70-72. Bobby Wadkins, the brother of Lanny Wadkins, led the field on Thursday with a 68. By Friday, the lead had shifted to Raymond Floyd and Lanny Wadkins. Bernhard Langer and Tom Watson were not far behind. Defending Champion Bob Tway opened with a 78. Seven club professionals made the cut, which was set at 151, one of the highest in the Championship's history. They included Fred Funk, the University of Maryland golf coach, who shot a 69 in the opening round. He eventually tied for 47th place.

On Saturday, Seve Ballesteros was pleased to find himself two strokes behind the leaders After finishing with a double bogey, birdie, and bogey, he celebrated his newfound calm: "My attitude is better, isn't it? I used to be a 24 handicap on that, now I'm almost a professional." By dinnertime, D. A. Weibring and Mark McCumber were in the lead.

Nelson went into the fourth round tied for seventh place and had trouble convincing his two sons, Drew and Josh, to come onto the course because of the extreme heat. "They were not interested in golf," Nelson explained. "On the first playoff hole with Wadkins, the crowd was chanting, 'Larry, Larry, Larry,' and it was really emotional. I think my children realized then that the sport is really cool." Nelson shot even par on Sunday and tied with Wadkins, who ended with a 73. His best shot of the day came on the 17th when he made a 20-foot birdie putt.

Had Scott Hoch made his eight-foot putt, he would have taken the title outright. Instead, though four under par for the day, he three-putted and tied for third. Ballesteros' chances evaporated when he scored an eight on the third hole. Mark McCumber, who led after five holes, lost five strokes to par by the turn. A birdie on the final hole would have put him in the playoff with Nelson and Wadkins. Floyd ended with an 80, and Greg Norman posted 79-79 on the weekend.

Nelson and Wadkins began the playoff on the 10th hole, and Wadkins missed a six-foot par putt and took a bogey, while Nelson made his. Nelson's 287 was the highest score in a major since the 1975 U.S. Open, won by Lou Graham at Medinah. The victory also gave him a berth on the Ryder Cup team. Nelson explained, "So in winning the PGA in 1987, I actually got two tournaments for the price of one."

In advance of the 1988 PGA Championship, course architect Pete Dye predicted that the wind would be the great equalizer, but it never materialized. Six golfers, including Scott Verplank, David Edwards, Gil Morgan, Doug Tewell, Bob Tway, and Andy Magee, lived or played at Oak Tree Golf Club in Edmond, Okla-

"THIS IS A GREAT THRILL. I'VE WON ONE OF THE GREATEST CHAMPIONSHIPS ON ONE OF THE MOST DIFFICULT GOLF COURSES AGAINST ONE OF THE HARDEST FIELDS I COULD IMAGINE."
—LARRY NELSON, 1987

homa, and were assumed to have some advantage over the rest of the field. Only Edwards, Tway, Magee, and Tewell made the cut. The course, called by *Golf Digest* one of the hardest in the world, had a course rating of 76.9, which was the highest in the country for a par 71. Its slope rating of 148 was second only to Pine Valley's 152. The greens were cut to slow them down to 9.3 on the Stimpmeter, and the rough was minimized. Aware of the course's reputation, The PGA of America elected not to modify the holes, but switched nine and 18 for the convenience of the spectators. The golfers that week did not seem to notice and consistently shot some of the lowest rounds in the history of The PGA Championship.

Journeyman golfer Jeff Sluman from Rochester, New York, won the event with a 65 in the fourth round, one stroke off the course record, in the searing Oklahoma heat. Former PGA President James Ray Carpenter expressed the sentiment of the spectators that week: "All of us little guys love to see the little guys win." To capture his first major victory, the five-foot-seven-inch Sluman, who once called himself "135 pounds of liquid dynamite," came from three strokes behind on Sunday to defeat Paul Azinger by three strokes. Sluman re-

At PGA National in 1987, three of the game's best players made the cut.

A sea of names helps identify the players on the practice range in 1988.

membered the fifth hole, where he holed his wedge from 115 yards for an eagle, as the turning point in the round. Afterward, Azinger confessed, "I thought Jeff must be as nervous as I was and something would happen to him. Boy, was I wrong."

There were four holes in one recorded during the week: by Gene Sauers and Raymond Floyd on the eighth hole; David Edwards on the 13th hole; and Azinger on the fourth. The cut, set at two over par, eliminated Jack Nicklaus, Arnold Palmer, Lee Trevino, Fuzzy Zoeller, Bernhard Langer, and Scott Simpson from the field. At the age of 30, Sluman recorded the second-lowest winning total in the Championship's history with a 272. Bobby Nichols had set the record with a 271 in 1964. Sluman also became the first player to make a major his first victory since Jerry Pate won the 1976 U.S. Open at the Atlanta Athletic Club. At the trophy ceremony, Sluman, who had been winless on the tour for six years, reflected on the victory, "It's a

great feeling to win a major. I can't imagine what Jack Nicklaus feels like, winning 20."

Mike Reid left the 1989 PGA Championship a disappointed man. Earlier in the year, he had lost the lead on the 14th hole at the Masters. At Kemper Lakes Golf Club, he led for all but the final two holes and finally lost to Payne Stewart. But Stewart did not have time to feel sorry for his friend; he had just birdied four of the last five holes to capture his first major. Stewart did not win as much as Reid lost. Nicknamed "Radar," Reid had not three-putted a green once and had only missed three fairways until the last three holes on Sunday. In contrast, Stewart made a 15-foot putt for par on the 13th hole, a 25-foot putt for birdie on the 14th, an 18-footer for birdie on the 16th, and a 12-footer for birdie on the 18th. Stewart was eight strokes behind after the first round, seven behind after the second, and six behind after the third.

Jeff Sluman achieved the most significant victory of his career at the 1988 PGA.

THE GOLF CHANNEL IS BORN

Before the 1990 PGA Championship at Shoal Creek, Arnold and Winnie Palmer were invited to stay with their friends, Joseph and Kay Gibbs. Throughout the week, they discussed the possibility of starting a television channel devoted specifically to golf. The next year, Gibbs, a successful cable entrepreneur since 1982, commissioned a Gallup survey to measure the feasibility of a 24-hour golf channel. In November 1991, Palmer signed on as chairman of the enterprise and helped attract sponsors. The first show aired on January 17, 1995. The first tournament, the Dubai Desert Classic, was broadcast two days later. During that first year, *Golf Academy Live,* which featured top PGA teaching professionals, premiered. On April 1, 1996, the Golf Channel launched its web site, www.thegolfchannel.com. In 2003, the network reached nearly 60 million homes worldwide and included such popular shows as *Golf Central.*

David Manougian, president of The Golf Channel, with co-founder Arnold Palmer.

Payne Stewart birdied four of the last five holes to win the 1989 Championship.

The second hole at Kemper Lakes in 1989.

The grand stand at Shoal Creek in 1990.

Shoal Creek, shown in 1990, also hosted the Championship in 1984.

For the third time, The PGA Championship was played at a public golf course. At the 10-year-old Kemper Lakes, 40 miles northwest of Chicago, golfers carded low numbers throughout the week because rain had softened the course, and the wind was calm. The course, which had never hosted a major, was ranked as one of "America's 100 Greatest Courses" by *Golf Digest* only four years after it opened. At 7,217 yards, it was the longest course site at sea level used by The PGA of America for the Championship.

On Thursday, Reid and Leonard Thompson led the field with 66s. But they had to share the spotlight with Arnold Palmer, who, just shy of his 60th birthday, shot a 31 on the front nine and took a share of the lead after 16

> "THE PGA WAS THE ICING ON THE CAKE. MAN, WHEN YOU WIN A MAJOR CHAMPIONSHIP, YOU'VE DONE SOMETHING."
> —LEE TREVINO, 1990

holes. Defending Champion Jeff Sluman, who was paired with Palmer and Larry Nelson, said, "It was great to watch him. It was like Ponce de Leon out there." Thunderstorms delayed the second round, but Reid retained the lead by two strokes over Craig Stadler and Leonard Thompson.

Reid's 70 on Saturday prompted him to exclaim, "Maybe I'm not supposed to be leading the PGA, but the Cubs aren't supposed to be leading the league, either." But Reid could not sustain his momentum on Sunday. On the 16th hole, his drive landed in the water, and he ended up with a bogey. He followed that with a double bogey on 17. On the 18th, his 5-iron shot landed seven feet from the cup, and he seemed poised to tie Stewart and force a playoff. Reid barely missed it left and had to settle for second place.

Afterward, he joked with reporters, "Where can you go around here to have a good cry?" But Stewart had nothing to cry about. In the scorers' tent he said, "I was wondering when my time could come."

One of the most important moments in The PGA Championship's history involved the 1990 event, scheduled for play at Shoal Creek in Birmingham, Alabama. In the late 1980s, civil rights groups began scrutinizing membership policies at country clubs, and The PGA of America found itself embroiled in one of the most visible controversies in recent memory.

The site of the 1984 PGA Championship and a popular course among the players, few expected Shoal Creek to become a litmus test for equity in golf. In June, two months before the event, Hall Thompson, the founder, responded to a reporter's questions about the club's membership policies. In the *Birmingham Post-Herald* he was quoted as saying that the club did not have any black members because "that's just not done in Birmingham, Alabama." Outraged by Thompson's comments, the National Association for the Advancement of Colored People (NAACP) and the Southern Christian Leadership Conference (SCLC) threatened to picket the club and the Championship. Corporate sponsors Lincoln-Mercury, Honda, Toyota, and IBM pulled more than $2 million worth of advertisements from ESPN and ABC. After a hailstorm of controversy reverberated through the golf world, the club finally agreed to integrate. On July 31, Shoal Creek offered black insurance executive Louis J. Willie a membership.

Wayne Grady outlasted Fred Couples in the fourth round of the 1990 PGA.

Seizing on the opportunity to make some important changes, on August 7, two days before the Championship was to begin, The PGA of America adopted a policy that eliminated clubs with discriminatory membership policies from consideration as future sites. PGA President Patrick Rielly explained, "The PGA recognizes that private clubs have a legal right to determine their own membership policies. But, as a leader in golf, The PGA also recognizes its obligations to foster and promote equal opportunity in the game." The PGA Tour, USGA, Senior PGA Tour, and Ladies Professional Golf Association (LPGA) quickly followed The PGA of America's lead. PGA Tour Commissioner Deane Beman warned potential hosts of PGA Tour events to integrate or risk obsolescence. USGA President C. Grant Spaeth decided to scrutinize policies of clubs of future USGA sites and withdraw bids to sites that did not meet certain standards.

Golf Magazine reported that the Senior PGA Tour and the LPGA declared that a private club would not be considered for tournaments unless its membership was integrated or moving in that direction. Some players, familiar with Gary Player's experience with anti-apartheid protesters at the 1969 PGA Championship, were worried about how the controversy might affect the event. Two weeks before the Championship, Arnold Palmer called Rielly to inquire about safety procedures. It turned out that he had nothing to worry about.

Two days after The PGA of America adopted its new policy, 151 players gathered in Alabama to compete for the $1,350,000 purse. They found a course that had been doctored by Jack Nicklaus, who lengthened some of the holes and deepened the bunkers. Australian Wayne Grady, runner-up in the 1989 Brit-

ish Open, shot 72-67-72-71–282, six under par and captured his first major championship. His closest competitor, Fred Couples, had a one-stroke lead through 66 holes, but bogeyed the next four, mostly because he was struggling with his putter. Only Grady, Couples, and Gil Morgan broke par for the entire tournament, largely because of the thick rough and blistering heat. By comparison, at the 1984 PGA Championship, 32 players finished under par. Grady's score at the event six years earlier would have placed him in a tie for 13th.

At the awards ceremony, Grady's fatigue was evident: "If I don't seem too excited, believe me I am. It was just such a grind. This was the longest day of my life." But he was not too tired for a good joke. When asked what Payne Stewart said to him on the green, Grady deadpanned, "He just asked me for a kiss, but I said no." Grady won $225,000 and became the seventh international player and third Australian, after Jim Ferrier and David Graham, to win the Championship. Upon receiving the trophy he said, "No matter how hard you scratch it now, you're not going to get my name off that trophy."

Nick Faldo's caddy, Fannie Sunesson, during the 1990 Championship.

Bob Tway won in 1986 with a birdie on the 72nd hole.

A junior golf clinic hosted by The PGA of America at the 2003 Championship.

THE GROWTH OF THE GAME

Shoal Creek in 1990 left an important legacy for The PGA of America and the world of golf. Ten years after the controversy, Jim Awtrey, the chief executive officer of The PGA, observed, "What Shoal Creek caused was not just a reflection about country clubs, but an inquiry into every part of golf." Former PGA President Pat Rielly agreed that it brought about some important changes. "I think the game was the winner," he said. "The makeup of the game really changed." And it has grown. As part of The PGA's mission to promote interest in the game of golf and grow participation, The PGA of America has developed programs for everyone—young and old; the physically and mentally challenged; beginners, intermediate, and expert players; and people from all social and ethnic backgrounds. The PGA offers diversity scholarships to students who attend schools that offer degrees in professional golf management and helps support the National Minority College Golf Championship. The primary role of every PGA professional is teaching, making learning the game a fun experience, introducing the game to people from all walks of life with various skill levels, and creating programs that will help to increase golf participation. Since 1991 alone, spending on player development programs and growth-of-the-game initiatives has totaled more than $33 million. The PGA of America and its more than 28,000 men and women professionals are instrumental in providing golf instruction and enjoyment of the game to millions of amateurs throughout the country. Now, as former PGA President Tom Addis once explained, golf "is a game for everybody."

CHAPTER EIGHT

GLORY'S LAST SHOT

John Daly's incredible performance at Crooked Stick Golf Club in 1991 began a new era, one in which the Championship experienced the improbable to the sublime, sometimes in the same event. Writing in *Golf Magazine*, Cameron Morfit captured the essence of the event, "The PGA is the break-through major that either confirms the greatness of a player or spins the golf world on a crazy tangent."

Jim Nantz, the lead golf host for CBS Sports, explained what made the decade so exciting: "We caught magic in a bottle the first year we broadcast The PGA Championship with John Daly in 1991, and it has been a tremendous Championship every year since." Daly expected to watch the Championship on television because he had failed to qualify and stood 14th on the list of alternates. A graduate of the South African and Hogan Tours, Daly, at 25, had never played in The PGA Championship, but a remarkable series of circumstances, detailed by Robert Sommers in *Golf Anecdotes*, was about to change everything.

Gene Sarazen, although eligible at the age of 89, declined to play. Masashi "Jumbo" Ozaki withdrew because of an injury, and Rodger Davis of Australia declined the invitation to avoid interrupting his European schedule. An injured Ronan Rafferty of Ireland declined because of the impending birth of his child.

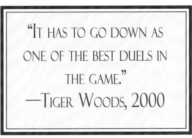

"IT HAS TO GO DOWN AS ONE OF THE BEST DUELS IN THE GAME."
—TIGER WOODS, 2000

Crooked Stick's head professional, Jim Ferriell, was too busy. Mark James and Lee Trevino withdrew. Marco Dawson shot a 74 in the Buick Open and fell to 10th alternate, just behind Daly.

Three of the nine alternates moved into The PGA field, then Gibby Gilbert withdrew, giving place to a fourth alternate. A shoulder injury took Paul Azinger out of the running, giving place to a fifth alternate. Nick Price withdrew because his wife, Sue, was expecting, giving the place to Bill Sander, the sixth alternate. When Sander declined, seventh alternate Mark Lye turned it down because he had not practiced, giving the place to Brad Bryant. Bryant, the eighth alternate, elected instead to visit his mother-in-law, who had recently had a bad fall. That left John Daly.

Once identified as the next alternate to get into the field, but still without confirmation that he would play, Daly packed his new BMW and drove seven-and-a-half hours with his girlfriend from Memphis to Indianapolis on Wednesday evening. When he arrived at midnight, there was a message from Ken Anderson, a PGA official in charge of the field, awaiting him at the front desk of their hotel. Daly was in the event. The next day, he teed off without a practice round, on a course that he had never seen and with a caddie that he had never met. He averaged 303

John Daly on the ninth hole in the third round in 1991.

yards off the tee and shot 69-67-69-71–276 to beat Bruce Lietzke by three strokes. Former PGA President Dick Smith claimed that Daly "literally destroyed the golf course." He hit the ball so far off the tee that Dan Jenkins joked in *Golf Digest*, "He stood near Indianapolis, took the clubhead around Rhode Island, then swung it back through Texas and finished in Georgia."

Daly's opening 69 did not garner him much attention, mostly because Ian Woosnam and Kenny Knox shot 67s. In addition, Thomas Weaver, a spectator, was killed by lightning just as he was about to get into his car. That tragic incident put a damper on the opening day.

Daly played the 445-yard 18th on Friday by hitting a driver and then a 7-iron to eight feet. His prodigious length brought him notice, but he showed that he could play from any vantage point on the course. The only blemish on Saturday's round came when several fans who were watching the event on television called to inform The PGA of America that Daly had violated Rule 8-2b of the *Rules of Golf*. It appeared that his caddie, Jeff "Squeaky" Medlen, who was supposed to loop for Nick Price that week, had touched the flagstick on the 11th green on the line of Daly's putt. After reviewing the videotape, The PGA concluded there was no infraction, and Daly's birdie on the hole stood. Saturday night, at an NFL exhibition game, Daly was given a standing ovation when his presence was announced over the loudspeaker. On Sunday, he closed with a 71.

Not afraid to show his excitement and responding with enthusiasm to the crowd's cheers, Daly became an everyman hero, a dark horse who was not even on the same track as the rest of the field when the race began. Like Jock Hutchison in 1920, both golfers failed to qualify, were entered as alternates at the last possible moment, and won the Championship. At the trophy ceremony, he revealed how much of a rookie he was, "I had no idea all these exemptions were involved in winning this thing. I just came here to play golf and got lucky and won. Everybody

knows I'm a Cinderella story." But he also showed heart, donating $30,000 of the prize money to establish a scholarship for the children of the spectator who was killed on the first day. Daly's win prompted Dan Jenkins to declare, "He's the greatest thing to come out of Memphis since Elvis." His victory energized the golf world, proving that anything can happen. The PGA Champions that followed would agree.

At Bellerive Country Club in St. Louis, Missouri, for the 1992 PGA Championship, Nick Price claimed his first major after 15 years as a professional. Born in 1957, in Durban, South Africa, Price served two years in the Rhodesian (now Zimbabwean) air force as a fighter pilot and began playing on the European tour as an amateur in 1975. He was a steady player, a student of David Leadbetter and not prone to heroics. For the next two years he dominated professional golf.

Bellerive, founded in 1897 as the Field Club of St. Louis, played host to the 1953 Western Open that was won by Dutch Harrison. Due to the course's proximity to Lambert International Airport, a military jet crashed on the 13th green in 1957, prompting the membership to seek another location. In 1960, the new Robert Trent Jones Sr.–designed course was ready for play; five years later, it hosted the U.S. Open. In advance of the 1992 PGA Championship, Jones was hired once again to oversee renovations. A new dual-pipe irrigation system was installed, and new greens were built on the third and 13th holes. For the first time in many years, the players were greeted by beautiful weather. With temperatures in the low 80s, players joked with PGA Vice President Gary Schaal that he had scheduled the year's last major "under blizzard conditions."

Gene Sauers and Craig Stadler shared the lead with 67s on Thursday, and Nick Faldo, Jay Don Blake, and Brian Claar looked like they might contend. Price, who declared "it's the guys who don't make mistakes who win," was three behind with a 70. He would repeat that score on Friday, losing a stroke to Sauers, who continued his pace with a 69. Defending Champion John Daly survived the 36-hole cut by one stroke. With a 72-78, Jack Nicklaus was not so lucky. For the first time in his career, he missed the cut in three straight majors. Price's 70-70 did not foreshadow what was to come.

On Saturday, Price made his move when he sank a birdie putt on the 12th hole that measured 105 feet. His 68 in the third round put him two strokes off the lead. Sauers shot a 70. Nick Faldo essentially ended his chances with a 76, and despite posting a 67 on Sunday, he finished tied for second. Sauers would also fade in the final round with a 75 that left him tied with Faldo, John Cook, and Jim Gallagher Jr. Saturday night, David Leadbetter said to Price, "Nick, look at that leader board. No Seve, no Watson. You can win this thing."

In his final round, Price started with 10 straight pars. His only serious threat came when John Cook chipped in on 16, but Price stayed in the running with a birdie. On 17, he made par with a putt from 12 feet and won by a three-stroke margin.

Though Gene Sauers led for 59 holes, Nick Price took home the Wanamaker Trophy in 1992.

Price, who was within three strokes of winning the British Open in 1982 and 1988, broke through at the 1992 PGA Championship.

In celebrating his first major championship Price described his reaction. "It feels really good," he said. "It feels like a monkey off my back. A whole troop of monkeys." The 1992 title helped revitalize his career. In both 1993 and 1994, he was named PGA Tour Player of the Year.

Two years after Price won in St. Louis, he repeated as PGA Champion in 1994 at Southern Hills, winning by six strokes. It was the largest margin of victory in The PGA Championship since Jack Nicklaus won by seven strokes 14 years earlier. Ranked number one in the world when he arrived in Tulsa, Price had won the British Open a month earlier. His back-to-back victories in the Open and The PGA had not been achieved since Walter Hagen in 1924.

The quality of Price's ball striking at Southern Hills brought acclaim from his fellow competitors. "He's a man in full flight," said Ben Crenshaw. "Striking the ball, I'd say he's been as good as anyone since Ben Hogan and Byron Nelson. God, he's magnificent to watch." John Cook echoed Crenshaw's adulation. "Nick has been scary for a long time now. He's Hogan Era. He's Nelson Era." Corey Pavin said, "I don't know what can slow Nick down. He's playing the best golf in the world."

Tied for the lead after the first round with Colin Montgomerie, who also posted a 67, Price pulled ahead on Friday with a 65 and stayed there. After the second round, he was five strokes ahead of the field. On Saturday, the rest of the contenders wasted their opportunities to catch him. Jay Haas, who was within one stroke of the lead, took a triple bogey on 15. Corey Pavin was within two

An idle threat at the 1994 Championship.

strokes, then double-bogeyed 14, and Phil Mickelson was within three shots and double-bogeyed 15. Price played conservatively, shot a 70, and hung on to his three-stroke lead. As they were leaving the course, players and spectators alike were surprised to see him back on the practice range, hitting balls with David Leadbetter. On Sunday, Price birdied the third and fourth holes and sank a curling 25-foot putt on the eighth hole to solidify a six-stroke lead.

While Price dominated the field, Arnold Palmer sang his swan song. After 37 attempts, Palmer missed the cut after shooting 79-74. His last putt in a PGA Championship covered 20 feet for a par on the 18th hole. As he arrived at the green, the crowd gave him a three-minute standing ovation. "The crowds . . . they can be a very moving thing," Palmer said. "It's nice to know they care about you."

Sports writers alternately called the 1993 PGA Championship at Inverness Club in Toledo, Ohio, a "pressure cooker" and "titanic struggle." Gary Van Sickle, writing for *Golf World*, wrote, "You have to get fired from your job and rehired two or three times within a couple of hours, so you can understand the kind of emotional roller coasters that Azinger and Norman rode." Greg Norman seemed fated to win, until Paul Azinger tied him on the final green. Forced into a sudden-death playoff, Norman three-putted the second hole and became the second player in history to lose playoffs in all four major championships, a bit of a dubious honor.

To get to the playoff, Azinger birdied four of the last seven holes to shoot a 68 to Norman's 69. Norman, who had eight straight rounds in the 60s in two consecutive majors, took his loss in stride. "I'll be fine," he said later. "I'm not going to cry over this or be despondent. When I look back, I've turned my career around in a phenomenal way this year." Azinger seemed much more agitated by his win, "My heart was beating so hard and so fast, my eyes were flashing like neon."

The British Open and The PGA in 1994 gave Nick Price two consecutive major victories.

Fifty-seven players broke par on the first day, and Lanny Wadkins holed a 9-iron from the rough for eagle on the 11th hole to lead with a 65. Or so it seemed. Late finisher Scott Simpson shot a 64 just as the sun was dipping below the horizon. He tied Bob Tway's record set in the 1986 PGA Championship. But Simpson's record was erased on Friday when Vijay Singh shot a 63—the 15th player to do so in a major—and took a two-stroke lead over Wadkins and Steve Elkington.

Darrell Kestner, a club professional from Deepdale Golf Club in Manhasset, New York, made headlines Saturday with an improbable double eagle. His wife, Margie, was asked by The PGA of America to carry a video camera around the course to provide amateur footage for a film they were producing. After nine holes, Kestner became worried that the battery would die and asked Margie to turn off the camera. An hour later, he regretted his decision. On the 13th hole, his second shot landed in the hole, making it the first "albatross" in PGA Championship history.

Bob Denney of The PGA of America explained that "Inverness' final hole formed an amphitheater for arguably the best leader board in a PGA Championship." The top 10 (including ties) after the third round included six players who had won a combined 19 major championships. Leading the way was 1993 British Open Champion Greg

The intersection of Sunset and Fairfax Streets in Los Angeles in 1995.

Norman, a stroke better than Paul Azinger; Vijay Singh; eight-time major winner Tom Watson; Bob Estes; three-time U.S. Open winner Hale Irwin; and 1977 PGA Champion Lanny Wadkins. Lurking two strokes back was five-time major winner Nick Faldo, Dudley Hart, 1987 U.S. Open Champion Scott Simpson, and Brad Faxon.

Azinger opened the week with 69-66, and Norman shot two 68s. On Friday, Azinger had seven birdies on the second nine, five of them in a row. Saturday's round did not disappoint the galleries. More than a dozen players were within three strokes of the lead throughout the afternoon. When it ended, 17 were within four strokes. Norman holed a 45-foot pitch on the 10th hole on his way to a 67 and the lead. Wadkins holed out from the fairway for an eagle, and Tom Watson chipped in twice. Later Davis Love III said, "It was one of the most exciting days of golf I've seen in a long time."

On Sunday, Tom Watson missed two short putts on one and three and fell out of contention. Hale Irwin and Bob Estes shot over par, and even Norman seemed to falter. Azinger, running on pure adrenaline, tied Norman on the 17th hole, which meant that Norman had to birdie 18 to win. At the last moment, his putt spun out of the hole for a tie. The players rode

> "ONE COULD ARGUE THAT DURING THIS DECADE THE PGA CHAMPIONSHIP HAS BEEN THE MOST EXCITING OF THE FOUR MAJORS."
> —CLIFTON BROWN, 2003

At Riviera in 1995, Steve Elkington broke The PGA's 72-hole record by two strokes.

back to the 18th tee to begin the first playoff since Larry Nelson won in 1987. They tied on 18, and then moved to continue on 10, where Azinger's par finally won. An exhausted Azinger had trouble raising the Wanamaker Trophy above his head. What appeared to be fatigue a month later turned out to be lymphoma in his right shoulder blade. He successfully fought the cancer and came back to play at Southern Hills in 1994, although he was unable to make the cut.

The 1995 PGA Championship was played at Riviera Country Club, a course that hosted not only the 1948 U.S. Open and the 1983 PGA Championship, but many Los Angeles Opens. Construction on the course began in 1926 at a cost of nearly $250,000, the second-most expensive layout at the time next to Yale University Golf Course, which was double the price. Riviera

had an impressive membership that included W. C. Fields, Clark Gable, Douglas Fairbanks, and Dean Martin. Designed by George C. Thomas, it was the course upon which Babe Didrikson Zaharias gave Katharine Hepburn putting lessons before her role in *Pat and Mike* and where Ben Hogan and Sam Snead coached Glenn Ford on the set of *Follow the Sun*. Before the Championship, the greens were rebuilt by Ben Crenshaw and Bill Coore and sodded with a grass known as Crenshaw Bent. Despite the temperate conditions, the greens were, according to Gary Van Sickle in *Golf World*, "semi-bare, on life support, bumpier than the Slauson Cutt-Off and looking like the home of the National Lawn Dart Finals."

Multiple records were set in California that week. Steve Elkington and Colin Montgomerie shot the lowest 72-hole total

A Zinger of a Championship

Bob Denney, The PGA's manager of media relations, recalled escorting a vanquished Greg Norman and the Champion, Paul Azinger, to the clubhouse following the 1993 PGA Championship. "Norman elected to walk up the fairway back to the clubhouse, keeping his right arm on his son's left shoulder. A nearby golf cart was missing a key, and Norman was patient at a time when he had the right to be testy. Seconds later, an official appeared with a new golf cart. I rode behind Norman and his son, while spectators near the clubhouse applauded and yelled encouragement all the way to the media center. An hour later, following Azinger's post-round news conference, I carried the Wanamaker Trophy ahead of the Champion into a clubhouse reception. Azinger was first toasted by PGA officials and then headed upstairs for taped interviews. 'That was a great approach to the 10th hole,' I said, hauling the trophy up the steps. 'What was it?' 'A pitching wedge,' Azinger said, smiling broadly. 'Wasn't it pure?'"

in The PGA Championship and the lowest in any major played in the United States. The field also set the lowest course average score, 71.09, for the Championship. Brad Faxon set a record for the lowest final round in The PGA Championship with a 63. His 28 was the lowest nine-hole score in the history of the Championship. Although not a record, five players—Elkington, Montgomerie, Jeff Maggert, Bob Estes, and Steve Lowery—shot all four rounds in the 60s.

The course gave up a 63 to Michael Bradley on Thursday, and Mark O'Meara shot 64, a score matched by Jim Gallagher Jr. Bradley could not keep the pace and shot 73-73-74 in the next three rounds to finish tied for 54th. On Friday, Ernie Els moved

Australian Steve Elkington prevented an all-American sweep of the majors in 1995.

into a tie for the lead with O'Meara, and they both ended the day 11 under par. Steve Elkington's 68-67 moved him into a tie for fourth. The cut was set at 142, and 72 players advanced. On Saturday, Els shot a 66 and stood three strokes ahead of Mark O'Meara and Jeff Maggert.

Before the Championship, Jack Burke Jr., whose remarkable short game helped him win the 1956 PGA Championship, gave a much-needed putting lesson to Elkington, who used to take a 350-mile train ride as a child to Sydney each week to work with instructor Alex Mercer. After Elkington barely missed winning the British Open, Burke scolded him, "Your putting was pathetic. Here's why and here's what you need to change." Burke worked on improving Elkington's release, and he had 14 fewer putts than Montgomerie after four rounds. "It's not the strongest part of my game," said Elkington, "but I putted brilliantly this week."

In order to be in a position where his putts mattered, Elkington shot a 64 on Sunday. He came from six strokes behind third-round leader Els, who was struggling off the tee and on the greens. Elkington hit 16 greens in regulation, birdied seven of the holes, and parred the rest. Montgomerie's final round of 65 included birdies on the last three holes to put him in a playoff with Elkington. The players went back to the tee at 18 to begin the first playoff hole, and both golfers reached the green in regulation, although from different angles. They both faced 20-foot putts for birdie. Elkington sank his, and Montgomerie did not. "The thing I couldn't get out of my mind on the back nine was that if I win this tournament, I'm going to go down in history," said Elkington. "In the playoff, one of us is going to be in history and the other one isn't. That was a real neat feeling." His 267 tied Greg Norman's score in the 1993 British Open as the lowest in major championship history, and Elkington went on to win the coveted Vardon Trophy for the player with the lowest adjusted scoring average for the year. A few years earlier, Elkington had considered giving up golf because severe allergies made it difficult for him to play. Fortunately, sinus surgery in May 1994 kept him on the tour.

A nearly identical playoff scenario developed the following year at Valhalla Golf Club in Louisville, Kentucky, and the 18th hole was again center stage. In Norse mythology, Valhalla is a palace where fallen heroes rest for eternity. At the 1996 PGA Championship, it was anything but peaceful.

Designed by Jack Nicklaus, the course was ranked 51st on the "America's 100 Greatest Courses" list published by *Golf Digest*. Prior to the Championship, Jim Awtrey and course owner Dwight Gahm agreed that The PGA of America would eventually purchase Valhalla and bring the Championship to Louisville on a regular basis. It turned out to be a good decision. The 1996 event sold out a year in advance, and the 2000 PGA Championship would be one of the most watched in history.

> "I WOULDN'T TRADE THAT MAJOR FOR ANY
> OTHER IN THE WORLD."
> —MARK BROOKS, 1996

With a field that included 81 of the top 100 ranked players in the world, local favorite Kenny Perry hoped to bring glory home by opening with a 66 to take the first-round lead. Defending Champion Steve Elkington was one behind with 67. Sixty players were unable to finish their rounds because of rain. Phil Mickelson repeated his Thursday 67 on Friday and held the lead by three strokes. If he managed to play at that level, he would have become the first left-handed player since Bob Charles, the 1963 British Open Champion, to capture a major. Mark Brooks' 68-70 kept him in the hunt, four strokes off the lead. Vijay Singh made a hole in one on the 14th hole, and finished with a 69 and a tie with Brooks. Jack Nicklaus, the course architect, and 67 other players missed the cut.

On Saturday, another Kentucky native and left-hander, Russ Cochran, posted a bogey-free 65, the low round of the day and a course record. Later, he said of the round, "With so many friends pulling for you, you put your heart and soul in every shot." Building on his first two rounds of 68 and 72, he eased into the lead to the delight of the local fans. Brooks and Singh were two strokes off in second. Mickelson dropped back after a 74 on Saturday and eventually finished tied for eighth. Nick Price, the 1992 and 1994 PGA Champion, shot 68-71-69, just one stroke behind Brooks and Singh.

Perry started Sunday with seven straight pars, to which he added back-to-back birdies at eight and nine and two additional birdies on 11 and 13. With a 12-foot putt on the 14th hole, he took sole possession of the lead. "The crowd was going ballistic," Perry recalled later. "My heart was racing." It may have

been racing too much, because Perry bogeyed the 18th hole—one of the easiest on the course that week—and made the biggest mistake of his career. After his round, he sat in the CBS television booth, donned a headset to chat with Jim Nantz and Ken Venturi, and watched as Mark Brooks scrambled from a greenside bunker to make a birdie and force a playoff. Instead of heading to the practice tee to warm up, Perry stayed for more than half an hour in the booth. When he finally asked PGA officials if he had time to hit some balls, they told him he was due on the tee. Realizing his mistake, he confessed, "I was probably caught up in the moment with all the people. Learned a good lesson, I guess. It's a hard one."

Mark Brooks birdied the final regulation hole to force a playoff against Kenny Perry in 1996.

Although Brooks had struggled at times during the week—making 12 bogeys and one double bogey—his 23 birdies and one eagle offset his mistakes. On the first playoff hole, the par-5 18th, Brooks reached the green in two shots and made his second putt for birdie. Perry once again found the left rough off the tee and was laying five when Brooks putted out for the victory. Perry did not bother to putt out and pocketed his ball. "I just kept plodding along," said Brooks. "I was taught early on that you can only take care of what you're doing and what everybody else is doing is irrelevant." By December, Brooks had three victories, a third-place finish on the money list, and the best year of his career.

Winged Foot's West Course, a club outside New York City designed by Albert Warren Tillinghast, was a suitable setting in 1997 for Davis Love III's first major victory. It boasted a strong connection to The PGA and the Championship. Claude Harmon, who was a semifinalist in the 1945 event, served as head professional at Winged Foot from 1945 to 1977. For many years, he seemed to run a farm team for young golf professionals. Jack Burke Jr., the 1956 Champion who helped Steve Elkington win in 1995, worked as an assistant professional at the course. Jack Lumpkin, Davis Love's teacher, held the same job from 1960 to 1961. Dave Marr, the 1965 Champion and the son of a club professional, also worked there.

Former PGA Champion John Daly shared the lead with Love after both players shot first-round 66s on a course that was rated 74.5, with a slope of 140. But later, Daly confessed to Jim Nantz that he "didn't have the mental strength" to be a serious contender. A 73 on Friday sent Daly back into the pack, and Love encountered some problems on his way to a one-over-par 71. Defending Champion Mark Brooks missed the cut and became the first golfer in the modern era to win a major and then miss the cut in all four majors the next year.

Justin Leonard caught Love on Saturday by shooting a 65, hitting 14 fairways and 15 greens on a course set-up that rewarded consistency. Phil Blackmar said of the rough, "I catch fish in water that is more shallow than the rough is here." Daly's 77-70 on Saturday and Sunday put him out of the running. Masters Champion Tiger Woods, who was greeted by Evander Holyfield on the first tee on Friday, did not shoot a single round in the 60s and finished tied for 29th.

Love, a crowd favorite in 1997, won at Winged Foot with a score of 269.

Facing page: Davis Love III finds his first major at the end of the rainbow.

Waiting for his afternoon tee time, Love showed how nervous he really was: "I ironed my shirt four or five times and packed my suitcase as neatly as I've ever packed it." On Sunday, Love and Leonard were paired, and the Championship began to look more like match than stroke play. Love took a four-stroke lead after four holes. By the turn, it looked as though Love had the event in hand after shooting a 32 to Leonard's 37. Leonard, who had won the British Open a month earlier, trimmed the lead from five strokes to three after he birdied and Love bogeyed the 12th hole. After both golfers parred the 13th, Love was not pushed again. He shot a 66 in the fourth round to win by five strokes. As Bill Fields of *Golf World* reported, "Two rainbows arched over the course, as if scripted by Frank Capra himself," as Love walked to the 18th hole. Penta, Love's mother, said of their appearance, "He knows his dad was with him." When fans, players, and officials are asked about the 1997 Championship, they always mention that moment.

> "I NEVER GET TIRED OF BEING INTRODUCED AS THE REIGNING PGA CHAMPION."
> —DAVIS LOVE III, 1997

By winning The PGA Championship, the 33-year-old Love finally achieved a lifelong dream. His victory also paid homage to his father, who had taught him the game and was killed in a plane crash in 1988. Davis Love II had played in a U.S. Open sectional qualifier at Winged Foot in 1960 with a hand that he had injured helping to rescue a woman trapped in a car accident. Prior to the 1997 Championship, Love's agent told PGA President Ken Lindsay, "Of all the majors, he wants to win The PGA Championship because of his father." Love's victory at Winged Foot was celebrated by golf fans and the thousands of members of The PGA. He remembered, "They were touched by it, and they felt they were a part of it because, ultimately, it is their Championship."

Tiger Woods, the first-round leader at the 1998 PGA Championship, made the most auspicious entry to professional golf in the history of the game in 1996 and then won the Masters in 1997. Thereafter, he became the favorite to win everything from golf tournaments to presidential elections. *Golf Digest* reported that when he arrived at Sahalee Country Club in 1998 with Mark O'Meara, Woods was greeted by a police officer by name at the entrance gate and welcomed to the course. Then the officer turned to O'Meara and asked, "Can I help you, sir?"

With his opening 66, a course record, and a two-stroke lead, Woods appeared on track to add another major to his precociously lengthy résumé. He was using a putter that he had found in O'Meara's garage and sank six putts 15 feet or longer. Yet, he knew what awaited him, "Three more rounds in a major is an eternity." On Friday, he shot a 72.

Sahalee, located 25 miles east of Seattle, was the first club to host The PGA Championship in the Pacific Northwest since Ben Hogan won it in 1946 at Portland Golf Club. The course, whose name means "high, heavenly ground" in the Chinook language, opened in 1969. Paul Runyan, the 1934 and 1938

The seventh hole at Sahalee in 1998 measured 421 yards.

PGA Champion, served as Sahalee's first professional. Listed on "America's 100 Greatest Courses," published by *Golf Digest*, since 1977, Rees Jones modified it slightly in advance of the 1998 Championship. Kerry Haigh, The PGA's managing director of tournaments, reported that the sixth and 18th holes were shortened to par 4s. The course featured narrow fairways that were shaded by tall Douglas firs, and the greens registered 11.6 on the Stimpmeter and did not need much tampering. Lee Janzen joked, "I think the best way to prepare for this course would have been to go to a big city, like New York, and play down Fifth Avenue."

> "OF COURSE, IT'S THE ONE MAJOR
> CHAMPIONSHIP I HAVEN'T WON AND
> IT'S NO. 1 ON MY LIST."
> —TOM WATSON, 1991

The field, including 85 of the top 100 ranked players in the world, was packed with talent. Twenty-five club professionals rounded out the group. Scott Williams, a club professional from nearby Redmond, Washington, stepped up to the tee on the first day and was so overwhelmed with emotion that he could not start. Former PGA President Will Mann remembered that Byron Nelson, who was sitting in a chair nearby, walked over to the young man, put his hand on his shoulder, and said, "Son, you can do this."

Vijay Singh was headed to the top of the leader board after posting a 66 on Friday to complement his first-round, even-par 70. Steve Stricker added a 68 to his opening 69 and trailed Singh by a stroke. The 36-hole cut eliminated Justin Leonard, Payne Stewart, David Duval, Stuart Appleby, and Lee Janzen from the field. Earlier in the week, Appleby, who shot 77-73, gave a tearful press conference in which he detailed the car accident in London that killed his wife, Renay, three weeks earlier. Stricker shot 66 on Saturday to Singh's 67, and they were tied going into the final round.

Singh and Stricker started the fourth round four strokes ahead of the field. At the sixth hole, Stricker fell behind by a shot. At 11, what looked like a disaster for Singh turned into an opportunity. His 3-wood second shot to the green hit a tree, but the ball miraculously bounced onto the green, 25

A FRONT ROW SEAT

Dick Murphy, a district director of The PGA of America and the recently retired head professional at Peachtree Golf Club in Atlanta, was assigned to follow John Daly and Kenny Knox on the final day of the 1991 PGA Championship at Crooked Stick. He remembered the experience vividly. "A few moments stand out to me. On the first hole, a tight par 4, Daly hit an iron off the tee, and it hit the trees to the left. He hit an L-wedge 125 yards, knocked a limb off of a tree, and the ball still carried into the back bunker. It just showed how powerful his swing was. On the fourth hole, I was walking with him, and he asked me, 'How am I doing?' I replied, 'You're doing great.' And he seemed so sincere. The main thing I remember, though, was that he played really fast. Daly was not out there to waste time. He seemed to be on automatic pilot."

Vijay Singh shot 271 to beat Steve Stricker in 1998 and capture his first major victory.

feet from the flag. Singh made a two-putt birdie, added another birdie at 15, and parred the last three holes. Stricker birdied 15 to stay within reach, but a bogey at 17 ended his chances. He ended in second place, two shots behind Singh. Former Champion Steve Elkington shot four rounds in the 60s and finished three strokes behind Singh for third. Defending Champion Davis Love III called the course "tricky" and tied for seventh place. Hometown favorite Fred Couples tied for 13th.

Known for his relentless practicing, Singh spent much of the week on the practice tee at Sahalee, delighting crowds by hitting balls that cleared the back fence. Nick Price said of his rival, "I don't even know if Mr. Hogan practiced as hard as Vijay did." When learning to play golf, Singh patterned his swing after photographs of Tom Weiskopf that he found in old magazines. He turned professional at the age of 19 and served as a club professional in Malaysia and Borneo. His first win on The PGA Tour came at the Buick Classic in 1993.

"I would rather hit balls than sit in a hotel room," said Singh. "You just have to stand out there and keep hitting until you find the right swing." His practice paid off; he only had one three-putt in 72 holes. Prior to 1998, his best finish in The PGA Championship was in 1993, when he placed fourth. Singh, who had won tournaments in 13 different countries, became the 10th player in the last 11 years to capture their first major title at The PGA. The repeat winner was Nick Price.

In the 1992 *PGA Championship Journal*, Tim Rosaforte asked a question that, in retrospect, might seem amusing to golf fans: "Will anyone ever dominate the game again?" In trying to answer it, he quoted Jack Nicklaus as saying, "I think it's going to be more difficult to dominate. But somebody's going to come to the front, really get confident and go for a few years." That somebody was Tiger Woods.

The 1999 PGA Championship came to Medinah Country Club, host of three U.S. Opens, in 1949, 1975, and 1990, and the 1939

In the 1920s, the Shriners from Chicago's Medinah Temple built the country club resort and hired Tom Bendelow to design the golf course.

Tiger Woods triumphed over one of the strongest fields ever assembled in a major in 1999.

Western Open. Designed by Tom Bendelow and dedicated by the Ancient Arabic Order of Nobles of the Mystic Shrine of North America (the Shriners) in 1928, the No. 3 course had undergone four revisions, the last of which cost more than $1 million in 1990. Tommy Armour, the 1930 PGA Champion, was the club professional at Medinah from 1933 to 1934. On the eve of the 1999 PGA Championship, the course was ranked 19th on the "America's 100 Greatest Courses" list published by *Golf Digest*. Four-inch bluegrass rough surrounded the greens, and 4,161 trees lined the course, one of which played a starring role in Sergio Garcia's action-packed round on Sunday.

Although Woods won, Garcia stole the show. On the 16th hole on Sunday, he almost stole the lead. His 3-wood off the tee went through the fairway, and the ball landed between the exposed roots of a large tree. "I had a shot, but I had to hit a big slice," he said. With a 6-iron and 189 yards to go, he closed his eyes and swung. "I opened my eyes and saw the ball was going at the green and I was pretty excited." As he rushed up the hill and leaped into the air for a better view, Garcia could see that his ball came to rest 50 feet from the flag. The fact that he missed his birdie putt and settled for par was eclipsed by the previous shot. Ryder Cup Captain Ben Crenshaw was stunned, saying, "I don't think anybody has ever seen a shot like that."

The first three days of the Championship were sedate by comparison. Garcia's 66 set the pace and was 23 strokes better than his opening round at the British Open earlier in the summer at Carnoustie. Garcia's drives averaged 313 yards, and he hit 15 greens in regulation on Thursday. Woods opened with a 70-67. On Friday, Garcia's 73 put him two strokes behind Woods. Jay Haas, who shot a 67, was the second-round leader. Woods shot a 68 on Saturday, and found himself tied with Mike Weir, who had a 69. Garcia had a 68 and was down by two.

On Sunday, Woods had four birdies in the first 11 holes. But, as he explained, "A five-shot lead can evaporate pretty quickly. If I make a couple of mistakes; they make a couple of birdies, and, boom, we're tied. That's exactly what happened. I made a couple of mistakes." His three-putt for bogey on the 12th hole cost him a stroke. The drama, though, really did not begin until Garcia birdied the next hole and Woods carded a double-bogey. Woods bogeyed 16, and that trimmed his lead to one stroke. He saved par with an eight-foot putt on 17, and rolled in a four-foot putt on 18 for the win. On his way to capturing his second major title, Woods shot an 11-under total of 277.

In his discussion about the battle between Garcia and Woods on Sunday, Steve Eubanks observed in his book *At the Turn,* "Their combined age wouldn't have qualified them for the senior tour, yet they were two of the most dynamic players in his-

tory, providing just the kind of top-notch duel everyone hoped would come from Tiger and [David] Duval." It electrified the crowd, especially the teenage girls who constantly shouted, "We love you Sergio." Jerry Higginbotham, Garcia's caddie, clearly noticed: "I've been out here a long time, and I've never heard anything like it." One great finish deserved another.

On Sunday, August 20, 2000, Kentucky's Valhalla Golf Club became the site of one of the most thrilling tournament finishes in modern golf history. Earlier that summer, Tiger Woods captured the U.S. Open and British Open titles, taking his first steps toward winning golf's four majors in a row. At Valhalla, Woods and Bob May were tied after both made birdie putts on the 18th hole in the final round, sending the event into a playoff. Late in the afternoon, they began the first three-hole aggregate score playoff in the Championship's history.

Sergio Garcia was the crowd's favorite at Medinah.

Garcia leaping into the air to see his shot after hitting from behind a tree on the 16th hole during the 1999 Championship.

On the first hole, the par-4 16th, Woods started with a birdie, putting him one stroke ahead of May. On the 17th hole, they both made memorable par saves, leaving the par-5 18th hole to decide the Championship. Woods hit his drive left, and the ball bounced off a sycamore tree and came to a rest to the left of the cart path. His approach shot landed in the left rough, and his third shot drifted into a green-side bunker. This was May's big chance. His drive crossed the fairway and landed in the left rough; unfortunately, his approach shot found the right rough. His third shot caught the ridge of the horseshoe-shaped green and stopped 40 feet from the hole. Woods hit his bunker approach to within two feet, and May narrowly missed his birdie attempt to lose the Championship by one stroke. Reflecting on his $900,000 victory, Woods declared, "This was probably one of the greatest duels I've ever had in my life. Birdie for birdie, shot for shot, we were going right at each other. That's as good as it gets."

In 2000, Woods and May dueled through the final round, finishing in a three-hole playoff.

Tiger came to Valhalla hoping to be the first golfer since Ben Hogan in 1953 to win three professional majors in a single year. On his way to shooting 66-67-70-67, he faced some stiff competition. Woods and Scott Dunlap, who was suffering from a cold, were at the top of the leader board on Thursday. Woods' round included seven birdies and one bogey. On Friday, Woods ended with a one-stroke lead over Dunlap, and Bob May shot a 66. When Jack Nicklaus, who was paired with Woods on the first two days, was asked if he had any advice for the young golfer, he replied, "Any advice? I'd ask him for a lesson."

On Saturday, Davis Love III came within three strokes of Woods, and José Maria Olazabal shot a 63. Woods shot a 70, barely holding onto a one-stroke lead over May and Dunlap. On Sunday, in front of 33,000 fans, Woods fell back by two strokes after the first six holes, but he played the last 12 in seven under par. *Sports Illustrated* reported, "May played like a champion. Woods played like a god." When May sank an 18-foot putt on 18, Woods was not to be upstaged. He made his six-footer, also for birdie, prompting the first three-hole playoff of this kind in the Championship's history.

Woods became the first golfer since Denny Shute in 1937 to win back-to-back PGA Championships. Bob May, who had played for years in Europe, had never won a PGA Tour event. The two men grew up 20 minutes from each other in southern California. May, seven years older than Woods, was such a dominant force in junior golf that Woods once told his parents, "I just wanted to hopefully one day win as many tournaments as he did."

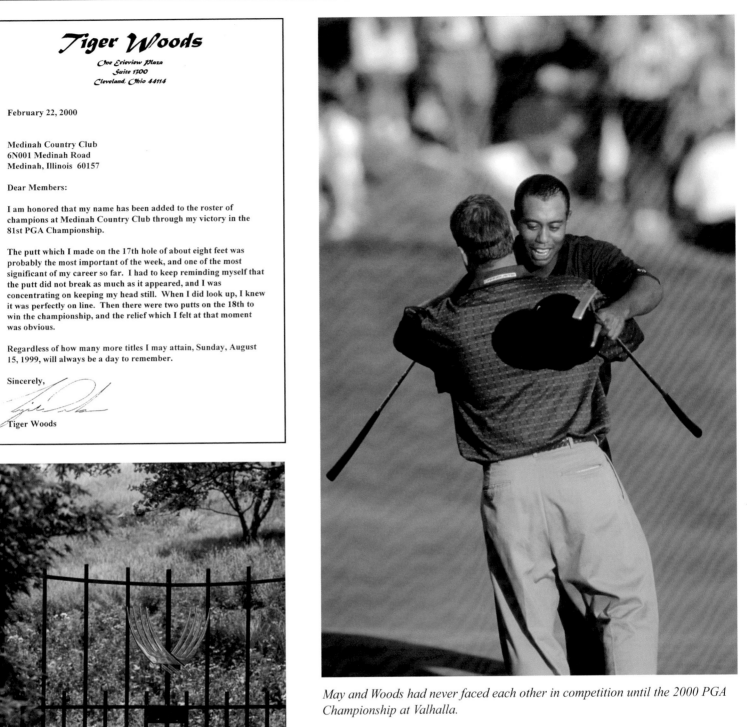

Tiger Woods

One Erieview Plaza
Suite 1300
Cleveland, Ohio 44114

February 22, 2000

Medinah Country Club
6N001 Medinah Road
Medinah, Illinois 60157

Dear Members:

I am honored that my name has been added to the roster of
champions at Medinah Country Club through my victory in the
81st PGA Championship.

The putt which I made on the 17th hole of about eight feet was
probably the most important of the week, and one of the most
significant of my career so far. I had to keep reminding myself that
the putt did not break as much as it appeared, and I was
concentrating on keeping my head still. When I did look up, I knew
it was perfectly on line. Then there were two putts on the 18th to
win the championship, and the relief which I felt at that moment
was obvious.

Regardless of how many more titles I may attain, Sunday, August
15, 1999, will always be a day to remember.

Sincerely,

Tiger Woods

May and Woods had never faced each other in competition until the 2000 PGA Championship at Valhalla.

"THE DUEL BETWEEN TIGER WOODS
AND BOB MAY WAS THE GREATEST BLOW-
BY-BLOW GOLF I'VE EVER SEEN."
—M. G. ORENDER, 2003

It seems fitting, that just as the 1990s opened with a Cinderella story, that three of the four PGA Championships of the new millennium would continue the trend. At the Highlands Course of the Atlanta Athletic Club in 2001, the PGA assembled one of the best fields in golf —95 of the top 100 ranked players were competing. On the 18th hole on Sunday, David Toms, who achieved All-America honors from Louisiana State University and had never won a major, made one of the most difficult decisions of his career. Locked in an epic battle with Phil Mickelson, Toms, whose drive left him 214 yards from the hole, elected to lay up. Despite audible groans from the crowd, the 34-year-old hit a wedge about 130 yards to give him an ideal

distance for a lob wedge to the green. From 88 yards, Toms' third shot landed about 12 feet from the hole. Mickelson barely missed his birdie putt and tapped in for par. Toms stood over his, hit his putt confidently, and watched the ball fall into the hole.

After the first round, Grant Waite of New Zealand took the lead with a 64; eight players, including Phil Mickelson and David Duval, were tied for second. On Friday, Shingo Katayama and Toms were at the top of the field with a 64 and 65, respectively. Tiger Woods struggled to make the cut with a 67 on Friday to go with his 73 on Thursday. On Saturday, Mickelson was leading until Toms aced the par-3 15th hole. Because records prior to World War II are unreliable, he is assumed to be the first golfer

Jack Nicklaus walking off the 18th green to a standing ovation in 2000, after he shot 77-71 and missed the cut.

Phil Mickelson lining up a putt in the 2001 Championship, where he was runner-up to David Toms.

to make a hole in one in a major championship in which he also emerged victorious. Toms, a veteran of the Nike Tour, had won four times in the past six years, only topping the leader board once before in a major. Earlier that summer at the British Open he was second after the second round. He had missed the cut in three of his four previous PGA Championship appearances. His score of 265, 15 under par, was the lowest in PGA Championship history.

The golfer who captured the imagination of the crowds in the hot Atlanta sun acted like a Japanese version of Lee Trevino. With his cowboy hat, infectious exuberance, and five woods in his bag, Katayama bounced balls off walls and skipped them over water hazards, all the while playing to the crowd. At 28, he had won nine tournaments in his six years on the Japan Golf Tour. On Saturday, Katayama's approach shot on the difficult 18th hole skipped off the surface of the lake, leapt over a two-foot wall, and landed on dry ground. When asked why, with a downhill lie in the deep rough, he did not lay up, he replied, "I thought it was my lucky day."

Rich Beem's improbable win in 2002 at Hazeltine National Golf Club near Minneapolis reminded many of John Daly's surprise win 11 years earlier. Beem, who six years before the event was selling stereo equipment and cell phones for $7 an hour, defeated Tiger Woods and Justin Leonard in a great finish. A former assistant professional at El Paso Country Club and son of Larry Beem, a longtime PGA professional, Beem was not afraid to show his nerves, drinking Pepto-Bismol before stepping up to the tee. He

The Atlanta Athletic Club, Bobby Jones' home club, hosted the 2001 Championship.

David Toms, after laying up on the 18th hole, hits his approach shot at the Atlanta Athletic Club in 2001.

carried his Magnolia Hi-Fi identification card with him to remind himself of his past. It was only his fourth appearance in a major, and he was about to stymie Woods' second attempt to win three majors in a single year. As Beem said early in the week, "I had nothing to lose."

Designed by Robert Trent Jones Sr., Hazeltine opened for play in 1962 and hosted the 1966 U.S. Women's Open and the 1970 and 1991 U.S. Opens. In 2002, the club added The PGA Championship to its roster. Revamped by Trent Jones' son, Rees, before the 1991 Open, it proved to be a tough test. On Thursday, Fred Funk and Jim Furyk opened with 68s and shared the lead. By Friday evening, five players were crowded at the top, including Beem and Justin Leonard. Defending Champion David Toms missed the cut by three strokes, but two club professionals, Dave Tentis and Don Berry, made it.

PGA President Jack Connelly remembered a decision before the third round of the 2002 Championship that reflected The PGA's commitment to fairness. After a terrible storm that came through on Friday night, the rules committee decided to move the tee up nearly 60 yards on the 16th hole on Saturday morning because Kerry Haigh thought most of the players would not be able to carry the creek and reach the fairway. They were grateful for the decision on a hole that Fred Funk called "one of the scariest I've seen."

On Saturday, in gusty winds that measured 30 miles per hour, Leonard, a Texan accustomed to such conditions, took a three-stroke lead over Beem with a 69, the best round of the day. Funk was four strokes back, and Woods was five. Beem, stunned to find himself in second place, modestly said in the interview room, "Guys like me aren't supposed to contend in majors." He was playing against one of the strongest fields, including 98 of the top 100 players, ever assembled.

Beem's charge on Sunday seemed to eclipse Leonard, the 1997 British Open Champion, who faded into the pack with a 77. Leonard's problems began with a bogey on the second hole and continued on the eighth with a double bogey. A disappointed Leonard explained, "I just made a couple of bad swings at the wrong time, and couldn't get it turned around in the middle of the round. Today I obviously threw a huge opportunity away, and that stings—and it will sting for a while." On the back nine

The Atlanta Athletic Club attracted nearly a quarter of a million spectators in 2001.

Shingo Katayama stole the show in Atlanta in 2001.

Toms' decision to lay up paid off handsomely in 2001.

Spectators trying to get a look at the action on the final hole in 2001.

on Sunday, Beem came alive. On the 11th hole, he hit his second shot to within six feet of the cup and made his putt for an eagle. This gave him a three-stroke lead over Woods. But Woods was not ready to give up. He birdied the last four holes, and declared, "I gave it absolutely everything I had." But it wasn't enough. Beem won by one stroke. In interviews later, Beem said, "This is the second-coolest thing to happen to me next to getting married. I fought so hard out there . . . and it paid off. I'm giddy.

That's the perfect word for me. Giddy." In 1998, Beem finished third in The PGA's Assistant Professional Championship and won a check for $3,000; five years later, he took home nearly $1 million.

Shaun Micheel, a 34-year-old professional from Memphis, had not won a PGA Tour event in his 163 starts when he captured the Wanamaker Trophy in 2003. In fact, he was best known for his heroics off the golf course. While on a trip with fellow professional Doug Barron to a TC Jordan Tour event on June 30, 1993, Micheel was sitting in a New Bern, North Carolina, hotel parking lot when he witnessed a 1990 Pontiac Grand Am fly over an embankment and splash into the Neuse River. Not a strong swimmer, he stripped to his boxer shorts, jumped on a concrete wall, and leaped into five feet of water. Micheel rescued Julia O'Neil Gibbs, 76, and Harold Mann, 68, with assistance from two male bystanders who pulled the elderly couple to safety. Micheel may be the only PGA Champion to have been awarded the Sons of Confederate Veterans Award for Bravery. He was certainly going to need some courage to face the field assembled at Oak Hill.

The club was the site of Jack Nicklaus' fifth and final victory in The PGA Championship in 1980, where he tied Walter Hagen's record of five wins. Oak Hill, a Donald Ross design, had hosted some of the most important events in golf in the past two decades—the 1980 PGA Championship, the 1984 Senior U.S. Open, the 1989 U.S. Open, the 1995 Ryder Cup matches, and the 1998 U.S. Amateur—and it proved a difficult challenge. After Thursday's round, television announcer Jim Huber explained, "The course was exactly what we expected—very tough. If you didn't hit the fairway, you were in trouble, and if you didn't

> "SOMEDAY I'LL TELL MY GRANDKIDS I PLAYED IN THE SAME TOURNAMENT AS TIGER WOODS."
> —TOM WATSON, 2000

putt well you were in trouble." Although Davis Love III replaced Tiger Woods as the week's favorite, the smart money was on a dark horse. In 2003, the Masters, U.S. Open, and British Open were all won by players who were not household names. Ben Curtis' improbable win at Royal St. George's Golf Club a month earlier made it seem as if anything was possible.

Former two-time PGA Champion Larry Nelson withdrew on Monday because of an injured hip, which gave his spot to fellow Atlantan Billy Andrade. The former Wake Forest star had played on the tour since 1987 and started the week as the seventh alternate. Although Robert Allenby highlighted his first round with a hole in one on the 11th hole, Phil Mickelson, playing in his 42nd major, and Rod Pampling, playing in his first PGA Championship, were at the top of the leader board with 66s. Andrade birdied the final hole and was only one stroke off

Chris Borders, the general manager of the Atlanta Athletic Club, being congratulated in 2001 by PGA President Jack Connelly.

In 2002, Rich Beem became the 12th champion in the last 15 years to win the PGA as his first major title.

the lead. Masters Champion Mike Weir and Lee Janzen shot 68s. Defending Champion Rich Beem shot an 82. Tiger Woods hit only five fairways, made one birdie, and finished with a 74. This was the sixth time he had opened in a major without breaking par. Only 12 players were under par.

On Friday, David Duval, who made just four cuts in 18 starts in 2003, left the course early, on the fifth hole, to nurse his ailing back. Aaron Baddeley came late, after his scheduled starting time, and was assessed a two-stroke penalty. Micheel birdied four of the last five holes and shot a 68, giving him a two-stroke lead over Andrade and Weir. Mickelson double-bogeyed the fifth and seventh holes and shot a 75, and Pampling ended only one stroke better. Ernie Els opened with 70-71 and moved into a tie for fifth. Love shot a 75 to go with his opening 74 and missed the cut.

> "IT'S THE HIGHLIGHT OF MY CAREER."
> —DAVID TOMS, 2001

On Saturday, Chad Campbell, a 29-year-old professional from Texas who had 13 wins on the Hooters Tour and three wins on the Buy.com Tour, shot a 65 to tie for the lead. He shared the honors with Micheel, who bogeyed the final three holes to lose his four-stroke lead. Campbell was playing in his seventh major, Micheel in his third. Mike Weir was three strokes back and said he felt a little like Seabiscuit, referring to the horse that beat Triple Crown winner War Admiral at Pimlico in 1938. Phil Mickelson's 72 put him seven strokes behind the leaders, and Billy Andrade was five strokes back. Tiger Woods two-putted for a bogey on the 18th for a 73 in the third round. After 54 holes, he was 13 strokes behind. Of the 19 players at the top, only four had won a major.

Sunday's round became a head-to-head duel between Micheel and Campbell. During the CBS broadcast, Lanny Wadkins said, "If someone can mount any kind of charge, these two men will really feel the heat." But no one did, and it looked like a match-play finish. Campbell was three over par on the front nine. Micheel three-putted the 15th, while Campbell birdied it, putting Micheel only one stroke in the lead. When Micheel hit into the rough on 17 and made a bogey, he set the stage for a finish that rivaled the battle between Greg Norman and Bob Tway in 1986. On the 18th hole, Micheel's first shot landed on the left side of the fairway, in the first cut of the rough. When asked about it later, he explained his state of mind at that moment: "I had a perfect yardage into 18. I was just trying to hit somewhere on the green." Micheel's second shot, a 7-iron from 175 yards, was ideal. The ball skipped three times and stopped two inches from the hole. Immediately afterward, announcer Dick Enberg exclaimed, "Did he ever produce glory's last shot!" Without a single win to his name, he added The PGA Championship to his résumé. It was the first time since 1969 that the four majors were won by first-time major winners. Micheel became the seventh player to win The PGA Championship in his first attempt.

When Tom Kerrigan stepped up to the first tee at Siwanoy Country Club in 1916, he never could have imagined that The PGA Championship would become one of the most coveted titles in the history of the game. But he would be pleased to know that it has not strayed too far from its roots. Although it has grown into one of the most-watched sporting events in the world, it still pays homage to the professionals who helped build it. As predicted by the *New York Times* on October 11, 1916, it has brought out some of the finest matches ever contested on the golf courses of America, and it will continue to do so.

Shaun Micheel was ranked 169 in the world when he won in 2003.

PASSING THE TORCH

Keith Reese, the head golf professional at Valhalla Golf Club, recalled the pairing of Tiger Woods and Jack Nicklaus in the first two rounds of the 2000 PGA Championship: "The most powerful moment was the play of the final hole of the second round when Jack needed an eagle to make the cut and Tiger was tied for the lead. As the players walked off the 18th tee, Tiger and Jack discussed how much they enjoyed the last two days, and Tiger said, 'Well let's finish it off the right way.' What followed will forever be etched in my mind. Jack laid up his second shot on the par-5 18th. Needing to hole his third shot, he hit a tremendous pitch, barely missing his badly needed eagle. Tiger wedged his bunker shot onto the green and stared down the birdie putt that would give him the 36-hole lead. Tiger made his birdie putt, and Jack pointed to Tiger and gave him an approving thumbs up, as if to signify the passing of the torch to the one who will most likely surpass Nicklaus' great achievement."

"IF YOU WIN THE PGA CHAMPIONSHIP, YOU
KNOW YOU'VE BEATEN THE BEST OF THE BEST.
YOU'VE BEATEN THE BEST FIELD IN THE WORLD ON
THE WORLD'S BEST GOLF COURSES."
—LANNY WADKINS, 2002

Appendix A
The PGA Championship Record Book

Year	Winner	Score	Runner-Up	Site	Yardage	Dates	Total Purse
1916	James M. Barnes	1-up	Jock Hutchison	Siwanoy Country Club, Bronxville, New York	6,251	Oct. 9-14	$2,580
1917	No Championship because of World War I						
1918	No Championship because of World War I						
1919	James M. Barnes	6 and 5	Fred McLeod	Engineers Country Club, Roslyn, New York	6,262	Sept. 15-20	$2,580
1920	Jock Hutchison	1-up	J. Douglas Edgar	Flossmoor Country Club, Chicago, Illinois	6,110	Aug. 17-21	$2,580
1921	Walter Hagen	3 and 2	James M. Barnes	Inwood Country Club, Far Rockaway, New York	6,600	Sept. 26-Oct. 1	$2,580
1922	Gene Sarazen	4 and 3	Emmett French	Oakmont Country Club, Oakmont, Pennsylvania	6,707	Aug. 12-18	$2,580
1923	Gene Sarazen	38 holes	Walter Hagen	Pelham Country Club, Pelham Manor, New York	6,419	Sept. 23-29	$3,600
1924	Walter Hagen	2-up	James M. Barnes	French Lick Springs, French Lick, Indiana	6,173	Sept. 15-20	$6,830
1925	Walter Hagen	6 and 5	William Mehlhorn	Olympia Fields Country Club, Olympia Fields, Illinois	6,490	Sept. 21-26	$6,330
1926	Walter Hagen	5 and 3	Leo Diegel	Salisbury Golf Links, Garden Hills, New York	6,750	Sept 20-25	$11,100
1927	Walter Hagen	1-up	Joe Turnesa	Cedar Crest Country Club, Dallas, Texas	6,371	Oct. 31-Nov. 5	$15,441
1928	Leo Diegel	6 and 5	Al Espinosa	Five Farms Course, Baltimore Country Club, Baltimore, Maryland	6,622	Oct. 1-6	$10,400
1929	Leo Diegel	6 and 4	Johnny Farrell	Hillcrest Country Club, Los Angeles, California	6,438	Dec. 2-7	$5,000
1930	Tommy Armour	1-up	Gene Sarazen	Fresh Meadows Country Club, Flushing, New York	6,815	Sept. 8-13	$10,300
1931	Tom Creavy	2 and 1	Denny Shute	Wannamoisett Country Club, Rumford, Rhode Island	6,583	Sept. 7-14	$7,200
1932	Olin Dutra	4 and 3	Frank Walsh	Keller Golf Course, St. Paul, Minnesota	6,686	Aug. 31-Sept. 4	$7,200
1933	Gene Sarazen	5 and 4	Willie Goggin	Blue Mound Country Club, Milwaukee, Wisconsin	6,270	Aug. 8-13	$7,200
1934	Paul Runyan	38 holes	Craig Wood	Park Club of Buffalo, Williamsville, New York	6,579	July 24-29	$7,200
1935	Johnny Revolta	5 and 4	Tommy Armour	Twin Hills Country Club, Oklahoma City, Oklahoma	6,035	Oct. 18-23	$7,820
1936	Denny Shute	3 and 2	Jimmy Thomson	Pinehurst Country Club, Pinehurst, North Carolina	6,879	Nov. 17-22	$9,200
1937	Denny Shute	37 holes	Harold McSpaden	Pittsburgh Field Club, Aspinwall, Pennsylvania	6,665	May 26-30	$9,200
1938	Paul Runyan	8 and 7	Sam Snead	Shawnee Country Club, Shawnee-On-Delaware, Pennsylvania	6,656	July 10-16	$10,000
1939	Henry Picard	37 holes	Byron Nelson	Pomonok Country Club, Flushing, New York	6,354	July 9-15	$10,600

Year	Winner	Score	Runner-Up	Site	Yardage	Dates	Total Purse
1940	Byron Nelson	1-up	Sam Snead	Hershey Country Club, Hershey, Pennsylvania	7,017	Aug. 26-Sept. 2	$11,050
1941	Vic Ghezzi	38 holes	Byron Nelson	Cherry Hills Country Club, Denver, Colorado	6,888	July 7-13	$10,600
1942	Sam Snead	2 and 1	Jim Turnesa	Seaview Country Club, Atlantic City, New Jersey	6,590	May 23-31	$7,550
1943	No Championship because of World War II						
1944	Bob Hamilton	1-up	Byron Nelson	Manito Golf and Country Club, Spokane, Washington	6,400	Aug. 14-20	$14,500
1945	Byron Nelson	4 and 3	Sam Byrd	Moraine Country Club, Dayton, Ohio	6,625	July 9-15	$14,700
1946	Ben Hogan	6 and 4	Ed Oliver	Portland Golf Club, Portland, Oregon	6,524	Aug. 19-25	$17,700
1947	Jim Ferrier	2 and 1	Chick Harbert	Plum Hollow Golf Club, Detroit, Michigan	6,907	June 18-24	$17,700
1948	Ben Hogan	7 and 6	Mike Turnesa	Norwood Hills Country Club, St. Louis, Missouri	6,467	May 19-25	$17,700
1949	Sam Snead	3 and 2	Johnny Palmer	Hermitage Country Club, Richmond, Virginia	6,677	May 25-31	$17,700
1950	Chandler Harper	4 and 3	Henry Williams Jr.	Scioto Country Club, Columbus, Ohio	7,032	June 21-27	$17,700
1951	Sam Snead	7 and 6	Walter Burkemo	Oakmont Country Club, Oakmont, Pennsylvania	6,882	June 27-July 3	$17,700
1952	Jim Turnesa	1-up	Chick Harbert	Big Spring Country Club, Louisville, Kentucky	6,620	June 18-25	$17,700
1953	Walter Burkemo	2 and 1	Felice Torza	Birmingham Country Club, Birmingham, Michigan	6,465	July 1-7	$20,700
1954	Chick Harbert	4 and 3	Walter Burkemo	Keller Golf Course, St. Paul, Minnesota	6,652	July 21-27	$20,700
1955	Doug Ford	4 and 3	Cary Middlecoff	Meadowbrook Country Club, Northville, Michigan	6,701	July 20-26	$20,700
1956	Jack Burke Jr.	3 and 2	Ted Kroll	Blue Hill Country Club, Canton, Massachusetts	6,634	July 20-24	$40,000
1957	Lionel Hebert	2 and 1	Dow Finsterwald	Miami Valley Golf Club, Dayton, Ohio	6,773	July 17-21	$42,100
1958	Dow Finsterwald	276	Billy Casper	Llanerch Country Club, Havertown, Pennsylvania	6,710	July 17-20	$39,388
1959	Bob Rosburg	277	Jerry Barber, Doug Sanders	Minneapolis Golf Club, St. Louis Park, Minnesota	6,850	July 30-Aug. 2	$51,175
1960	Jay Hebert	281	Jim Ferrier	Firestone Country Club, Akron, Ohio	7,165	July 21-24	$63,130
1961	Jerry Barber	277*	Don January	Olympia Fields Country Club, Olympia Fields, Illinois	6,722	July 27-31	$64,800
1962	Gary Player	278	Bob Goalby	Aronimink Golf Club, Newtown Square, Pennsylvania	7,045	July 19-22	$69,400
1963	Jack Nicklaus	279	Dave Ragan	Dallas Athletic Club, Dallas, Texas	7,046	July 18-21	$80,900
1964	Bobby Nichols	271	Jack Nicklaus, Arnold Palmer	Columbus Country Club, Columbus, Ohio	6,851	July 16-19	$100,000
1965	Dave Marr	280	Billy Casper, Jack Nicklaus	Laurel Valley Golf Club, Ligonier, Pennsylvania	7,090	Aug. 12-15	$149,700
1966	Al Geiberger	280	Dudley Wysong	Firestone Country Club, Akron, Ohio	7,180	July 21-24	$149,360

YEAR	WINNER	SCORE	RUNNER-UP	SITE	YARDAGE	DATES	TOTAL PURSE
1967	Don January	281*	Don Massengale	Columbine Country Club, Denver, Colorado	7,436	July 20-24	$148,200
1968	Julius Boros	281	Bob Charles, Arnold Palmer	Pecan Valley Country Club, San Antonio, Texas	7,096	July 18-21	$150,000
1969	Ray Floyd	276	Gary Player	NCR Country Club, Dayton, Ohio	6,915	August 14-17	$175,000
1970	Dave Stockton	279	Bob Murphy, Arnold Palmer	Southern Hills Country Club, Tulsa, Oklahoma	6,962	August 13-16	$200,000
1971	Jack Nicklaus	281	Billy Casper	PGA National Golf Club, Palm Beach Gardens, Florida	7,096	February 25-28	$202,440
1972	Gary Player	281	Tommy Aaron, Jim Jamieson	Oakland Hills Country Club, Bloomfield Hills, Michigan	7,054	August 3-6	$224,087
1973	Jack Nicklaus	277	Bruce Crampton	Canterbury Golf Club, Cleveland, Ohio	6,852	August 9-12	$225,000
1974	Lee Trevino	276	Jack Nicklaus	Tanglewood Golf Club, Clemmons, North Carolina	7,050	August 8-11	$225,000
1975	Jack Nicklaus	276	Bruce Crampton	Firestone Country Club, Akron, Ohio	7,180	August 7-10	$225,000
1976	Dave Stockton	281	Raymond Floyd, Don January	Congressional Country Club, Bethesda, Maryland	7,054	August 12-16	$250,950
1977	Lanny Wadkins	282*	Gene Littler	Pebble Beach Golf Club, Pebble Beach, California	6,804	August 11-14	$250,750
1978	John Mahaffey	276*	Jerry Pate, Tom Watson	Oakmont Country Club, Oakmont, Pennsylvania	6,989	August 3-6	$300,240
1979	David Graham	272*	Ben Crenshaw	Oakland Hills Country Club, Bloomfield Hills, Michigan	7,014	August 2-5	$350,600
1980	Jack Nicklaus	274	Andy Bean	Oak Hill Country Club, Rochester, New York	6,964	August 7-10	$376,400
1981	Larry Nelson	273	Fuzzy Zoeller	Atlanta Athletic Club, Duluth, Georgia	7,070	August 6-9	$401,600
1982	Raymond Floyd	272	Lanny Wadkins	Southern Hills Country Club, Tulsa, Oklahoma	6,862	August 5-8	$451,800
1983	Hal Sutton	274	Jack Nicklaus	Riviera Country Club, Pacific Palisades, California	6,946	August 4-7	$600,000
1984	Lee Trevino	273	Lanny Wadkins, Gary Player	Shoal Creek Country Club, Birmingham, Alabama	7,145	August 16-19	$700,300
1985	Hubert Green	278	Lee Trevino	Cherry Hills Country Club, Englewood, Colorado	7,145	August 8-11	$702,000
1986	Bob Tway	276	Greg Norman	Inverness Club, Toledo, Ohio	6,982	August 7-10	$801,100
1987	Larry Nelson	287*	Lanny Wadkins	PGA National Golf Club, Palm Beach Gardens, Florida	7,002	August 6-9	$900,000
1988	Jeff Sluman	272	Paul Azinger	Oak Tree Golf Club, Edmond, Oklahoma	7,015	August 11-14	$1,000,000
1989	Payne Stewart	276	Andy Bean, Mike Reid, Curtis Strange	Kemper Lakes Golf Club, Hawthorn Woods, Illinois	7,217	August 10-13	$1,200,000

YEAR	WINNER	SCORE	RUNNER-UP	SITE	YARDAGE	DATES	TOTAL PURSE
1990	Wayne Grady	282	Fred Couples	Shoal Creek Country Club, Birmingham, Alabama	7,145	August 9-12	$1,350,000
1991	John Daly	276	Brucke Lietzke	Crooked Stick Golf Club, Carmel Indiana	7,295	August 8-11	$1,400,000
1992	Nick Price	278	John Cook, Nick Faldo	Bellerive Country Club, St. Louis, Missouri	7,148	August 13-16	$1,400,000
1993	Paul Azinger	272*	Greg Norman	Inverness Club, Toledo, Ohio	7,024	August 12-15	$1,700,000
1994	Nick Price	269	Corey Pavin	Southern Hills Country Club, Tulsa, Oklahoma	6,824	August 11-14	$1,700,000
1995	Steve Elkington	267*	Colin Montgomerie	Riviera Country Club, Pacific Palisades, California	6,956	August 10-13	$2,000,000
1996	Mark Brooks	277*	Kenny Perry	Valhalla Golf Club, Louisville, Kentucky	7,144	August 8-11	$2,400,000
1997	Davis Love III	269	Justin Leonard	Winged Foot Golf Club, Mamaroneck, New York	6,987	August 14-17	$2,600,000
1998	Vijay Singh	271	Steve Stricker	Sahalee Country Club, Redmond, Washington	6,906	August 13-16	$3,000,000
1999	Tiger Woods	277	Sergio Garcia	Medinah Country Club, Medinah, Ilinois	7,401	August 12-15	$3,000,000
2000	Tiger Woods	270*	Bob May	Valhalla Golf Club, Louisville, Kentucky	7,167	August 17-20	$5,000,000
2001	David Toms	265	Phil Mickelson	Atlanta Athletic Club, Duluth, Georgia	7,213	August 16-19	$5,200,000
2002	Rich Beem	278	Tiger Woods	Hazeltine National Golf Club, Chaska, Minnesota	7,355	August 15-18	$5,500,000
2003	Shaun Micheel	276	Chad Campbell	Oak Hill Country Club, Rochester, New York	7,134	August 14-17	$6,000,000

* denotes playoff

APPENDIX B
A HISTORY OF THE SEASON'S FINAL MAJOR:
A TRAVELING EXHIBITION

A History of the Season's Final Major is a traveling exhibition that tells the story of The PGA Championship from the very first playing of the event in 1916 at Siwanoy Country Club to the most recent victory. Composed of nearly 90 panels, it is the only museum exhibition that focuses exclusively on one of golf's four major championships. Each Championship is represented, and a wide variety of artifacts are on display, from Walter Hagen's walking stick to Gene Sarazen's niblick to Jack Nicklaus' putter.

The exhibition debuted at the Louisville Slugger Museum on June 8, 2000, and it travels to the cities that are hosting The PGA Championship. To date, it has appeared at the Atlanta History Center (2001), the Mall of America (2002), and the Rochester Museum and Science Center (2003). Curated by The PGA of America, it is constantly being updated as a new Champion is crowned each year.

Each exhibition panel consists of two photographs of The PGA Champion and a bronze plaque offering a detailed description of the year's event. Each Champion is asked to donate a signature artifact to the exhibition. Visitors will see Henry Picard's 1939 putter, the straw hat worn by Sam Snead in 1942, the Chicago Bears hat Payne Stewart wore at the 1989 presentation ceremony, and Tiger Woods' famous red shirt from the 2000 Championship at Valhalla. For more information about the exhibition, contact The PGA of America Communications Department at 561-624-8400.

APPENDIX C
THE PGA HISTORICAL CENTER

When 35 charter members of The Professional Golfers' Association of America gathered in New York City on January 17, 1916, they established goals to elevate the standards of their profession and ensure the future of golf. The charter members' collective dream to build the game for future generations comes to life in The PGA Historical Center at PGA Village in Port St. Lucie, Florida.

Opened on February 27, 2003, this single-floor, 8,300-square-foot museum and library brings together the elements that make up golf's international landscape. The PGA of America operated The PGA World Golf Hall of Fame in Pinehurst, North Carolina, from 1984 to 1993. The Association then loaned many pieces of memorabilia to the World Golf Hall of Fame near St. Augustine, Florida. Those collections are now housed at The PGA Historical Center and open to the public.

The Center's showcase is the Probst Library, one of the world's premier golf collections of both periodicals and hardbound books. The library includes more than six thousand hardcover books, more than three thousand handbooks and yearbooks, and more than six hundred volumes of bound periodicals. The library is named for Colonel R. Otto Probst (1896–1986), an engineer from South Bend, Indiana, who began collecting golf periodicals and books in the 1930s. The collection features monographs dating from the 18th century and periodicals from the mid-19th century on instruction, art, biography, golf club histories, essays, equipment, fiction, history, humor, poetry, records, reference manuals, and travelogues.

Adjoining the Probst Library is a room containing rare books on golf, including the first published Scottish Acts of Parliament of 1566, covering, in retrospect, the reigns of King James I through Mary Queen of Scots. The manuscript includes the first known printed reference to golf. In 1457, James II prohibited his subjects from playing golf because it prevented training in archery, vital to the defense of the kingdom. The Acts were later relaxed in 1501 with the Treaty of Glasgow, and James IV had his own clubs made and began playing the game.

In addition, the Historical Center tells the story of golf in America through a variety of exhibitions under a large rotunda. *The PGA Timeline*, documenting the evolution of the world's largest working sports organization, is divided into four 25-year sections. The original minutes from the birth of The PGA in 1916, golf clubs from such notable golfers as Walter Hagen and Jim Barnes, and a program from a Red Cross charity tournament profile the remarkable individuals who pioneered teaching methods that are still in use today. *The History of PGA Magazine* tells the story of the oldest continuous golf publication in the United States, which celebrated its one thousandth issue in August 2003. There are additional exhibitions on The PGA Championship, the Ryder Cup Matches, and other PGA of America competitions. Replicas of golf's Grand Slam trophies from the Masters, U.S. Open, British Open, and PGA Championship are housed in the center of the rotunda.

The Center also features a one-of-a-kind gallery displaying art, ceramics, sculpture, trophies, glassware, games and toys, early golf training aids, early equipment, and a replica of a clubmaker's bench from the 19th century.

The PGA Historical Center hosts the PGA Golf Professional Hall of Fame and a Wall of Fame in a courtyard setting that honors both PGA members and significant contributors to the Association. The south portico of the center overlooks a putting green that is an interactive area where visitors are challenged to use replicas of early golf equipment to master their putting stroke.

The Center is open to the public summer weekends from 10 A.M. to 4 P.M. and daily from fall through Easter Sunday. It is accessible to researchers, by special appointment, year-round. The PGA of America, founded in 1916, is a not-for-profit organization that promotes the game of golf while continuing to enhance the standards of the profession. The Association is comprised of more than 28,000 men and women PGA Professionals who are dedicated to growing participation in the game of golf.

For information or for volunteer opportunities, call 800-800-GOLF or access www.pga.com. The PGA Historical Center is located at 8559 Commerce Center Drive in Port St. Lucie, Florida, 34986. Telephone: 772-370-5410.

Renown architect Donald Ross' workbench on display.

INDEX

PHOTO CREDITS

All photographs included in this book are courtesy of The PGA of America with the following exceptions:

Allsport USA, 192

Associated Press International, 58

Atlanta History Center, 15 (both)

Baltimore Country Club, 33

Cleveland Plain Dealer, iv

Corbis, 8, 12, 27, 59, 62 (both), 63, 64, 71, 73, 104, 130, 131, 132, 203 (right)

Richard Dole for The PGA of America, 182 (bottom), 184, 188

Steven J. Gilbert for The PGA of America, 190 (both), 191 (top), 193

Chandler Harper, 96

Hershey Community Archives, 68

Historical Society of Pennsylvania, 6

Rusty Jerret for The PGA of America, 199

Jeff McBride for The PGA of America, 152, 167, 171, 178, 179, 180 (top)

Gary Newkirk for the PGA, 191 (bottom)

New York Historical Society, 4 (bottom)

Montana Pritchard for The PGA of America, Table of Contents, 20 (left), 194, 195, 197, 198 (both), 200, 201, 202, 203 (left), 204 (bottom), 205 (right), 206 (both), 207 (bottom), 208, 210 (both), 212, 221, back cover

Keith Reese at Valhalla Golf Club, 214

United States Golf Association, 50

Wannamoisett Country Club, 44